ARCTIC OCEAN

W9-COF-241

Spitsbergen

Franz Josef Land

Severnaya
Zemlya

New Siberian
Islands

Laptev Sea

East Siberian Sea

Chukchi Sea

Novaya
Zemlya

Kara
Sea

Central
Siberian
Plateau

Chersky Range

Kolyma

Bering
Strait

Barents
Sea

Yenisey

Lena

Bering
Sea

Lake
Ladoga

Lake
Onega

West
Siberian
Plain

Siberia

Kamchatka

Aleutian
Basin

ASIA

Aleutian Islands
Aleutian Trench

Volga

Ob'

Lake Baikal

Amur

Sea of
Okhotsk

Sakhalin

Kuril-Kamchatka Trench

Emperor Seamounts

European Plain

Irtysh

Altai
Mountains

Gobi

Manchurian
Plain

Hokkaido

Northwest
Pacific
Basin

Dnieper

Don

Ural Mountains

Lake
Balkash

Tien Shan

Sea of
Japan/
East Sea

Honshu

PACIFIC

Black Sea

Mount
Elbrus
△5,642 m (18,510 ft)

Aral Sea

Caspian
Sea

Kunlun Mountains

Yellow River

Yangtze

Kyushu

Bonin Trench

OCEAN

Danube

Caucasus

Anatolia

Zagros Mountains

Amu Darya

Hindu Kush

K2 △
8,611 m
(28,251 ft)

Plateau
of Tibet

East
China
Sea

Micronesia

an Sea

Euphrates
Tigris

Syrian
Desert

Persian
Gulf

Indus

Thar
Desert

Mount Everest
8,848 m (29,029 ft)

Himalayas

Ganges

Taiwan

Philippine
Sea

Mariana
Islands

Libyan Desert

Red Sea

Arabian
Peninsula

Arabian
Sea

Deccan

Mekong

South
China
Sea

Philippine Islands

Mariana Trench

Central
Pacific
Basin

ICA

Nile

Gulf of Aden

Horn of
Africa

Arabian
Basin

Western Ghats

Eastern Ghats

Bay of
Bengal

Caroline Islands

North
Fiji
Basin

Ethiopian
Highlands

Maldive
Islands

Sri Lanka

Malay
Peninsula

Borneo

East Indies

Melanesia

Ubangi

Lake
Victoria

△ Kilimanjaro
5,895 m
(19,340 ft)

Somali
Basin

New
Guinea △
Mount Wilhelm
4,509 m (14,793 ft)

Solomon Islands

Congo
Basin

Great Rift Valley

Seychelles

INDIAN

Sumatra

Celebes

Tonga

Lake
Tanganyika

Ninetyeast Ridge

Java

Java Trench

Timor
Sea

Arafura
Sea

Coral
Sea

Vanuatu

Fiji

Lake
Nyasa

OCEAN

New
Caledonia

New Hebrides
Trench

Zambezi

Mozambique Channel

Madagascar

Mauritius
Réunion

Great Sandy
Desert

Great Dividing Range

Great Barrier Reef

Lord Howe Rise

Kermadec Trench

Kalahari
Desert

AUSTRALIA

Drakensberg

Great Victoria
Desert

Darling

Murray

North
Island

Cape of
Good Hope

Southwest Indian Ridge

Wharton
Basin

Great
Australian Bight

Southeast Indian Ridge

New
Zealand

Bass Strait

South
Island

South Australian
Basin

Tasmania

Tasman
Sea

Kerguelen
Plateau

Enderby Plain

South Indian Basin

Davis Sea

HERN OCEAN

ANTARCTICA

OUR WORLD IN PICTURES
COUNTRIES OF THE WORLD

OUR WORLD IN PICTURES

COUNTRIES OF THE WORLD

WRITTEN BY **ANDREA MILLS**

DK | Penguin Random House

DK LONDON
Senior Editor Carron Brown
Senior Designer Sheila Collins
Editors Georgina Palffy, Anna Streiffert Limerick,
Selina Wood, Sam Kennedy, Vicky Richards, Kelsie Besaw
US Editors Jennette ElNaggar, Heather Wilcox
US Executive Editor Lori Cates Hand
Senior Cartographic Editor Simon Mumford
Cartography Leanne Kelman, Ed Merritt, Martin Sanders
3-D Illustrators Adam Benton, Adam Brackenbury, Simon Mumford
Managing Editor Francesca Baines
Managing Art Editor Philip Letsu
Production Editor Kavita Varma
Senior Production Controller Jude Crozier
Jacket Design Development Manager Sophia MTT
Publisher Andrew Macintyre
Associate Publishing Director Liz Wheeler
Art Director Karen Self
Publishing Director Jonathan Metcalf

DK DELHI
Senior Editor Sreshtha Bhattacharya
Senior Art Editor Shreya Anand
Editors Upamanyu Das, Shambhavi Thatte
Art Editors Noopur Dalal, Sifat Fatima, Baibhav Parida
Assistant Art Editor Bhavnoor Kaur
Cartographic Editor Parnika Bagla
Senior Cartographers Subhashree Bharati,
Mohammad Hassan, Zafar-ul-Islam Khan
Cartographer Ashif
Manager Cartography Suresh Kumar
Project Picture Researcher Deepak Negi
Assistant Picture Researcher Geetika Bhandari
Picture Research Manager Taiyaba Khatoon
Managing Editor Kingshuk Ghoshal
Managing Art Editor Govind Mittal
Senior DTP Designers Pawan Kumar, Jagtar Singh
DTP Designers Mohd Rizwan, Ashok Kumar
Pre-production Manager Balwant Singh
Production Manager Pankaj Sharma
Jacket Designers Suhita Dharamjit, Tanya Mehrotra

First American Edition, 2020
Published in the United States by DK Publishing
1450 Broadway, Suite 801, New York, NY 10018

Copyright © 2020 Dorling Kindersley Limited
DK, a Division of Penguin Random House LLC
21 22 23 24 10 9 8 7 6 5 4 3 2
003–310480–Nov/2020

All rights reserved.
Without limiting the rights under the copyright reserved above,
no part of this publication may be reproduced, stored in or introduced into
a retrieval system, or transmitted, in any form, or by any means (electronic,
mechanical, photocopying, recording, or otherwise), without the prior
written permission of the copyright owner.
Published in Great Britain by Dorling Kindersley Limited

A catalog record for this book is available from the Library of Congress.
ISBN 978-1-4654-9150-3

DK books are available at special discounts when purchased in bulk
for sales promotions, premiums, fund-raising, or educational use.
For details, contact: DK Publishing Special Markets,
1450 Broadway, Suite 801, New York, NY 10018
SpecialSales@dk.com

Printed and bound in Latvia

For the curious
www.dk.com

MIX
Paper from
responsible sources
FSC™ C018179

This book was made with Forest Stewardship Council™ certified paper—
one small step in DK's commitment to a sustainable future.
For more information go to www.dk.com/our-green-pledge

CONTENTS

*Spiral aloe,
Lesotho*

*Andros rock iguana,
The Bahamas*

Blue and yellow macaw, Brazil

Baseball, Cuba

Chihuahua, Mexico

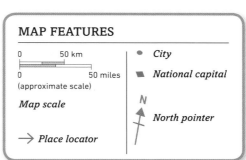

MAP FEATURES

0 — 50 km
0 — 50 miles
(approximate scale)

Map scale

→ *Place locator*

● *City*

■ *National capital*

N *North pointer*

Olive oil, Spain

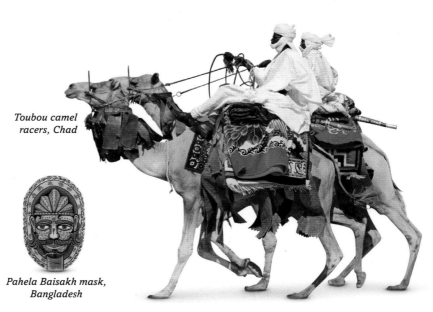

Toubou camel racers, Chad

Traditional copperware, Cyprus

Curanto, Chile

Pahela Baisakh mask, Bangladesh

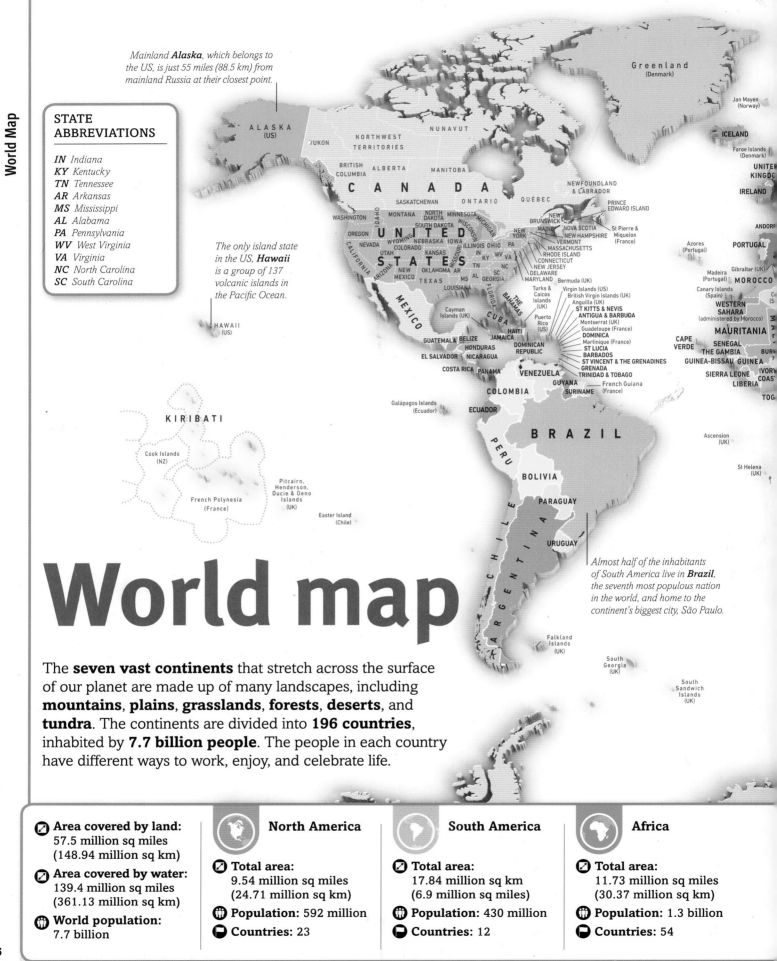

World Map

STATE ABBREVIATIONS

IN Indiana
KY Kentucky
TN Tennessee
AR Arkansas
MS Mississippi
AL Alabama
PA Pennsylvania
WV West Virginia
VA Virginia
NC North Carolina
SC South Carolina

*Mainland **Alaska**, which belongs to the US, is just 55 miles (88.5 km) from mainland Russia at their closest point.*

*The only island state in the US, **Hawaii** is a group of 137 volcanic islands in the Pacific Ocean.*

*Almost half of the inhabitants of South America live in **Brazil**, the seventh most populous nation in the world, and home to the continent's biggest city, São Paulo.*

World map

The **seven vast continents** that stretch across the surface of our planet are made up of many landscapes, including **mountains**, **plains**, **grasslands**, **forests**, **deserts**, and **tundra**. The continents are divided into **196 countries**, inhabited by **7.7 billion people**. The people in each country have different ways to work, enjoy, and celebrate life.

⬀ **Area covered by land:**
57.5 million sq miles
(148.94 million sq km)

⬀ **Area covered by water:**
139.4 million sq miles
(361.13 million sq km)

👥 **World population:**
7.7 billion

North America

⬀ **Total area:**
9.54 million sq miles
(24.71 million sq km)

👥 **Population:** 592 million

📋 **Countries:** 23

South America

⬀ **Total area:**
17.84 million sq km
(6.9 million sq miles)

👥 **Population:** 430 million

📋 **Countries:** 12

Africa

⬀ **Total area:**
11.73 million sq miles
(30.37 million sq km)

👥 **Population:** 1.3 billion

📋 **Countries:** 54

6

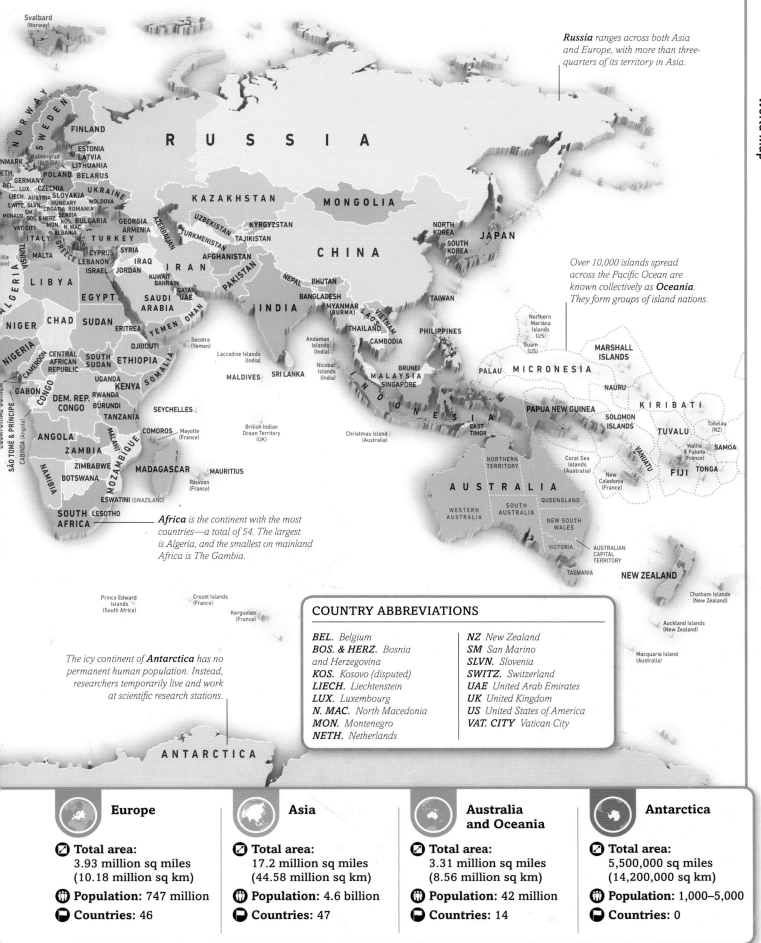

Russia ranges across both Asia and Europe, with more than three-quarters of its territory in Asia.

Over 10,000 islands spread across the Pacific Ocean are known collectively as *Oceania*. They form groups of island nations.

Africa is the continent with the most countries—a total of 54. The largest is Algeria, and the smallest on mainland Africa is The Gambia.

The icy continent of *Antarctica* has no permanent human population. Instead, researchers temporarily live and work at scientific research stations.

COUNTRY ABBREVIATIONS

BEL. Belgium
BOS. & HERZ. Bosnia and Herzegovina
KOS. Kosovo (disputed)
LIECH. Liechtenstein
LUX. Luxembourg
N. MAC. North Macedonia
MON. Montenegro
NETH. Netherlands

NZ New Zealand
SM San Marino
SLVN. Slovenia
SWITZ. Switzerland
UAE United Arab Emirates
UK United Kingdom
US United States of America
VAT. CITY Vatican City

Europe
- **Total area:** 3.93 million sq miles (10.18 million sq km)
- **Population:** 747 million
- **Countries:** 46

Asia
- **Total area:** 17.2 million sq miles (44.58 million sq km)
- **Population:** 4.6 billion
- **Countries:** 47

Australia and Oceania
- **Total area:** 3.31 million sq miles (8.56 million sq km)
- **Population:** 42 million
- **Countries:** 14

Antarctica
- **Total area:** 5,500,000 sq miles (14,200,000 sq km)
- **Population:** 1,000–5,000
- **Countries:** 0

ASIA

ARCTIC
OCEAN

Beaufort
Sea

Ellesmere
Island

Banks
Island

Baffi

Victoria
Island

Bering
Sea

Aleutian Islands

Denali
(Mount McKinley)
6,190 m (20,310 ft)

ALASKA
(USA)

YUKON

NUNAVUT

Great
Bear
Lake

NORTHWEST
TERRITORIES

Great
Slave
Lake

Gulf of
Alaska

Haida
Gwaii

BRITISH
COLUMBIA

Rocky Mountains

ALBERTA

SASKATCHEWAN

MANITOBA

CANA

Lake
Winnipeg

HAWAII
(USA)

Hawaiian Islands

N

O'ahu

Hawai'i

0   100 km
0   100 miles
(approximate scale)

Vancouver
Island

WASHINGTON

OREGON   IDAHO

Missouri

MONTANA

NORTH DAKOTA

SOUTH DAKOTA

WYOMING

NEBRASKA

UNITED

COLORADO   KANSAS

OF AM

NEVADA   UTAH

CALIFORNIA

ARIZONA   NEW MEXICO

Baja California

MEXICO

NORTH
AMERICA

PACIFIC OCEAN

Greenland
(to Denmark)

Denmark Strait

Davis Strait

sland

Labrador Sea

ATLANTIC

OCEAN

NEWFOUNDLAND
AND LABRADOR

Hudson Bay

QUÉBEC

St Pierre & Miquelon
(to France)

PRINCE EDWARD ISLAND

NEW BRUNSWICK

NOVA SCOTIA

MAINE

ONTARIO

NEW HAMPSHIRE

VERMONT

MASSACHUSETTS
RHODE ISLAND
CONNECTICUT

Lake Superior

Lake Huron

Lake Ontario

NEW YORK

NEW JERSEY

MICHIGAN

Lake Erie

PENNSYLVANIA

DELAWARE

WISCONSIN

Lake Michigan

MARYLAND

N

0   500 km

0   500 miles

(approximate scale)

NESOTA

IOWA

ILLINOIS

INDIANA

OHIO

Ohio

WEST
VIRGINIA

VIRGINIA

TATES

MISSOURI

KENTUCKY

NORTH CAROLINA

RICA

Mississippi

TENNESSEE

SOUTH
CAROLINA

Anguilla
(to UK)

LAHOMA

ARKANSAS

ALABAMA

GEORGIA

British Virgin
Islands
(to UK)

ST KITTS & NEVIS

ANTIGUA & BARBUDA

Montserrat (to UK)

LOUISIANA

Virgin Islands
(to USA)

Guadeloupe (to France)

EXAS

MISSISSIPPI

FLORIDA

THE
BAHAMAS

Turks & Caicos
Islands
(to UK)

Puerto
Rico
(to USA)

DOMINICA

Martinique (to France)

DOMINICAN
REPUBLIC

ST LUCIA

BARBADOS

*Gulf of
Mexico*

CUBA

HAITI

GRENADA

ST VINCENT &
THE GRENADINES

TRINIDAD &
TOBAGO

JAMAICA

Navassa Island
(to USA)

Curaçao
(Neth.)

Bonaire
(to Neth.)

Cayman Islands
(to UK)

Guantanamo
Bay
(to USA)

Aruba
(Neth.)

Grande

*Caribbean
Sea*

SOUTH AMERICA

BELIZE

HONDURAS

GUATEMALA

NICARAGUA

PANAMA

EL SALVADOR

COSTA
RICA

Canada

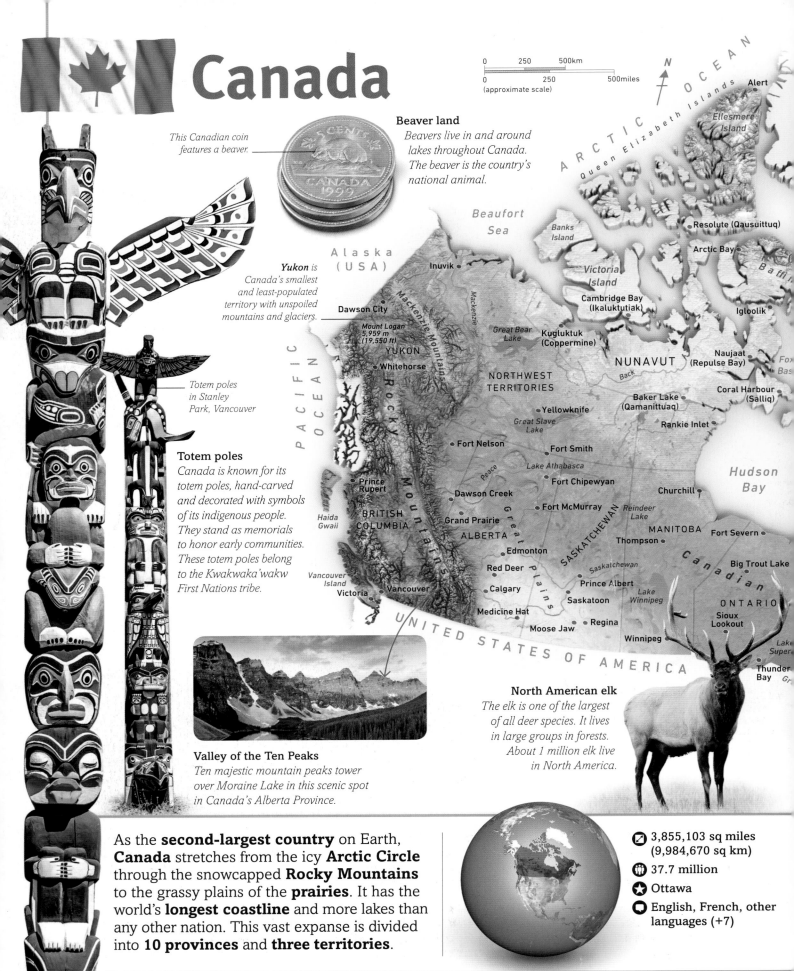

0   250   500km
0   250   500miles
(approximate scale)

This Canadian coin features a beaver.

Beaver land
Beavers live in and around lakes throughout Canada. The beaver is the country's national animal.

Yukon is Canada's smallest and least-populated territory with unspoiled mountains and glaciers.

Totem poles in Stanley Park, Vancouver

Totem poles
Canada is known for its totem poles, hand-carved and decorated with symbols of its indigenous people. They stand as memorials to honor early communities. These totem poles belong to the Kwakwaka'wakw First Nations tribe.

Valley of the Ten Peaks
Ten majestic mountain peaks tower over Moraine Lake in this scenic spot in Canada's Alberta Province.

North American elk
The elk is one of the largest of all deer species. It lives in large groups in forests. About 1 million elk live in North America.

Map labels

ARCTIC OCEAN
Queen Elizabeth Islands
Ellesmere Island
Alert
Resolute (Qausuittuq)
Arctic Bay
Baffin
Beaufort Sea
Banks Island
Victoria Island
Cambridge Bay (Ikaluktutiak)
Igloolik
Alaska (USA)
Inuvik
Mackenzie Mountains
Mackenzie
Great Bear Lake
Kugluktuk (Coppermine)
NUNAVUT
Naujaat (Repulse Bay)
Fox Bas
Dawson City
Mount Logan 5,959 m (19,550 ft)
YUKON
Whitehorse
NORTHWEST TERRITORIES
Back
Coral Harbour (Salliq)
Yellowknife
Great Slave Lake
Baker Lake (Qamanittuaq)
PACIFIC OCEAN
Fort Nelson
Fort Smith
Rankie Inlet
Lake Athabasca
Hudson Bay
Prince Rupert
Dawson Creek
Peace
Fort Chipewyan
Churchill
Haida Gwaii
BRITISH COLUMBIA
Grand Prairie
Fort McMurray
Reindeer Lake
Great Plains
ALBERTA
SASKATCHEWAN
MANITOBA
Fort Severn
Thompson
Edmonton
Canadian
Vancouver Island
Red Deer
Saskatchewan
Big Trout Lake
Vancouver
Calgary
Prince Albert
Lake Winnipeg
ONTARIO
Victoria
Medicine Hat
Saskatoon
Sioux Lookout
Moose Jaw
Regina
Lake Super
Winnipeg
Thunder Bay
UNITED STATES OF AMERICA
Gr

As the **second-largest country** on Earth, **Canada** stretches from the icy **Arctic Circle** through the snowcapped **Rocky Mountains** to the grassy plains of the **prairies**. It has the world's **longest coastline** and more lakes than any other nation. This vast expanse is divided into **10 provinces** and **three territories**.

- 3,855,103 sq miles (9,984,670 sq km)
- 37.7 million
- Ottawa
- English, French, other languages (+7)

Maple leaf
Maple trees grow across Canada. The country produces 75 percent of the world's maple syrup, made from the tree sap. A maple leaf can be seen on the Canadian national flag.

Inuit people
The indigenous inhabitants of northern Canada, the Inuit are well adapted to the cold. They often use a sled, called a qamutiik, to travel on snow.

Ice hockey
Canada's most popular sport is ice hockey. With 20 Olympic medals—13 of them gold—Canada is the most successful nation in this sport.

Niagara Falls
With a drop of 167 ft (51 m), this group of three majestic waterfalls is located at the borders of Canada and the US. About 30 million tourists visit Niagara Falls every year.

Baffin Bay

Davis Strait

Iqaluit (Frobisher Bay)

Cape Dorset

Hudson Strait

Ivujivik

Labrador Sea

Labrador

Nain

Kuujjuaq

Cartwright

NEWFOUNDLAND & LABRADOR

Goose Bay

St. Anthony

Churchill Falls

Kuujjuaq (Poste-de-la-Baleine)

Labrador

Gander
Newfoundland

St. Johns'

Laurentian Mountains

Kuujjuarapik (Poste-de-la-Baleine)

ukjuak ort arrison)

QUÉBEC Shield

Stephenville

Eastmain

ames Bay

Sept-Îles

Gulf of St. Lawrence

St. Lawrence

PRINCE EDWARD ISLAND

Moose Factory

NEW BRUNSWICK
Charlottetown

Timmins

Val d'Or

Québec

Fredericton

Moncton

Halifax

NOVA SCOTIA

ATLANTIC OCEAN

awa

Cobalt

Victoriaville

Montréal

udbury

OTTAWA

Lake Huron

Lake Ontario

Québec Province is the largest Canadian province and is home to most French speakers in Canada.

Toronto

Hamilton

London

Niagara Falls

CN Tower stands 1,814 ft (553 m) tall and has an observation deck overlooking Toronto.

Poutine
This dish of french fries covered in cheese curds and gravy started out in Québec Province and is now served throughout the country.

Toronto towers
Canada's largest city sits on the banks of Lake Ontario with a stunning backdrop of high-rise buildings and skyscrapers.

Geography: One-third is **frozen land** inside the Arctic Circle. Southern Canada has **mountains, grasslands, forests,** and **lakes.**

History: Canada was **officially founded** in 1867, although the **Inuit people** have inhabited it for about 5,000 years.

Culture: Despite the **cold climate,** Canadians love being in the great **outdoors, playing sports,** and going **hiking.**

Natural wonders: From the breathtaking **Rocky Mountains** to the dramatic **Niagara Falls,** Canada has spectacular scenery.

Wildlife: Canada is home to **brown bears, polar bears, seals, caribou, wolves, wolverines, elk,** and **whales.**

Food and drink: Most Canadians enjoy a **typical Western diet** of beef, chicken, fish, dairy products, and vegetables.

United States of America

Grizzly bear
The northwestern part of the US is known for wild populations of grizzly bears. They hunt salmon that are swimming upriver.

Hawaii
Located in the Pacific Ocean, the state of Hawaii is made up of 137 volcanic islands.

Ni'ihau • Kaua'i • Lihu'e
PACIFIC OCEAN
O'ahu
Honolulu
Moloka'i • Kahului
Mauna Kea • Maui
4,207 m (13,803 ft)
Hawai'i • Hilo

0 — 200 km
0 — 200 miles
(approximate scale)

Exploring space
The American company SpaceX has designed reusable rockets that make sending cargo and people into space more affordable. The Falcon 9 rocket launched astronauts voyaging to the International Space Station (ISS) in 2020.

Ukulele
This stringed instrument from Hawaii can play many styles of music, including jazz.

CANADA

PACIFIC OCEAN

Seattle • Spokane • Great Falls — Missouri River — Minot
Olympia • WASHINGTON — MONTANA — NORTH DAKO
Portland — Columbia River — Helena — Bismarck
Salem — Billings — SOUTH DAKO
Eugene — OREGON — IDAHO — Rapid City — Pierr
Boise — Snake River — Casper — Mount — NEBRASK
Twin Falls — WYOMING — Rushmore
Great — Salt Lake — Cheyenne
Reno • Elko — City — Denver
Sacramento — NEVADA — Great — UTAH — Colorado Sprin
San Francisco — Salt Lake — COLORADO — Pueblo
San Jose — Mount Whitney — Grand Canyon
Fresno — 4,421m — Amarillo
(14,505 ft) — Las Vegas
CALIFORNIA — Albuquerque • Santa Fe — Lubbock
San Bernardino — ARIZONA — NEW MEXICO — Roswell
Los Angeles — Phoenix
San Diego — Tucson — El Paso

Rocky Mountains
Cascade Range
Coast Ranges
Sierra Nevada Ranges
Colorado River
Great Basin
Great Plains

MEXICO

N

Football
Played since the 1880s, this fast-paced team game is now the most popular sport in the country.

D. CHESSER 44

RAMS 26

Iconic landmark
This famous sign overlooks Hollywood, the neighborhood in Los Angeles that is the center of the American film industry.

The **United States of America**, or **US**, stretches between the east and west coasts of the North American continent. Its **50 states** have a diverse range of **peoples**, **landscapes**, and **cultures**. The nation's **entertainment industry** and the **technology sector's** innovative products are popular around the world.

⬈ 3,796,742 sq miles
(9,833,517 sq km)

👥 332.6 million

★ Washington, DC

🗩 English, Spanish, other languages (+9)

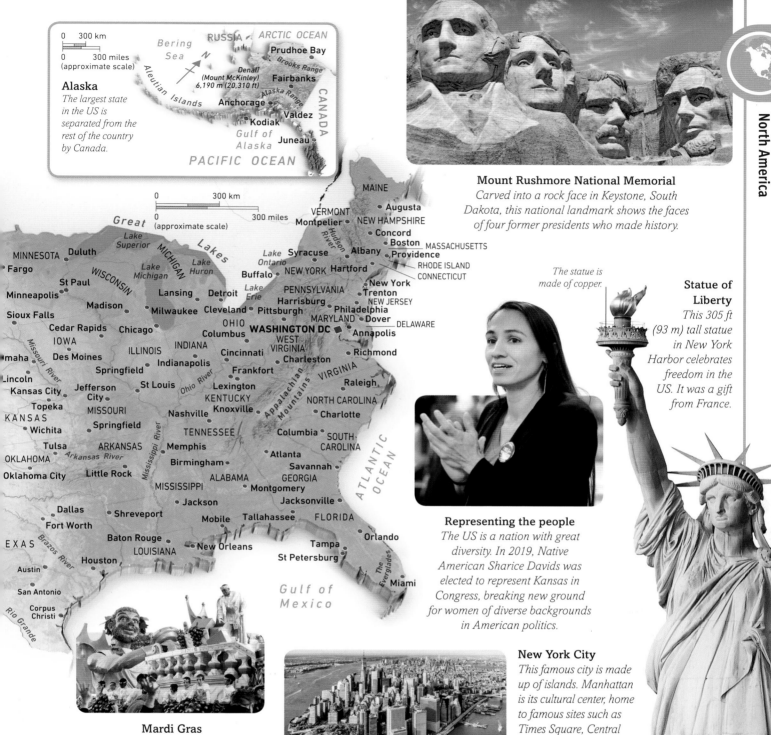

Alaska

Alaska
The largest state in the US is separated from the rest of the country by Canada.

0 300 km
0 300 miles
(approximate scale)

RUSSIA ARCTIC OCEAN
Bering Sea
Prudhoe Bay
Brooks Range
Denali (Mount McKinley) 6,190 m (20,310 ft)
Fairbanks
Alaska Range
Anchorage
CANADA
Valdez
Kodiak
Gulf of Alaska
Juneau
Aleutian Islands
PACIFIC OCEAN

Mount Rushmore National Memorial
Carved into a rock face in Keystone, South Dakota, this national landmark shows the faces of four former presidents who made history.

0 300 km
0 300 miles
(approximate scale)

Great Lakes
MINNESOTA Duluth
Fargo
Lake Superior
MICHIGAN
Lake Michigan
Lake Huron
WISCONSIN
Minneapolis St Paul
Madison
Sioux Falls
Cedar Rapids
Chicago
IOWA
Des Moines
maha
Omaha
Lincoln
Kansas City
Topeka
KANSAS
Wichita
Tulsa
OKLAHMA
OKLAHOMA
Oklahoma City
Dallas Shreveport
Fort Worth
EXAS
TEXAS
Brazos River
Austin
Houston
San Antonio
Corpus Christi
Rio Grande
Lake Ontario
Syracuse
Buffalo
Lansing Detroit
Lake Erie
Milwaukee Cleveland
OHIO
Columbus
ILLINOIS INDIANA
Springfield
Indianapolis
Cincinnati
St Louis
Frankfort
Ohio River
Lexington
KENTUCKY
Nashville Knoxville
TENNESSEE
Memphis
Springfield
ARKANSAS
Arkansas River
Little Rock
Birmingham
ALABAMA
MISSISSIPPI
Jackson
Mobile
Montgomery
Baton Rouge
LOUISIANA
New Orleans
Mississippi River
Missouri River
Jefferson City
MISSOURI
MAINE
Augusta
VERMONT NEW HAMPSHIRE
Montpelier Concord
Hudson River
Boston MASSACHUSETTS
Albany Providence
Hartford RHODE ISLAND
NEW YORK CONNECTICUT
New York
PENNSYLVANIA Trenton
Harrisburg NEW JERSEY
Philadelphia
Pittsburgh MARYLAND Dover
WASHINGTON DC DELAWARE
WEST VIRGINIA Annapolis
Charleston Richmond
VIRGINIA
Raleigh
NORTH CAROLINA
Charlotte
Columbia
SOUTH CAROLINA
Atlanta
Savannah
GEORGIA
Jacksonville
Tallahassee
FLORIDA
Orlando
Tampa
St Petersburg
The Everglades
Miami
ATLANTIC OCEAN
Gulf of Mexico

Representing the people
The US is a nation with great diversity. In 2019, Native American Sharice Davids was elected to represent Kansas in Congress, breaking new ground for women of diverse backgrounds in American politics.

The statue is made of copper.

Statue of Liberty
This 305 ft (93 m) tall statue in New York Harbor celebrates freedom in the US. It was a gift from France.

New York City
This famous city is made up of islands. Manhattan is its cultural center, home to famous sites such as Times Square, Central Park, and the Empire State Building.

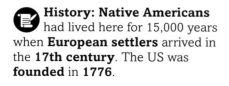

Mardi Gras
The Mardi Gras in New Orleans, the biggest carnival in the US, features colorful floats and parades.

Geography: The **Rocky Mountains** dominate the west, rising out of the **Great Plains**.

History: Native Americans had lived here for 15,000 years when **European settlers** arrived in the **17th century**. The US was **founded** in 1776.

Culture: This **multicultural country** celebrates many traditions, including **Thanksgiving** and **Halloween**.

Natural wonders: The **Grand Canyon** in Arizona and the **Florida Everglades** are examples of the country's natural beauty.

Wildlife: Coyotes, **cougars**, **bears**, **bison**, and **moose** are native to the US.

Food and drink: The US is famous for **fast foods** such as **burgers** and **hot dogs**.

Mexico

Monarch migration
Every year, millions of monarch butterflies travel more than 3,000 miles (4,800 km) from the US to Mexico.

Day of the Dead
In this annual festival, families and friends remember loved ones who have died. Altars, prayers, and parades with elaborate costumes and makeup mark the occasion.

This tiny dog breed is only 6–9 in (15–23 cm) high.

Chihuahua
The ancestor of this small dog was first bred in Mexico. It takes its name from the Mexican state of Chihuahua.

Map labels: Tijuana, Ensenada, Mexicali, Nogales, UNITED STATES OF AMERICA, Isla Guadalupe, Isla Cedros, Ciudad Juárez, Hermosillo, Chihuahua, Gulf of California, Lower California, Sierra Madre Occidental, Rio Conchos, Rio Grande, San Ignacio, Guaymas, Nuevo Laredo, Los Mochis, Gómez Palacio, Monterrey, Torreón, Matamoros, Culiacán, Durango, Laguna Madre, La Paz, Mazatlán, Zacatecas, San Luis Potosí, Ciudad Victoria, San Lucas Cape, Islas Tres Marías, Aguascalientes, Tepic, León, Ciudad Madero, Puerto Vallarta, Guadalajara, Querétaro, Lago de Chapala, Pico de Orizaba 5,636 m (18,491 ft), Isla Roca Partida, Isla San Benedicto, Isla Socorro, Colima, Manzanillo, Toluca, MEXICO CITY, Puebla, Verac, Sierra Madre Oriental, Oaxaca, Acapulco, Sierra Madre del Su, PACIFIC OCEAN

0 250 km
0 250 miles
(approximate scale)

Guatemala

Rigoberta Menchú
The human rights activist Rigoberta Menchú has focused on improving the lives of indigenous people and won the Nobel Peace Prize for her achievements in 1992.

Guatemala City
The country's capital sits almost 4,920 ft (1,500 m) above sea level. At the center of this ancient city lies the cathedral, which has survived many earthquakes.

Mayan pottery
The Maya are remembered for their pottery and ceramics, some of which are elaborately decorated.

Map labels: MEXICO, Lago Petén Itza, La Libertad, Flores, BELIZE, San Luis, Caribbean Sea, Volcán Tajumulco 4,220 m (13,850 ft), Huehuetenango, Cobán, Livingston, PACIFIC OCEAN, Quetzaltenango, Santa Cruz del Quiché, Salamá, Lago de Izabal, Puerto Barrios, Chimaltenango, GUATEMALA CITY, Zacapa, HONDURAS, Champerico, Chiquimula, Escuintla, Jutiapa, EL SALVADOR, San José

0 50 km
0 50 miles
(approximate scale)

- ⊘ 42,042 sq miles (108,889 sq km)
- 👥 17.2 million
- ★ Guatemala City
- ◯ Quiché, Mam, other languages (+3)

The **Central American nation** of **Guatemala** is located south of Mexico. It is known for its **volcanoes** and **rain forests** and for the **remains** of the ancient **Mayan civilization** that can still be found there.

Market shopping
Across Mexico, the best way to shop for everyday items, from fruit and vegetables to clothes, is at the local market.

Frida Kahlo
The 20th-century Mexican painter Frida Kahlo was known for her many self-portraits and works based on Mexican culture.

Tacos
A popular food is the traditional taco, a tortilla filled with spicy meat and veggies.

Chichén Itzá
At the center of the ancient Mayan city of Chichén Itzá is the Temple of Kukulcan, a monumental step pyramid.

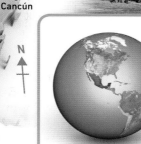

Gulf of Mexico

Yucatan Channel

Mérida

Chichén-Itzá

Cancún

Campeche

Yucatan Peninsula

Bay of Campeche

Carmen

Minatitlán

Chetumal

Villahermosa

BELIZE

Tuxtla

Comitán

GUATEMALA

Tapachula

N

- 758,449 sq miles (1,964,375 sq km)
- 128.6 million
- Mexico City
- Spanish, other languages (+8)

Mexico is the **third-largest country** in **North America**. Many **ancient civilizations** established cities here. Now tourists come to visit their **ruins** as well as the country's **magnificent beaches**.

Black orchid
The national flower of Belize is the black orchid. Native to Central America, this species thrives in tropical jungles and swamplands.

N

MEXICO

Corozal

Orange Walk

San Pedro

Doyle's Delight 1,124 m (3,688 ft)

BELMOPAN

Belize City

Turneffe Islands

San Ignacio

Great Blue Hole
Measuring 984 ft (300 m) wide and 407 ft (124 m) deep, this huge marine sinkhole on the Belize Barrier Reef is popular with divers.

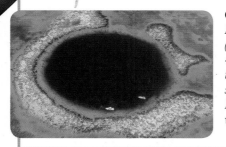

GUATEMALA

Maya Mountains

Dangriga

Punta Gorda

Barrier Reef

Caribbean Sea

0   50 km
0   50 miles
(approximate scale)

Belize

Garifuna Settlement Day
Celebrated on November 19, this public holiday marks the arrival of the Afro-Caribbean Garifuna people in Belize on this date in 1832. People parade through the streets, making music and dancing.

Lying on the **Caribbean Sea**, Belize is a small country on the eastern coast of **Central America**. It has **dense tropical forests** and a **coral barrier reef** nearly 186 miles (300 km) long.

- 8,867 sq miles (22,966 sq km)
- 399,600
- Belmopan
- English Creole, Spanish, other languages (+3)

El Salvador

Monumento al Divino Salvador del Mundo
This statue of Jesus Christ has stood in San Salvador since 1942.

Shelled swimmer
The world's largest turtle, the leatherback, is found off the coast of the country. It is named after the texture of its shell.

0   20 km
0   20 miles
(approximate scale)

Volcán de Santa Ana 2,381 m (7,812 ft)

GUATEMALA

HONDURAS

Santa Ana • Chalatenango
Ahuachapán •
SAN SALVADOR
Sonsonate • • Sensuntepeque
• Cojutepeque
Lake Ilopango • San Vicente • San Francisco Gotera
La Libertad • Zacatecoluca
• San Miguel
Usulután • La Unión

P A C I F I C   O C E A N

Gulf of Fonseca

Xuc dance
Originally created to celebrate sugar cane harvests, this lively folk dance is now performed at carnivals.

- 8,124 sq miles (21,041 sq km)
- 6.5 million
- San Salvador
- Spanish

This tiny country is the **most densely populated** in Central America, with most **people living around the central lakes**. It has **more than 20 active volcanoes** and often experiences **earthquakes**.

Honduras

GUATEMALA

Gulf of Honduras

Bay Islands
Roatán

• Puerto Cortés
• Tela • La Ceiba
San Pedro Sula • • Trujillo
Río Aguán
Santa Rosa de Copán • • Yoro
Cerro Las Minas 2,870 m (9,420 ft)
Brus Laguna
Nueva Ocotepeque •
Comayagua
• Juticalpa
La Esperanza • • La Paz
Río Patuca
Puerto Lempira
TEGUCIGALPA
• Yuscarán

EL SALVADOR

• Choluteca

NICARAGUA

Caribbean Sea

0   100 km
0   100 miles
(approximate scale)

Swan Islands

Scarlet macaw
The national bird of Honduras is the scarlet macaw, one of the world's largest parrots.

Ruins of Copán
Among the ruins are intricate stone carvings. This one shows the city's 13th ruler.

Growing bananas
Bananas have been a major export since the late 19th century, but some banana crops are destroyed by seasonal hurricanes.

- 43,278 sq miles (112,090 sq km)
- 9.2 million
- Tegucigalpa
- Spanish, other languages (+2)

Honduras sits between the **Caribbean Sea** to the north and the **Pacific Ocean** to the south. To the west of the country lie the **ruins** of the ancient **Mayan city** of **Copán**, which dates back to the **5th century**.

Costa Rica

High and low
Slow-moving sloths live high in the treetops of Costa Rica, while beetles and other bugs scurry around the forest floor.

Costa Rica is rich in **animal life**—more than **half a million species** live in the nation's **cloud forests**, **rain forests**, **mangrove swamps**, **arid plains**, and **tropical waters**. **Wildlife** is **protected** in one-third of the country.

- 19,730 sq miles (51,100 sq km)
- 5 million
- San José
- Spanish, other languages (+3)

Boruca people
An indigenous Costa Rican tribe, the Boruca people are known for their skilled carving of traditional wooden devil masks.

Map labels: NICARAGUA, La Cruz, Los Chiles, Liberia, Santa Cruz, Canas, Quesada, Cordillera, Puntarenas, Alajuela, SAN JOSÉ, Cartago, Limón, Central, Caribbean Sea, Cordillera de Talamanca, Quepos, Bribri, Cerro Chirripó 3,821 m (12,536 ft), Cortes, Drake, Golfito, PANAMA, PACIFIC OCEAN

Scale: 0 — 50 km / 0 — 50 miles (approximate scale)

Nicaragua

Ometepe Island
The largest island in Lake Nicaragua, Ometepe has two volcanoes, one of which towers over the surrounding waters.

Dennis Martínez
One of Nicaragua's best-known athletes is Dennis Martínez, a pitcher in Major League Baseball from the 1970s to 1990s.

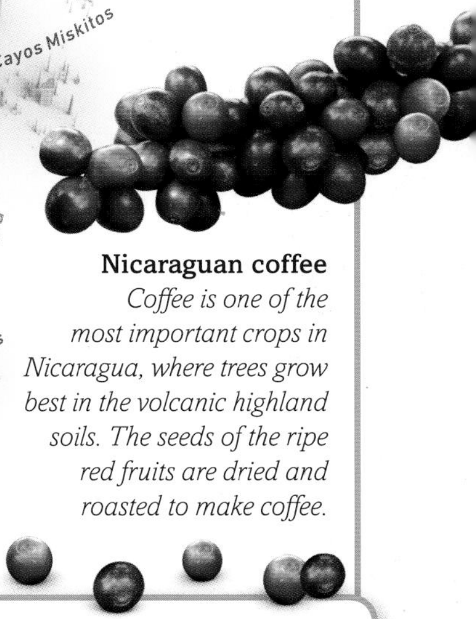

Map labels: HONDURAS, Mogotón 2,085 m (6,841 ft), Cayos Miskitos, Ocotal, Somoto, Puerto Cabezas, Cordillera Isabella, Potosí, Esteli, Jinotega, Chinandega, Matagalpa, Río Grande de Matagalpa, León, Mosquito Coast, Caribbean Sea, Boaco, Lake Managua, MANAGUA, Juigalpa, Río Escondido, Jinotepe, Granada, Corn Islands, Rivas, Bluefields, Lake Nicaragua, San Juan del Sur, San Carlos, COSTA RICA, Río San Juan, PACIFIC OCEAN

Scale: 0 — 50 km / 0 — 50 miles (approximate scale)

Nicaraguan coffee
Coffee is one of the most important crops in Nicaragua, where trees grow best in the volcanic highland soils. The seeds of the ripe red fruits are dried and roasted to make coffee.

- 50,336 sq miles (130,370 sq km)
- 6.2 million
- Managua
- Spanish, other languages (+2)

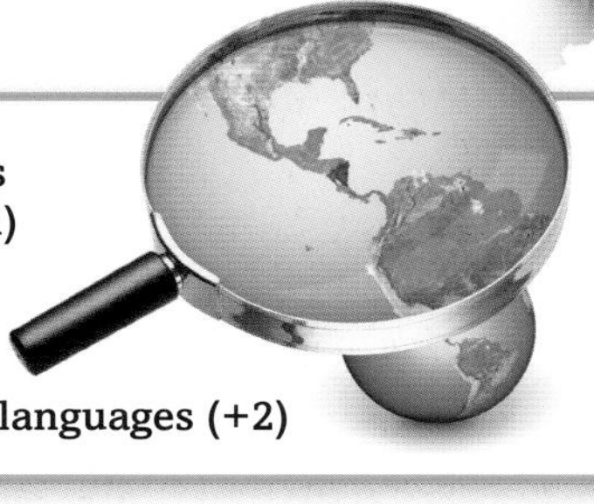

This Central American country has a **dramatic landscape** of **volcanoes** and **lakes**. **Lake Nicaragua**, which covers more than 3,000 sq miles (8,000 sq km), is the **largest**.

Panama

The blue and red represent the country's two main political parties.

About 14,000 ships pass through the canal every year.

Ocean shortcut
The Panama Canal opened in 1914. Some 50 miles (82 km) long, it allows shipping to avoid the lengthy and dangerous journey around South America.

Festive clothing
Girls in Panama are given their first *pollera* dress at the age of 16. Worn at festivals and celebrations, this decorative dress has colorful embroidery.

Map labels: COSTA RICA, Volcán Barú 3,475 m (11,401 ft), Almirante, Puerto Armuelles, David, Cordillera Central, Colón, Panama Canal, Lake Gatún, San Miguelito, PANAMA CITY, Aligandí, Serranía del Darien, Gulf of Darien, ATLANTIC OCEAN, PACIFIC OCEAN, Santiago, Penonomé, Chitré, Las Tablas, Península de Azuero, Gulf of Panama, Garachiné, El Real, COLOMBIA

0 100 km
0 100 miles
(approximate scale)

- 29,120 sq miles (75,420 sq km)
- 3.9 million
- Panama City
- English Creole, other languages (+3)

Known as the "**Crossroads of the Americas**," Panama lies on the **strip of land** linking **Central** and **South America**. An **artificial waterway** cuts across the country, linking the **Pacific** and **Atlantic oceans**.

Cuba

Colorful snail
Polymita snails are found only in the forests of Cuba.

The star symbolizes Cuba's independence from Spain in 1898 and the US in 1902.

Cuban capital
Havana is the biggest city in the Caribbean and a major port. The historic old town is very popular with tourists.

Map labels: Pinar del Río, Artemisa, HAVANA (LA HABANA), Matanzas, Cárdenas, Península de Zapata, Yucatan Channel, Nueva Gerona, Isla de la Juventud, Co...

Colorful houses with crumbling facades are common in Havana's older quarters.

Vintage cars
For years the import of cars to Cuba was banned. Many on the streets are vintage American cars, used as taxis.

Cuba is the **largest island** in the **Caribbean Sea**. It is also one of the few **socialist republics** in the world. **Tourism** and **agriculture** are its main industries, and **sugar**, **tobacco**, and **citrus fruits** are some of its **major exports**.

- 42,803 sq miles (110,860 sq km)
- 11.1 million
- Havana
- Spanish

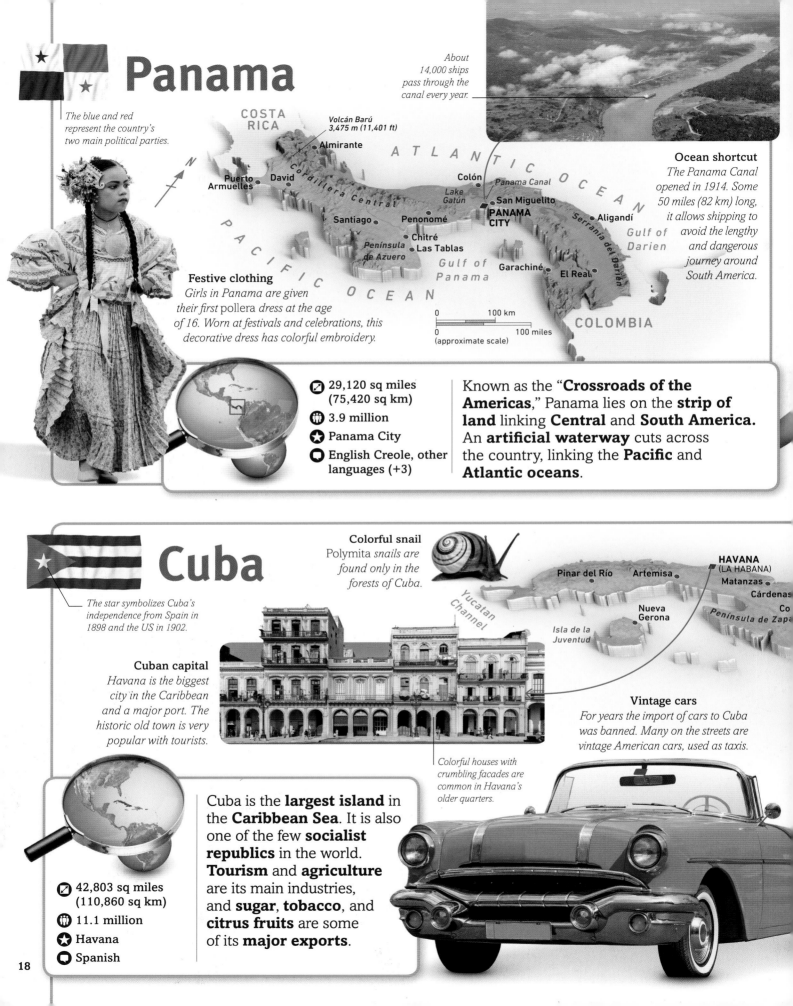

The Bahamas

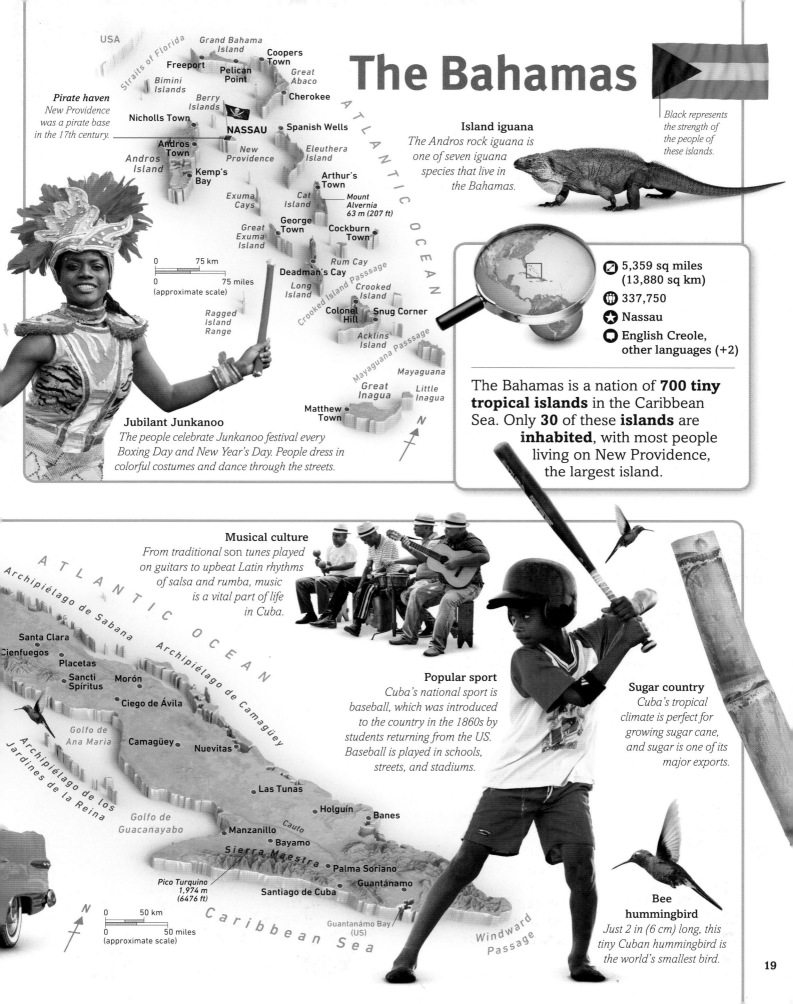

Black represents the strength of the people of these islands.

USA

Straits of Florida

Grand Bahama Island

Coopers Town

Freepor t

Pelican Point

Great Abaco

Bimini Islands

Berry Islands

Cherokee

Nicholls Town

NASSAU

Spanish Wells

ATLANTIC OCEAN

Andros Town

New Providence

Eleuthera Island

Andros Island

Kemp's Bay

Arthur's Town

Exuma Cays

Cat Island

Mount Alvernia 63 m (207 ft)

George Town

Cockburn Town

Great Exuma Island

Rum Cay

Deadman's Cay

Crooked Island Passsage

Long Island

Crooked Island

Ragged Island Range

Colonel Hill

Snug Corner

Acklins Island

Mayaguana Passsage

Mayaguana

Great Inagua

Little Inagua

Matthew Town

N

0 ——— 75 km
0 ——— 75 miles
(approximate scale)

Pirate haven
New Providence was a pirate base in the 17th century.

Jubilant Junkanoo
The people celebrate Junkanoo festival every Boxing Day and New Year's Day. People dress in colorful costumes and dance through the streets.

Island iguana
The Andros rock iguana is one of seven iguana species that live in the Bahamas.

- 5,359 sq miles (13,880 sq km)
- 337,750
- Nassau
- English Creole, other languages (+2)

The Bahamas is a nation of **700 tiny tropical islands** in the Caribbean Sea. Only **30** of these **islands** are **inhabited**, with most people living on New Providence, the largest island.

Musical culture
From traditional son tunes played on guitars to upbeat Latin rhythms of salsa and rumba, music is a vital part of life in Cuba.

ATLANTIC OCEAN

Archipiélago de Sabana

Archipiélago de Camagüey

Santa Clara

Cienfuegos

Placetas

Sancti Spíritus

Morón

Ciego de Ávila

Golfo de Ana Maria

Camagüey

Nuevitas

Archipiélago de los Jardines de la Reina

Las Tunas

Golfo de Guacanayabo

Holguín

Banes

Manzanillo

Cauto

Bayamo

Sierra Maestra

Palma Soriano

Pico Turquino 1,974 m (6476 ft)

Santiago de Cuba

Guantánamo

N

0 ——— 50 km
0 ——— 50 miles
(approximate scale)

Caribbean Sea

Guantánamo Bay (US)

Windward Passage

Popular sport
Cuba's national sport is baseball, which was introduced to the country in the 1860s by students returning from the US. Baseball is played in schools, streets, and stadiums.

Sugar country
Cuba's tropical climate is perfect for growing sugar cane, and sugar is one of its major exports.

Bee hummingbird
Just 2 in (6 cm) long, this tiny Cuban hummingbird is the world's smallest bird.

Jamaica

Caribbean Sea

Montego Bay • Montego Bay • Falmouth
Lucea • • • • St Ann's Bay
The Cockpit Country · Dry Harbour Mountains
Savanna-la-Mar •
Christiana •
Bluefields Bay · Mocho Mountains
Black River · Mandeville •
Black River • • May Pen
Old Harbour •
Caribbean Sea · Long Bay

N 0 — 20 km
0 — 20 miles
(approximate scale)

Jerk chicken
A favorite dish in Jamaica is this grilled chicken, which is marinated in a hot spice mix for a fiery flavor.

Marley is depicted here on the walls of the Bob Marley Museum in Kingston.

Birthplace of reggae
Reggae is a slow, rhythmic style of music that was born in Jamaica in the 1960s and quickly became popular worldwide. One of its best-known stars was singer and songwriter Bob Marley.

Super sprinter
Known as the "Lightning Bolt," the Jamaican sprinter Usain Bolt is the fastest man on Earth. He holds the 100 m world record with a time of 9.58 seconds.

Haiti

0 — 50 km
0 — 50 miles
(approximate scale)

ATLANTIC OCEAN
Île de la Tortue
Port-de-Paix •
Cap-Haïtien •
Gonaïves •
Fort-Liberté •
St-Marc •
Montrouis • Hinche •
N
Jérémie • Grande Cayemite Île de la Gonâve
Canal de St-Marc
Canal de la Gonâve
Massif de la Hotte
Cayes • **PORT-AU-PRINCE**
Port-Salut •
Jacmel •
Île-à-Vache
Caribbean Sea
Pic de la Selle 2,680 m (8,790 ft)
DOMINICAN REPUBLIC

Tap tap bus
Eye-catching painted buses called tap taps provide a taxi service for commuters in Port-au-Prince.

Citadelle Laferrière
This imposing fortress was built on Haiti's northern coast in the 19th century to protect the newly independent country against French invasion.

- ⤢ 10,714 sq miles (27,750 sq km)
- 👥 11.1 million
- ★ Port-au-Prince
- ⬤ French Creole, French

The Republic of Haiti occupies the **western third** of the **island of Hispaniola**. Once a French colony, it **gained independence** in **1804**. Devastated by an **earthquake** that struck close to the capital, **Port-au-Prince**, in 2010, this mountainous country is still recovering.

Blue mountains

Clouds of mist hang over Jamaica's longest mountain range. The plantations here produce some of the finest coffee in the world.

*The capital city of **Kingston** is surrounded by mountains on three sides.*

Blue Mountain Peak
2,256 m (7,402 ft)

Port Maria
Annotto Bay
warton
Port Antonio
Spanish Town
KINGSTON
Morant Bay
Portland Bight
Jamaica Channel
Magno
Blue Mountains

Jamaican roselle

Known for its health benefits, this flower is used to make sauces, salads, and herbal teas.

Girls' education

In the past, many Jamaican girls did not get an education, but now most girls go to school and more than a third enroll in college.

Caribbean hermit crab

These land crabs protect their soft bodies with the empty shells of other animals.

- 4,244 sq miles (10,991 sq km)
- 2.8 million
- Kingston
- English Creole, English

Jamaica is the **third-largest island** in the Caribbean, 146 miles (234 km) long and up to 50 miles (80 km) wide. With **beautiful beaches**, tourism is its main industry.

Dominican Republic

Dominican Carnival

February is a time for celebration in the Dominican Republic. The annual carnival sees colorful parades and performances that reflect local traditions.

Monte Cristi
Puerto Plata
Esperanza
Bisonó
Santiago
Dajabón
Samaná
Pico Duarte
3,098 m (10,164 ft)
La Vega
San Francisco de Macorís
HAITI
Cordillera Central
Río Yuna
Sabana de la Mar
Bonao
Pedro Santana
El Seibo
SANTO DOMINGO
Comendador
San Pedro de Macorís
La Romana
Higüey
Boca de Yuma
Jimani
Lake Enriquillo
Neiba
Baní
Barahona
Pedernales
Isla Saona
Caribbean Sea
N
Isla Beata

ATLANTIC OCEAN

0   50 km
0   50 miles
(approximate scale)

El Limón Waterfall

Surrounded by tropical rain forest, the El Limón near Samaná cascades more than 164 ft (50 m) to a pool popular with swimmers.

The Dominican Republic makes up the **eastern part** of **Hispaniola island**. This country has the **Caribbean's tallest mountain—Pico Duarte**—and its **lowest point, Lake Enriquillo**.

- 18,792 sq miles (48,670 sq km)
- 10.5 million
- Santo Domingo
- Spanish, French Creole

St. Kitts and Nevis

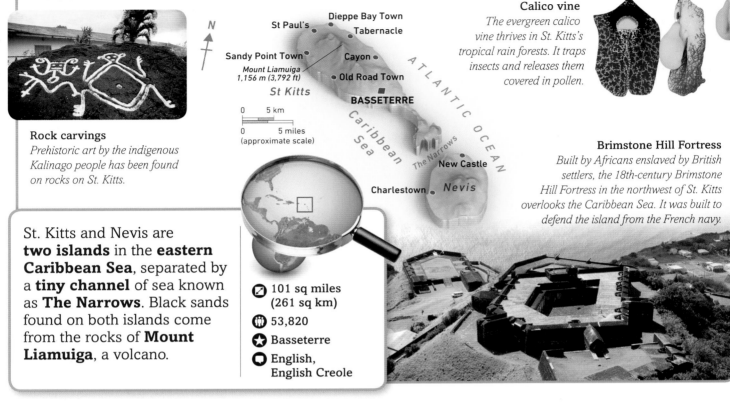

Rock carvings
Prehistoric art by the indigenous Kalinago people has been found on rocks on St. Kitts.

Calico vine
The evergreen calico vine thrives in St. Kitts's tropical rain forests. It traps insects and releases them covered in pollen.

St Paul's
Dieppe Bay Town
Tabernacle
Sandy Point Town
Cayon
Mount Liamuiga 1,156 m (3,792 ft)
Old Road Town
St Kitts
BASSETERRE
0   5 km
0   5 miles
(approximate scale)
ATLANTIC OCEAN
Caribbean Sea
The Narrows
New Castle
Charlestown
Nevis

Brimstone Hill Fortress
Built by Africans enslaved by British settlers, the 18th-century Brimstone Hill Fortress in the northwest of St. Kitts overlooks the Caribbean Sea. It was built to defend the island from the French navy.

St. Kitts and Nevis are **two islands** in the **eastern Caribbean Sea**, separated by a **tiny channel** of sea known as **The Narrows**. Black sands found on both islands come from the rocks of **Mount Liamuiga**, a volcano.

- 101 sq miles (261 sq km)
- 53,820
- Basseterre
- English, English Creole

Dominica

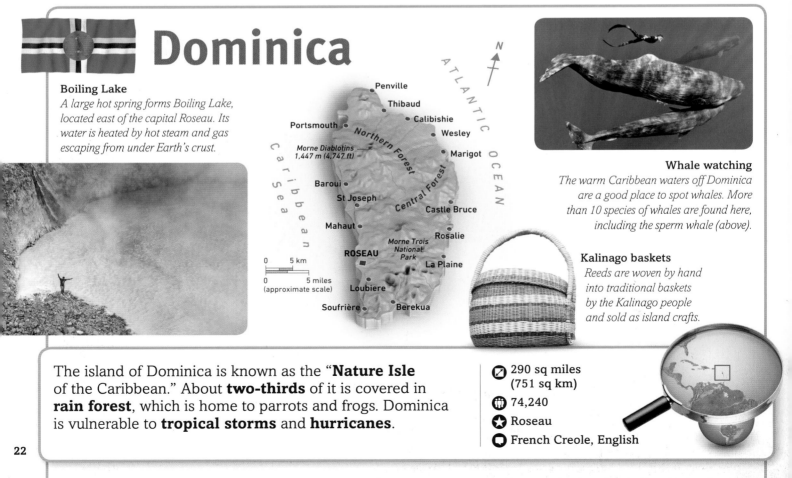

Boiling Lake
A large hot spring forms Boiling Lake, located east of the capital Roseau. Its water is heated by hot steam and gas escaping from under Earth's crust.

Penville
Thibaud
Portsmouth
Calibishie
Wesley
Morne Diablotins 1,447 m (4,747 ft)
Northern Forest
Marigot
Baroui
St Joseph
Central Forest
Castle Bruce
Mahaut
Rosalie
Morne Trois National Park
ROSEAU
La Plaine
Loubiere
Soufrière
Berekua
0   5 km
0   5 miles
(approximate scale)
Caribbean Sea
ATLANTIC OCEAN

Whale watching
The warm Caribbean waters off Dominica are a good place to spot whales. More than 10 species of whales are found here, including the sperm whale (above).

Kalinago baskets
Reeds are woven by hand into traditional baskets by the Kalinago people and sold as island crafts.

The island of Dominica is known as the "**Nature Isle of the Caribbean.**" About **two-thirds** of it is covered in **rain forest**, which is home to parrots and frogs. Dominica is vulnerable to **tropical storms** and **hurricanes**.

- 290 sq miles (751 sq km)
- 74,240
- Roseau
- French Creole, English

Antigua and Barbuda

Bird sanctuary
Codrington Lagoon National Park in Barbuda is a natural sanctuary for thousands of frigate birds.

The bright red throat pouch of the male frigate bird attracts females.

Goat Islands
Codrington
Palmetto Point
Barbuda
Spanish Point

ATLANTIC OCEAN

Caribbean Sea

- ⬈ 171 sq miles (443 sq km)
- 👥 98,180
- ⭐ St. John's
- 💬 English, English patois

St. John's is the capital and main port city of Antigua.

Two large islands and several smaller ones make up the **Caribbean nation** of Antigua and Barbuda. Antigua alone has **365 sandy beaches** and is a **major yachting center**. In 2017, Barbuda was badly damaged by powerful **Hurricane Irma**.

Antigua
Cedar Grove
ST JOHN'S
Five Islands Village
Boggy Peak 402 m (1,319 ft)
All Saints   Willikies
Urlings
English Harbour

0   10 km
0   10 miles
(approximate scale)

Guadeloupe Passage

Yacht regatta
The Antigua Classic Yacht Regatta began in 1967 at English Harbour. Today, the race attracts many yachts from around the world.

St. Lucia

Bustling city
Castries, the capital of St. Lucia, is a busy port visited by many cruise ships.

Two triangles on the flag symbolize the Pitons.

Julien Alfred
In 2018, the young sprinter Julien Alfred became the first athlete from St. Lucia to win a Youth Olympic medal.

St Lucia Channel

Caribbean Sea

ATLANTIC OCEAN

Gros Islet

0   5 km
0   5 miles
(approximate scale)

CASTRIES
La Ressource
Anse La Raye

The Pitons
Towering twin mountains known as the Pitons are a famous natural landmark in St. Lucia.

Gros Piton is the taller of the Pitons, standing 2,619 ft (798 m) high.

Mount Gimie 950 m (3,117 ft)
Soufrière
Micoud
Gros Piton 798 m (2,619 ft)
Laborie
Vieux Fort

St Vincent Passage

- ⬈ 238 sq miles (616 sq km)
- 👥 166,485
- ⭐ Castries
- 💬 English, French Creole

St. Lucia is known for **tall mountains**, **volcanic beaches**, and **coral reefs teeming with life**. This island's **economy** is dependent on **tourism**, **bananas**, and **coconuts**.

Barbados

The Barbadian flag depicts the trident belonging to Neptune, the Roman god of the sea.

0   8 km
0   8 miles
(approximate scale)

Global superstar
The Barbados-born pop singer Rihanna has sold millions of records across the world and won nine Grammy awards.

N

ATLANTIC OCEAN

- Checker Hall
- Speightstown
- Boscobelle
- Belleplaine
- Lower Carlton
- Mount Hillaby 340 m (1,120 ft)
- Holetown
- Bathsheba
- Endeavour
- Church Village
- Cave Hill
- Valley
- Wellhouse
- **BRIDGETOWN**
- Brerton
- Marchfield
- St Patricks
- Oistins
- Scarborough

ATLANTIC OCEAN

Beach life
Palm-fringed beaches and tropical seas attract millions of visitors to Barbados.

Barbados anole
An inhabitant of the island's rain forests, this green lizard blends in with leafy foliage.

Sharp claws help the anole cling to tree branches.

- 166 sq miles (430 sq km)
- 294,560
- Bridgetown
- Bajan, English

Barbados became a **British colony** in the 17th century and **gained independence in 1966**. With its **white-sand beaches** and **clear, turquoise waters**, this **sunny Caribbean island** is a popular tourist destination.

Grenada

0   10 km
0   10 miles
(approximate scale)

Fragrant spice
Grenada is one of the world's largest producers of nutmeg. This sweet spice, which features on the left side of the national flag, was introduced to Grenada by traders in 1843.

Caribbean Sea

- Carriacou
- Hillsborough
- Petite Martinique
- Ronde Island

ATLANTIC OCEAN

- Sauteurs
- Mount Saint Catherine 840 m (2,760 ft)
- Gouyave
- *Grenada*
- Grenville
- Seven Sisters Falls
- **ST GEORGE'S**

St. George's sits on a horseshoe-shaped harbor.

N

Cascading waterfalls
The Seven Sisters Falls are one of several natural wonders found in the Grand Etang National Park on Grenada island.

- 133 sq miles (344 sq km)
- 113,100
- St. George's
- English, English Creole

Grenada is as famous for its **spice production** as it is for its **scenic beaches**. This mountainous, tropical country is made up of **one large island**, Grenada, and **six smaller ones**.

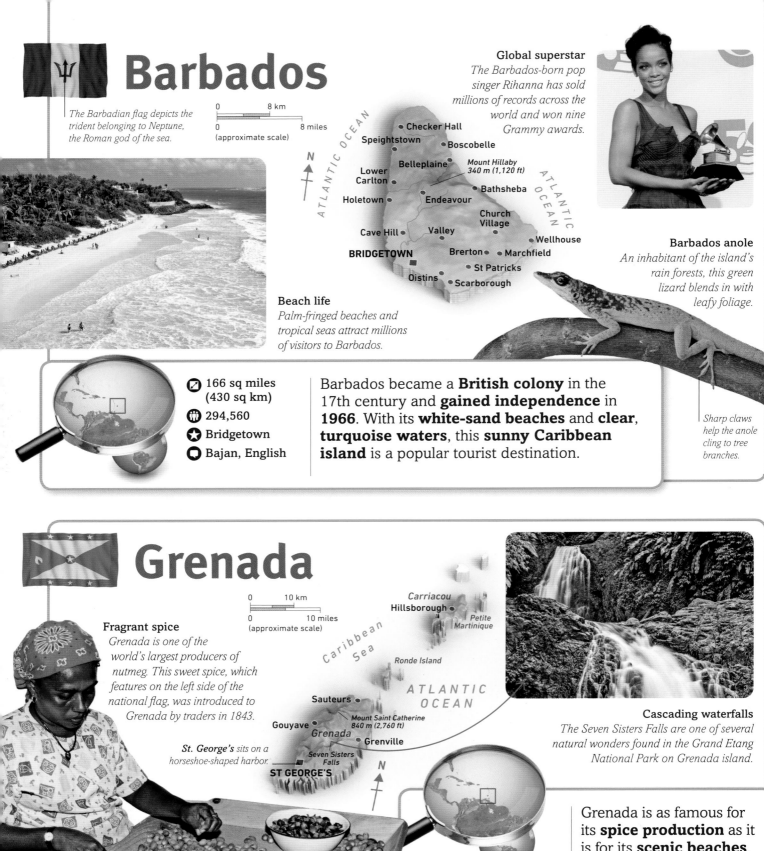

St. Vincent and the Grenadines

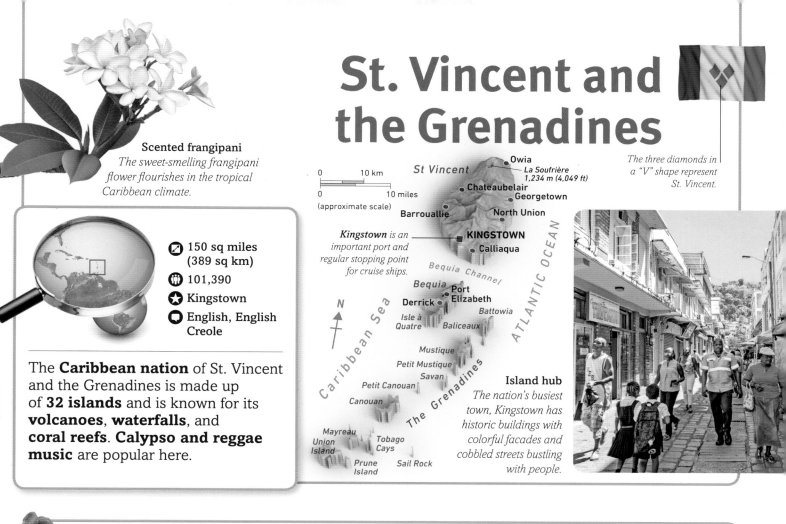

Scented frangipani
The sweet-smelling frangipani flower flourishes in the tropical Caribbean climate.

- ⤢ 150 sq miles (389 sq km)
- 👥 101,390
- ★ Kingstown
- 💬 English, English Creole

The **Caribbean nation** of St. Vincent and the Grenadines is made up of **32 islands** and is known for its **volcanoes**, **waterfalls**, and **coral reefs**. **Calypso and reggae music** are popular here.

The three diamonds in a "V" shape represent St. Vincent.

Kingstown is an important port and regular stopping point for cruise ships.

Island hub
The nation's busiest town, Kingstown has historic buildings with colorful facades and cobbled streets bustling with people.

Map labels: St Vincent, Owia, La Soufrière 1,234 m (4,049 ft), Chateaubelair, Georgetown, Barroualle, North Union, KINGSTOWN, Calliaqua, Bequia Channel, Bequia, Port Elizabeth, Derrick, Battowia, Isle à Quatre, Baliceaux, Mustique, Petit Mustique, Savan, Petit Canouan, Canouan, The Grenadines, Mayreau, Union Island, Tobago Cays, Prune Island, Sail Rock, Caribbean Sea, ATLANTIC OCEAN

Trinidad and Tobago

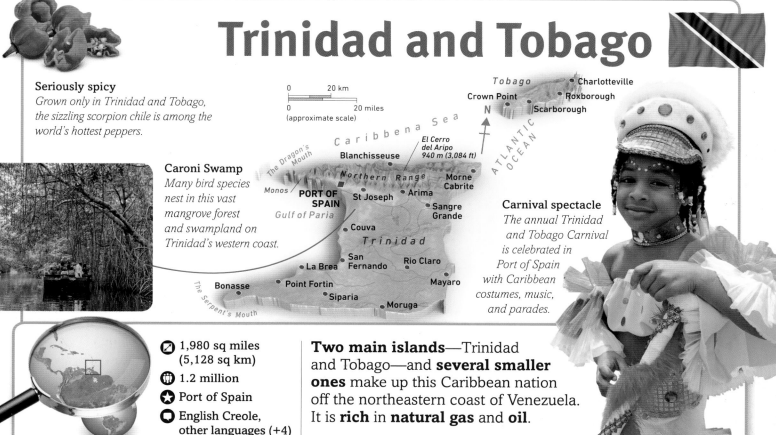

Seriously spicy
Grown only in Trinidad and Tobago, the sizzling scorpion chile is among the world's hottest peppers.

Caroni Swamp
Many bird species nest in this vast mangrove forest and swampland on Trinidad's western coast.

Carnival spectacle
The annual Trinidad and Tobago Carnival is celebrated in Port of Spain with Caribbean costumes, music, and parades.

Map labels: Tobago, Charlotteville, Crown Point, Roxborough, Scarborough, Caribbeana Sea, El Cerro del Aripo 940 m (3,084 ft), The Dragon's Mouth, Blanchisseuse, Northern Range, Morne Cabrite, Monos, PORT OF SPAIN, St Joseph, Arima, Sangre Grande, Gulf of Paria, Couva, Trinidad, San Fernando, Rio Claro, La Brea, Bonasse, Point Fortin, Mayaro, The Serpent's Mouth, Siparia, Moruga, ATLANTIC OCEAN

- ⤢ 1,980 sq miles (5,128 sq km)
- 👥 1.2 million
- ★ Port of Spain
- 💬 English Creole, other languages (+4)

Two main islands—Trinidad and Tobago—and **several smaller ones** make up this Caribbean nation off the northeastern coast of Venezuela. It is **rich** in **natural gas** and **oil**.

ATLANTIC OCEAN

Mouths of
the Amazon

French
Guiana
(to France)

SURINAME

GUYANA

Guiana Highlands

Amazon

Caribbean Sea

VENEZUELA

Llanos

Guiana

Amazon
Basin

B R

Lake
Maracaibo

NORTH
AMERICA

Gulf of
Panama

COLOMBIA

BOLIVIA

ECUADOR

PERU

Lake
Titicaca

Lago
Poopó

Gulf of
Guayaquil

A N D E S

Galápagos
Islands
(to Ecuador)

PACIFIC

SOUTH AMERICA

ATLANTIC OCEAN

N

0 ——————— 400 km
0 ——————— 400 miles
(approximate scale)

B R A Z I L

Represa de
Sobradinho

São Francisco

Brazilian Highlands

Planalto de
Mato Grosso

Gran Chaco

PARAGUAY

Paraná

URUGUAY

Pampas

ARGENTINA

Cerro Aconcagua
6,961 m (22,838 ft)

A N D E S

C H I L E

O C E A N

Patagonia

Gulf of
San
Jorge

Falkland
Islands
(to UK)

Bahía
Grande

Isla de Chiloé

Cape
Horn

Venezuela

Angel Falls
With a spectacular drop of 3,212 ft (979 m), Angel Falls is the world's highest waterfall.

Iglesia de San Francisco
One of the best-known churches of Caracas, Iglesia de San Francisco is dedicated to Saint Francis of Assisi.

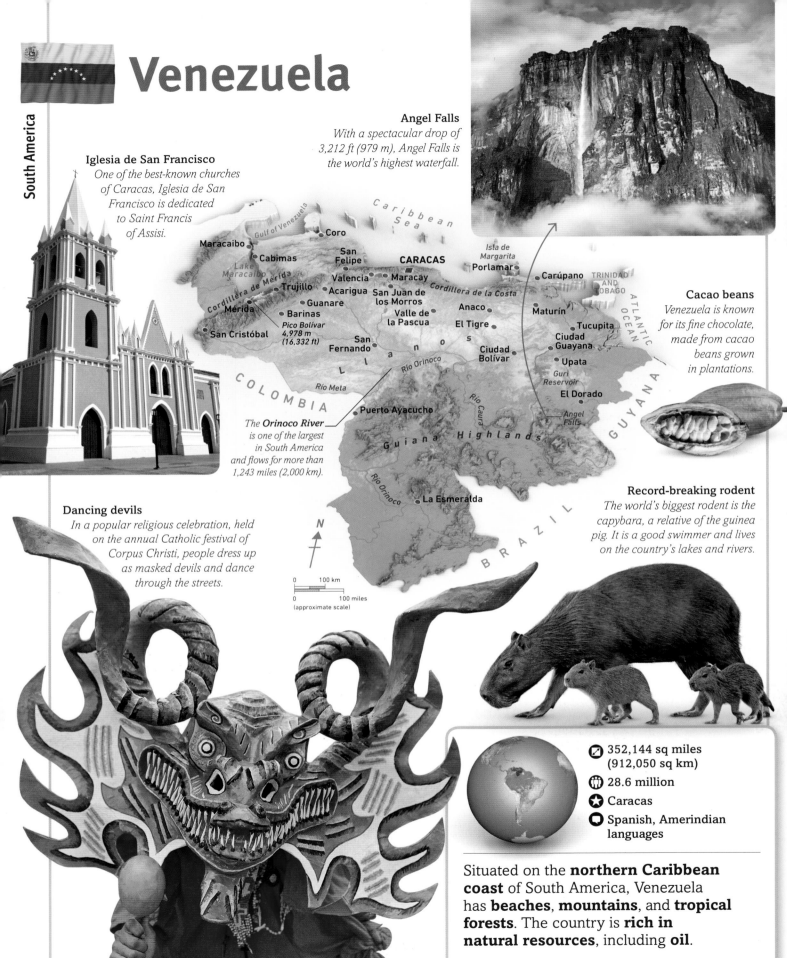

Cacao beans
Venezuela is known for its fine chocolate, made from cacao beans grown in plantations.

*The **Orinoco River** is one of the largest in South America and flows for more than 1,243 miles (2,000 km).*

Map labels
Gulf of Venezuela
Caribbean Sea
Coro
Maracaibo
Cabimas
San Felipe
Lake Maracaibo
CARACAS
Isla de Margarita
Porlamar
Carúpano
TRINIDAD AND TOBAGO
Valencia
Maracay
Cordillera de la Costa
ATLANTIC OCEAN
Cordillera de Mérida
Trujillo
Acarigua
San Juan de los Morros
Anaco
Maturín
Mérida
Guanare
Valle de la Pascua
El Tigre
Tucupita
Barinas
Ciudad Guayana
San Cristóbal
Pico Bolívar 4,978 m (16,332 ft)
San Fernando
Ciudad Bolívar
Upata
Llanos
Guri Reservoir
El Dorado
COLOMBIA
Río Meta
Río Orinoco
Angel Falls
GUYANA
Puerto Ayacucho
Río Caura
Guiana Highlands
Río Orinoco
La Esmeralda
BRAZIL

0   100 km
0   100 miles
(approximate scale)

N

Dancing devils
In a popular religious celebration, held on the annual Catholic festival of Corpus Christi, people dress up as masked devils and dance through the streets.

Record-breaking rodent
The world's biggest rodent is the capybara, a relative of the guinea pig. It is a good swimmer and lives on the country's lakes and rivers.

- 352,144 sq miles (912,050 sq km)
- 28.6 million
- Caracas
- Spanish, Amerindian languages

Situated on the **northern Caribbean coast** of South America, Venezuela has **beaches**, **mountains**, and **tropical forests**. The country is **rich in natural resources**, including **oil**.

Suriname

Squirrel monkeys
The country's tropical rain forests are home to these tree-dwelling monkeys. They live in large groups and feed on fruit and insects.

Paramaribo is the largest city and home to almost half of the population.

ATLANTIC OCEAN

N

Nieuw Nickerie
Totness
Groningen
Nieuw Amsterdam
Apoera
Onverwacht
PARAMARIBO
Bakhuis
Brokopondo
Moengo
W.J. van Blommesteinmeer
Wilhelmina Mountains
Juliana Top
1,230 m
(4,035 ft)
Apetina
Oranje Mountains
Kwamalasamutu

Courantyne River
Maroni River
French Guiana (France)

G U Y A N A

0   50 km
0   50 miles
(approximate scale)

B R A Z I L

Creole people
The ancestors of the Creole people in Suriname came from Europe and Africa many generations ago. They speak a language called Sranan Tongo.

- ⬈ 63,251 sq miles (163,820 sq km)
- 👥 609,560
- ★ Paramaribo
- 🗣 Sranan (Creole), other languages (+7)

Among the **smallest countries** in South America, Suriname lies on the **northeastern coast** of the continent. Once a **Dutch colony**, it became **independent** in 1975.

Rhinoceros dung beetle
This large, rare beetle is named for the upright horns on its head. Unusually, both male and female beetles have horns.

Guyana

A toucan uses its enormous beak to reach for fruit.

Toco toucan
Native to South America, this brightly colored bird lives in Guyana's tropical rain forests. A weak flier, it hops from tree to tree for food.

VENEZUELA

Mabaruma
Matthews Ridge
Charity
GEORGETOWN
Bartica
New Amsterdam
Linden
Corriverton
Kamarang
Ituni
Mount Roraima
2,810 m (9220 ft)
Kurupukari
Annai
Lethem
Kanuku Mountains
Glendor Mountains
Acarai Mountains
Guiana Highlands

Cuyuni River
Pakaraima Mountains
Essequibo River

ATLANTIC OCEAN

S U R I N A M E

B R A Z I L

N

0   50 km
0   50 miles
(approximate scale)

- ⬈ 83,000 sq miles (214,969 sq km)
- 👥 750,200
- ★ Georgetown
- 🗣 English Creole, other languages (+4)

Located in northeastern South America, Guyana is mostly **tropical rain forest**. A former British colony, it gained **independence** in 1966. The country is the only one in South America with **English** as its **official language**.

Cricketing legend
Sir Clive Hubert Lloyd is a legendary Guyanese batsman who captained the West Indies to two Cricket World Cup victories in 1975 and 1979.

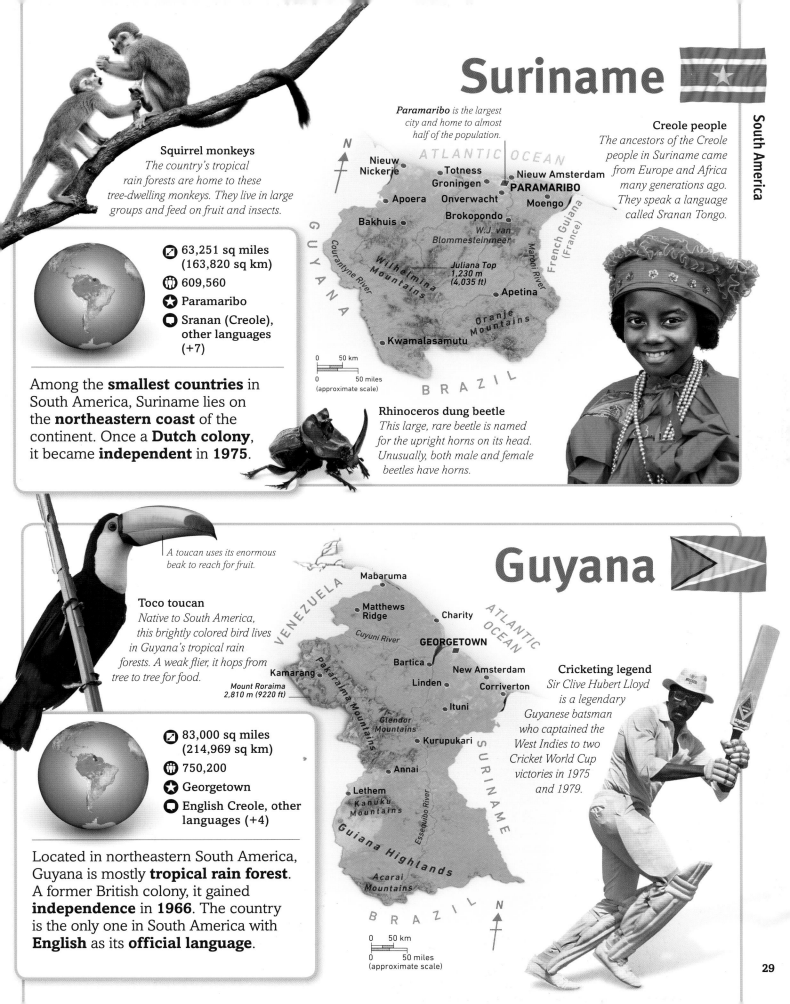

Colombia

River of colors
The river Caño Cristales in central Colombia is famous for the rare water plants that grow there. For a few months a year, these turn a spectacular bright red!

Changua
A soup made from eggs and milk called changua is a popular breakfast in the Andes region of the country.

Cotton-top tamarin
Native to the forests of northwestern Colombia, this small monkey takes its name from the fluffy white fur on its head.

Pico Cristóbal Colón
5,775 m (18,947 ft)

Santa Marta
Ríohacha
Barranquilla
Cartagena
Sierra Nevada de Santa Marta
Gulf of Darien
Valledupar
Sincelejo
Montería
PANAMA
Cúcuta
VENEZUELA
Río Atrato
Barrancabermeja
Bucaramanga
Quibdó
Medellín
PACIFIC OCEAN
Manizales
Tunja
Pereira
BOGOTÁ
Río Magdalena
Armenia
Cordillera Occidental
Cordillera Central
Cordillera Oriental
Río Meta
Puerto Carreño
Ibagne
Buenaventura
Villavicencio
Orocué
Cali
Neiva
ANDES
Río Guaviare
Popayán
Puerto Inírida
Tumaco
San José del Guaviare
Pasto
Florencia
Río Apaporis
Mitú
ECUADOR
Río Caquetá
Río Putumaya
PERU
BRAZIL
Amazon
Leticia

Local fruit sellers
For generations, brightly dressed fruit sellers known as palenqueras *have marketed their produce in the city of Cartagena. They carry fruit in big bowls balanced on their heads.*

Museum of Gold
The indigenous Muisca people of Colombia crafted fine figures and jewelry out of gold. The Museum of Gold in the city of Bogotá has more than 55,000 exhibits dating back hundreds of years.

National sport
This modern monument depicts Chaquén, the Muisca god of sports, playing the traditional throwing game of tejo.

The Andes Mountains and two rivers, the **Cauca** and the **Magdalena**, pass through Colombia. Among this country's major products are **coffee**, **bananas**, **emeralds**, and **coal**.

439,735 sq miles
(1,138,910 sq km)

49.1 million

Bogotá

Spanish, other languages (+3)

Ecuador

Root crop
A small root vegetable similar to a potato, called olluco, *grows in the Andes Mountains and is used in salads, soups, and stews in Ecuador.*

Quito old town
The Spanish founded Quito in the 16th century, building it on the former site of an Inca city. The modern city center has retained its historic Spanish architecture.

Galápagos iguanas
The Galápagos are home to land iguanas (pictured left) and unique marine iguanas that are able to swim and graze on algae.

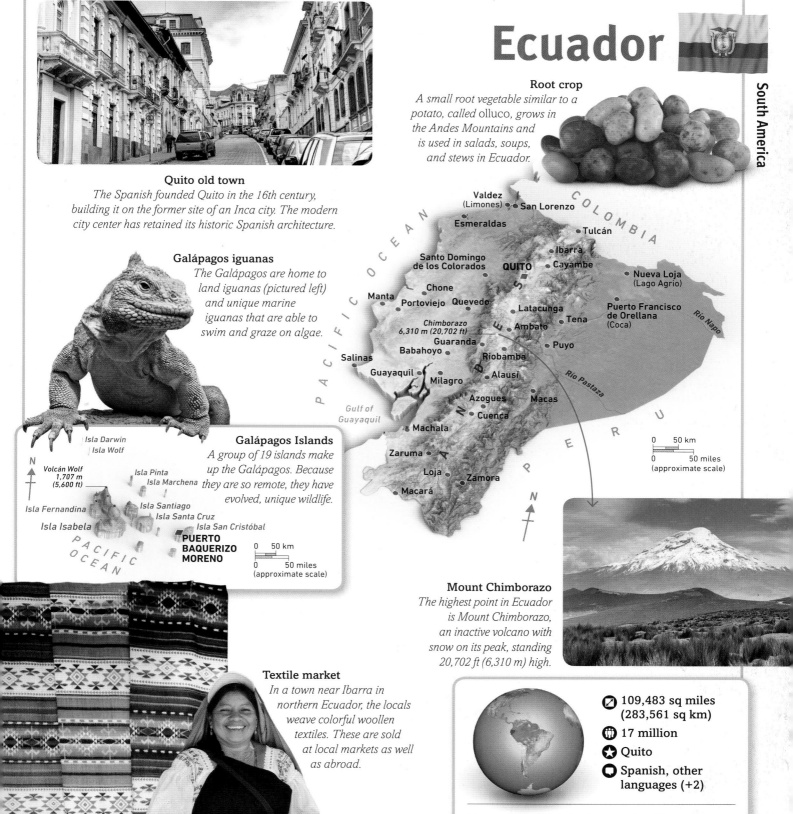

Galápagos Islands
A group of 19 islands make up the Galápagos. Because they are so remote, they have evolved, unique wildlife.

Isla Darwin
Isla Wolf
Volcán Wolf
1,707 m
(5,600 ft)
Isla Pinta
Isla Marchena
Isla Fernandina
Isla Santiago
Isla Santa Cruz
Isla Isabela
Isla San Cristóbal
PUERTO BAQUERIZO MORENO
PACIFIC OCEAN
N
0   50 km
0   50 miles
(approximate scale)

COLOMBIA
Valdez (Limones)
San Lorenzo
Esmeraldas
Tulcán
Ibarra
Santo Domingo de los Colorados
QUITO
Cayambe
Nueva Loja (Lago Agrio)
Chone
Manta
Portoviejo
Quevedo
Latacunga
Tena
Puerto Francisco de Orellana (Coca)
Río Napo
Chimborazo 6,310 m (20,702 ft)
Ambato
Guaranda
Babahoyo
Puyo
Salinas
Riobamba
Río Pastaza
Guayaquil
Milagro
Alausí
Azogues
Macas
Gulf of Guayaquil
Cuenca
Machala
Zaruma
Loja
Zamora
Macará
PACIFIC OCEAN
ANDES
PERU
N
0   50 km
0   50 miles
(approximate scale)

Mount Chimborazo
The highest point in Ecuador is Mount Chimborazo, an inactive volcano with snow on its peak, standing 20,702 ft (6,310 m) high.

Textile market
In a town near Ibarra in northern Ecuador, the locals weave colorful woollen textiles. These are sold at local markets as well as abroad.

⊘ 109,483 sq miles (283,561 sq km)
🏙 17 million
★ Quito
⬡ Spanish, other languages (+2)

Ecuador, which sits on the **Equator**, is marked by the Andes Mountains and low-lying **coastal regions**. Lying about 620 miles (1,000 km) to the west in the Pacific Ocean, the **Galápagos Islands** also belong to Ecuador.

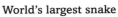

Brazil

World's largest snake
Weighing 550 lb (250 kg) and growing up to 16 ft (5 m) long, the green anaconda can be found in Brazil's Amazon rainforest and the wetlands called the Pantanal.

Modern masterpiece
This Roman Catholic cathedral in the capital city, Brasília, has room for 4,000 worshippers. It was designed by famous Brazilian architect Oscar Niemeyer.

The **Amazon rainforest** covers 1.2 million sq miles (3.2 million sq km) in Brazil.

0   200 km
0   200 miles
(approximate scale)

GUYANA
GUIANA Highland
VENEZUELA
COLOMBIA
Boa Vista
Pico da Neblina 3,014 m (9,888 ft)
Río Negro
Serra do Jatapu
Carvoeiro
Amazon
Manaus
A m a z o n   B a s i n
Río Juruá
Eirunepé
Rio Purus
Rio Madeira
Río Juruena
Porto Velho
Serra Cachimb
Rio Branco
Chapada dos Parecis
BOLIVIA
Mato Grosso
Cuiabá
Pantanal
Campo Grande
PERU
PARAGUAY
Paraná
ARGENTINA
Iguaçu Falls
Santa Maria
Porto Ale
Bagé
URUGUAY

Rio Carnival
The first carnival in Rio de Janeiro was held in 1723. Since then, this annual celebration has grown to become the world's largest street festival, attracting millions of visitors. Its parades feature performers in spectacular costumes, dancing to rhythmic samba beats.

Soccer fever
Brazilians love soccer. The country's national team has won the World Cup a record-breaking five times.

Covering almost half of **South America,** Brazil is the continent's **largest country**. It is named after the Brazilwood tree, growing in the **Amazon rainforest**, which spreads across **more than 35 percent** of the country. Abundant **natural resources** give Brazil a **strong economy**, and **coffee** and **soybeans** are important **agricultural exports**.

⬠ 3,287,957 sq miles (8,515,770 sq km)

👥 211.7 million

⭐ Brasília

💬 Portuguese, Amerindian languages, other languages (+4)

Indigenous peoples of the Amazon
The world's largest rain forest provides a home for hundreds of indigenous peoples. The Xingu, made up of many ethnic groups, live and fish by the Xingu River.

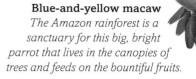

Blue-and-yellow macaw
The Amazon rainforest is a sanctuary for this big, bright parrot that lives in the canopies of trees and feeds on the bountiful fruits.

FRENCH GUIANA
ME
Planalto acanaquará
Macapá
mazon
Ilha de Marajó
ntarém
Belém
São Luís
Parnaíba
Rio Xingu
Tucuruí Reservoir
Fortaleza
Imperatriz
Teresina
Mossoró
Planalto da Borborema
Natal
Juazeiro do Norte
João Pessoa
Rio Tocantins
Sobradinho Reservoir
Recife
Palmas do Tocantins
Juazeiro
Espigão Mestre
Maceió
Chapada Diamantina
Aracaju
Rio São Francisco
Salvador
BRASÍLIA
Ilhéus
Goiânia
Brazilian Highlands
Serra do Espinhaço
Uberlândia
Uberaba
Araçatuba
Belo Horizonte
São Carlos
Vitória
Campinas
Serra da Mantiqueira
Campos dos Goytacazes
ucarana
Nova Iguaçu
Rio de Janeiro
São Paulo
Santos
Curitiba
ATLANTIC OCEAN
Florianópolis
Serra do Mar

Rio de Janeiro
Christ the Redeemer, the iconic 98 ft (30 m) tall statue, overlooks Rio and its beaches, including Copacabana, and the pointy Sugarloaf Mountain.

Coffee production
One-third of the world's coffee beans is grown in Brazil. Traditional producers toss the beans on mesh screens to separate the branches and leaves from the ripe fruit.

Acrobatic martial art
Capoeira is a martial-art form that combines self-defense, acrobatics, and dance. It was developed here in the 16th century by enslaved Africans.

Geography: The landscape includes the vast **Amazon rainforest** and the **Amazon River**, the world's second-longest river.

History: First inhabited by **indigenous peoples**, Brazil was a **Portuguese colony** from 1500 to 1825.

Culture: Brazil has a rich culture of **diverse religions**, **carnivals**, **dance**, and **music**, including styles such as *bossa nova* and *samba*.

Natural wonders: As well as its tropical rain forest, Brazil's natural beauty can be seen in the **Sugarloaf Mountain** and **Iguaçu Falls**.

Wildlife: About **10 million species** of animals, including **jaguars**, **piranhas**, and **tropical birds**, live in the rain forest.

Food and drink: The Brazilian menu is vast and varied, with **fish** and **meat stews**, **barbecued meat**, and **black beans**.

Bolivia

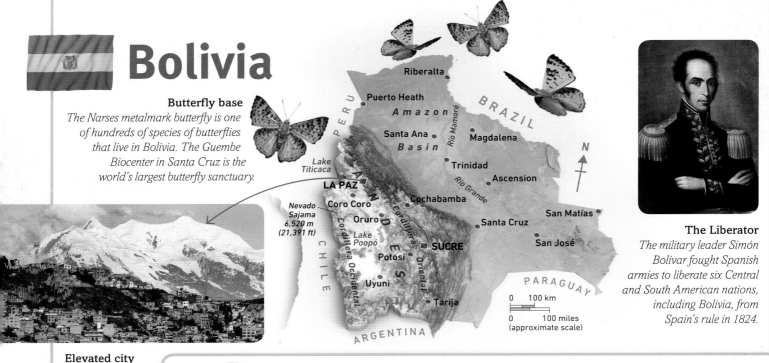

Butterfly base
The Narses metalmark butterfly is one of hundreds of species of butterflies that live in Bolivia. The Guembe Biocenter in Santa Cruz is the world's largest butterfly sanctuary.

The Liberator
The military leader Simón Bolívar fought Spanish armies to liberate six Central and South American nations, including Bolivia, from Spain's rule in 1824.

Elevated city
At a height of 11,975 ft (3,650 m), La Paz is the highest capital city on Earth.

- ⤢ 424,164 sq miles (1,098,580 sq km)
- 👥 11.6 million
- ★ Sucre and La Paz
- ⬡ Aymara, Quechua, Spanish

A **landlocked nation** in South America, Bolivia ranges from the **Andes Mountains** to the **Altiplano** (high plateau) and the **Atacama Desert** to the **Amazon rainforest**. On the border with Peru lies **Lake Titicaca**, the largest lake in South America.

Peru

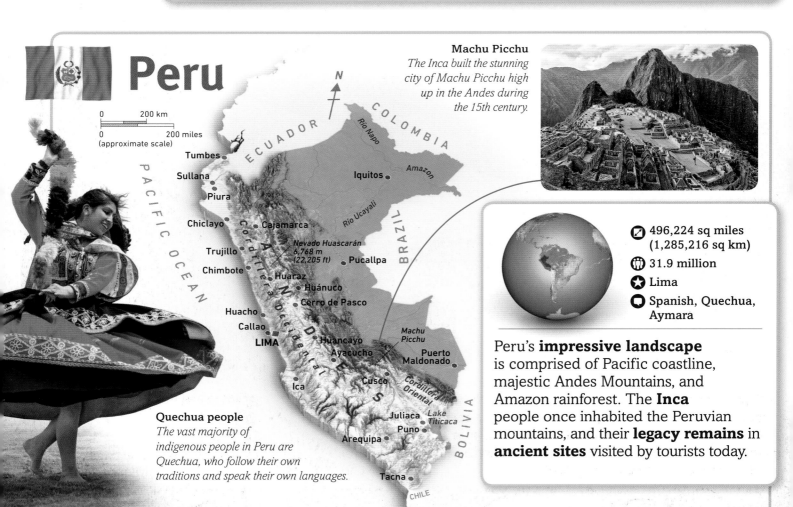

Machu Picchu
The Inca built the stunning city of Machu Picchu high up in the Andes during the 15th century.

Quechua people
The vast majority of indigenous people in Peru are Quechua, who follow their own traditions and speak their own languages.

- ⤢ 496,224 sq miles (1,285,216 sq km)
- 👥 31.9 million
- ★ Lima
- ⬡ Spanish, Quechua, Aymara

Peru's **impressive landscape** is comprised of Pacific coastline, majestic Andes Mountains, and Amazon rainforest. The **Inca** people once inhabited the Peruvian mountains, and their **legacy remains** in **ancient sites** visited by tourists today.

Rare blooms

The Atacama Desert is the driest place on Earth. It rains here only every six years or so, but when it does, seeds in the sand quickly germinate into blankets of colorful flowers.

Easter Island

This remote volcanic island is known as Rapa Nui *by its inhabitants.*

Mount Terevaka
510 m (1,673 ft)

Rano Raraku

Ahu Akivi

Ahu Tongariki

Hanga Roa

Rano Kau Volcano

PACIFIC OCEAN

N

0   6 km
0   6 miles
(approximate scale)

Chile

PERU
BOLIVIA
Arica
Iquique
Calama
Antofagasta

Atacama Desert

Cerro Ojos del Salado
6,880 m (22,572 ft)
Copiapó

0   200 km
0   200 miles
(approximate scale)

La Serena
Coquimbo

Viña del Mar
Valparaíso
SANTIAGO
Rancagua
Talca

Talcahuano
Concepción
Chillán

Temuco

Valdivia

Puerto Montt

Isla de Chiloé

Juan Fernández Islands

PACIFIC OCEAN

Archipiélago de los Chonos

Golfo de Penas

A N D E S

A R G E N T I N A

N

Punta Arenas

Strait of Magellan

Cape Horn   Drake Passage

Paranal Observatory

Located in the Atacama Desert, this observatory has some of the world's most powerful telescopes for observing the night sky.

Underground snack

Meaning "stony ground," this traditional Chilean dish of meat, fish, and vegetables is cooked on hot rocks inside a deep hole in the ground.

High-life llamas

The llama is a popular pack animal in Chile also kept for its wool. This domesticated hardy creature is able to live at high altitudes.

Stone statues

Chile's best-known landmarks are the stone figures of Easter Island. The moai *(meaning "statues") were carved from about 1000 CE onward.*

Mapuche people

About 10 percent of the Chilean population is indigenous Mapuche people. They make beautiful handcrafted textiles, including ponchos, to sell.

Stretching 2,670 miles (4,300 km), this South American nation is the world's **longest** and **thinnest country**. One side is bordered by the **Andes Mountains**, and the other is the **Pacific Ocean**, where **Easter Island** lies some 2,290 miles (3,680 km) away.

- 291,933 sq miles (756,102 sq km)
- 18.2 million
- Santiago
- Spanish, Amerindian languages

Argentina

The sun represents the May Revolution of 1810 when Argentina became independent from Spain.

Lionel Messi
Argentina is passionate about soccer. The captain of the national soccer team, Messi, has won the Ballon d'Or—the highest prize in the sport—a record-breaking six times.

0   200 km

0   200 miles
(approximate scale)

Cerro Aconcagua
6,959 m
(22,831 ft)

N

BOLIVIA

PARAGUAY

Gran Chaco

San Miguel de Tucumán

Santiago del Estero

Posadas

Paraná

BRAZIL

San Juan

Mendoza   Córdoba

Santa Fe

San Rafael   Concordia

Rosario

URUGUAY

BUENOS AIRES

La Plata

Neuquén   Río Colorado

Bahía
Blanca   Mar del
Plata

River
Plate

Río Salado

Río Negro

P a m p a s

C H I L E

*The capital **Buenos Aires** lies on the banks of the Plate River.*

Esquel

Rawson

Comodoro
Rivadavia

Gulf of
San Jorge

P a t a g o n i a

El Calafate

Bahía
Grande

ATLANTIC
OCEAN

Río Grande

Drake Passage

Ceibo flowers
The ceibo tree grows across the country, and its vibrant red flowers have been a national symbol since 1942.

Argentine tango
The tango is a dramatic style of Latin dance that began in Buenos Aires in the 19th century. It is now popular throughout the world.

Perito Moreno glacier
The 19-mile (30 km) long Perito Moreno glacier ends at the country's largest lake, Lago Argentina.

Empanadas
These popular baked pastries can be made with a variety of fillings. In Argentina, beef is a favorite.

Colorful La Boca
A traditional neighborhood of Buenos Aires, La Boca is famous for its colorful houses, street musicians, and bustling market stalls.

⤢ 1,073,518 sq miles
(2,780,400 sq km)

👥 45.5 million

★ Buenos Aires

⬡ Spanish, Italian, Amerindian languages

Argentina is the **second-largest country** in South America. In the center of the country is a **vast area of grassland** called **Pampas**. To the south lies a **drier region** known as **Patagonia**.

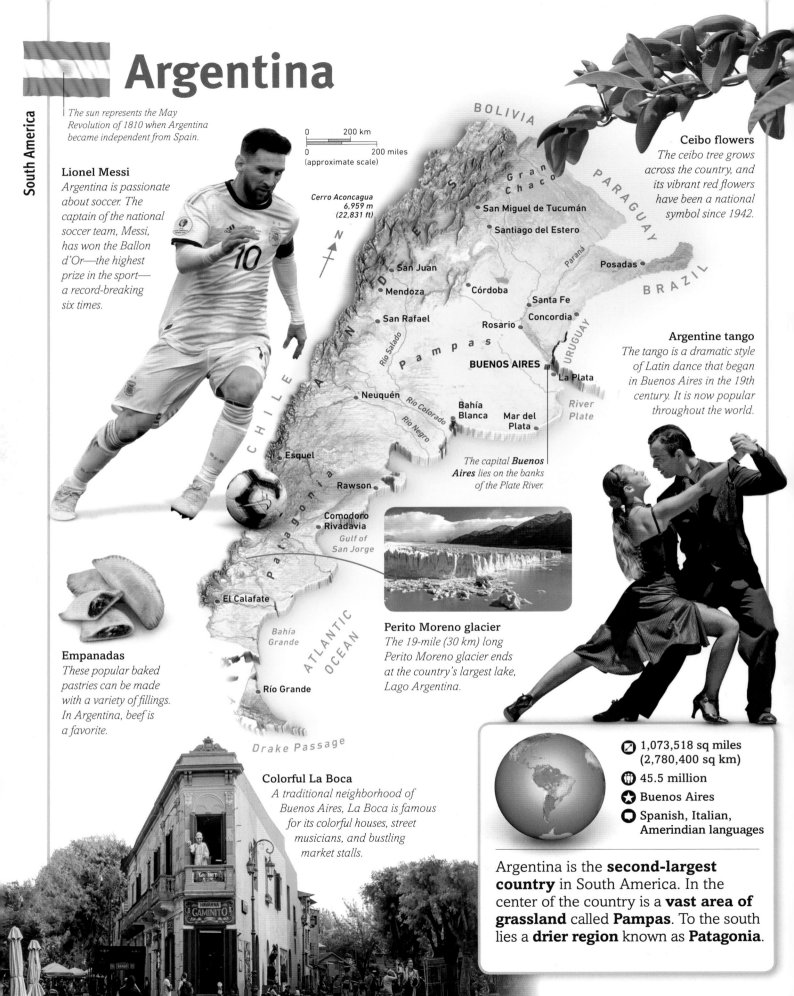

Paraguay

Paraguayan harp
First played by traditional folk musicians in rural areas of the country, the harp has become Paraguay's national instrument.

Ñandutí lace
The Spanish brought to Paraguay the traditional, handcrafted lace called Ñandutí, meaning "spiderweb." Today artisans use it to make embroidered clothing in eye-catching colors.

Yacaré caiman
Rivers and swamps are home to this caiman. It was once heavily hunted but is now a protected species.

BOLIVIA
Capitán Pablo Lagerenza
General Eugenio A. Garay
Chaco Boreal
Mariscal Estigarribia
Gran Chaco
ARGENTINA
BRAZIL
Pedro Juan Caballero
Concepción
Rosario
ASUNCIÓN
Villarrica
Caazapá
Pilar
San Juan Bautista
Paraná
Encarnación
Coronel Oviedo
Cordillera de Amambay
Salto del Guairá
Ciudad del Este
Cerro Tres Kandú 842 m (2,762 ft)

0   100 km
0   100 miles
(approximate scale)

⊘ 157,047 sq miles (406,752 sq km)
👥 7.2 million
★ Asunción
⬡ Guaraní, Spanish, German

Forests, hills, grasslands, and swamps are found across Paraguay, which is **landlocked** by **three countries.** The nation's **exports** include crops such as **cotton, coffee,** and **oilseeds.**

Uruguay

Hardy herders
Since the 18th century, horsemen called gauchos have herded cattle and sheep across the grassy plains of Uruguay.

The blue and white stripes symbolize the nine original regional departments of Uruguay.

ARGENTINA
Artigas
Rivera
Salto
Paysandú
Cuchilla de Haedo
Tacuarembó
Río Negro
Melo
BRAZIL
Fray Bentos
Mercedes
Duranzo
Treinta y Tres
Trinidad
Cuchilla Grande
San José de Mayo
Florida
Cerro Catedral 513 m (1,683 ft)
Colonia del Sacramento
Canelones
Santa Lucía
MONTEVIDEO
River Plate
Maldonado
ATLANTIC OCEAN

N

0   50 km
0   50 miles
(approximate scale)

Sea lion colony
One of South America's largest sea lion colonies is found in Cabo Polonio National Park on Uruguay's eastern coast.

Mate is traditionally drunk through a metal straw with a filter to keep out leaves.

Herbal brew
The national beverage of southern South America is mate, an herbal drink made from the dried leaves of the yerba mate tree.

The **second-smallest country** on the continent, Uruguay has a **beautiful coastline** and **fertile grasslands.** Half of the population live in the capital city of **Montevideo.**

⊘ 68,036 sq miles (176,215 sq km)
👥 3.4 million
★ Montevideo
⬡ Spanish

EUROPE

Mediterranean Sea

EGYPT

Nil
Del

TUNISIA

*Libyan
Desert*

LIBYA

Atlas Mountains

ALGERIA

Ahaggar

Tibesti

a

MOROCCO

ATLANTIC OCEAN

Madeira
(to Portugal)

Canary Islands
(to Spain)

S

a

h

r

NIGER

CHAD

Western
Sahara
(administered by Morocco)

*Massif
de l'Air*

*Lake
Chad*

a

MALI

S

a

h

e

l

MAURITANIA

*Taoudenni
Basin*

S

Niger

NIGERIA

BURKINA FASO

CAPE
VERDE

SENEGAL

BENIN

Niger

CAMEROON

CONG

THE GAMBIA

GUINEA

IVORY
COAST
(CÔTE D'IVORE)

GHANA

TOGO

GABON

GUINEA-
BISSAU

SIERRA
LEONE

EQUATORIAL
GUINEA

SAO TOME &
PRINCIPE

LIBERIA

Cabinda
(to Angola)

ATLANTIC OCEAN

AFRICA

ASIA

Nile

Red Sea

_Nubian
Desert_

ERITREA

SUDAN

DJIBOUTI

_Horn of
Africa_

_Ethiopian
Highlands_

ETHIOPIA

SOMALIA

Sudd

SOUTH SUDAN

KENYA

CENTRAL
AFRICAN
REPUBLIC

UGANDA

Great Rift Valley

_Kilimanjaro
5,895 m
(19,308 ft)_

_Lake
Albert_

_Lake
Victoria_

_Congo
Basin_

RWANDA

Congo

BURUNDI

_Lake
Tanganyika_

TANZANIA

DEM. REP.
CONGO

Great Rift Valley

_Lake
Malawi_

MALAWI

ANGOLA

ZAMBIA

Zambezi

ZIMBABWE

NAMIBIA

BOTSWANA

_Kalahari
Desert_

Namib Desert

LESOTHO

Orange River

SOUTH
AFRICA

_Cape of
Good Hope_

N

0   500 km

0   500 miles

(approximate scale)

SEYCHELLES

COMOROS

_Mayotte
(to France)_

MOZAMBIQUE

Mozambique Channel

MADAGASCAR

INDIAN OCEAN

MAURITIUS

_Réunion
(to France)_

ESWATINI
(formerly Swaziland)

Morocco

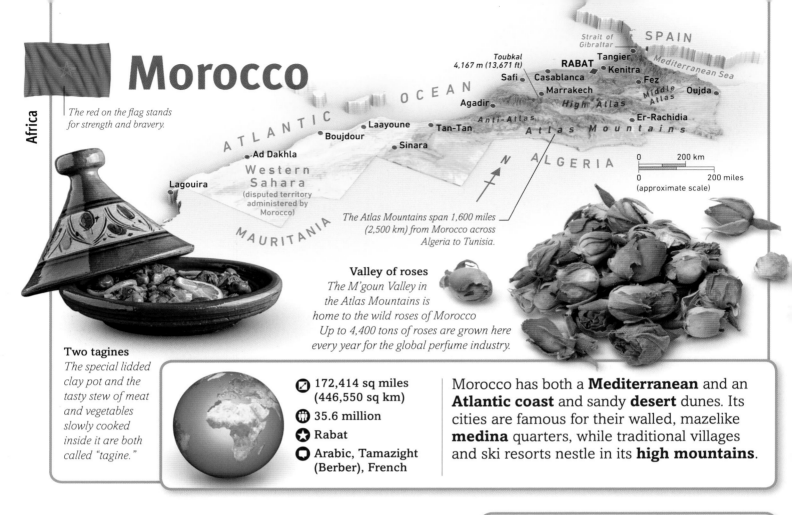

The red on the flag stands for strength and bravery.

Toubkal 4,167 m (13,671 ft)

ATLANTIC OCEAN

Strait of Gibraltar · SPAIN · Mediterranean Sea

Tangier · **RABAT** · Kenitra · Fez · Oujda

Safi · Casablanca · Marrakech · Middle Atlas

Agadir · High Atlas · Er-Rachidia

Laayoune · Tan-Tan · Anti-Atlas · Atlas Mountains

Boujdour · Sinara · ALGERIA

Ad Dakhla

Lagouira

Western Sahara (disputed territory administered by Morocco)

MAURITANIA

0 — 200 km
0 — 200 miles
(approximate scale)

The Atlas Mountains span 1,600 miles (2,500 km) from Morocco across Algeria to Tunisia.

Valley of roses
The M'goun Valley in the Atlas Mountains is home to the wild roses of Morocco Up to 4,400 tons of roses are grown here every year for the global perfume industry.

Two tagines
The special lidded clay pot and the tasty stew of meat and vegetables slowly cooked inside it are both called "tagine."

- ⬡ 172,414 sq miles (446,550 sq km)
- 👥 35.6 million
- ⭐ Rabat
- 🗣 Arabic, Tamazight (Berber), French

Morocco has both a **Mediterranean** and an **Atlantic coast** and sandy **desert** dunes. Its cities are famous for their walled, mazelike **medina** quarters, while traditional villages and ski resorts nestle in its **high mountains**.

Algeria

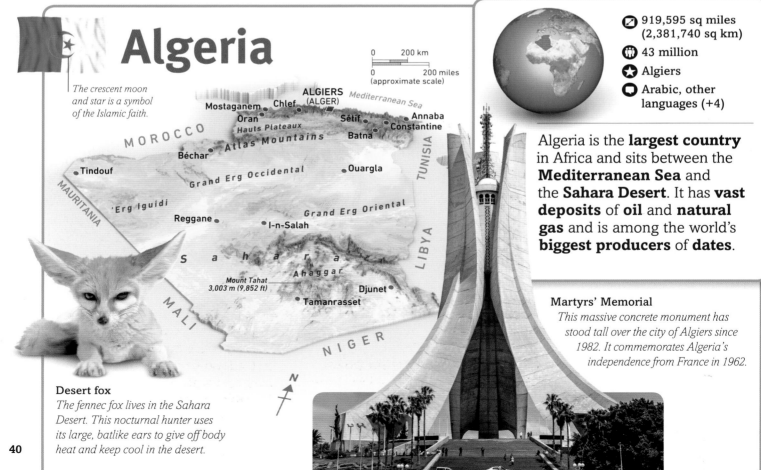

The crescent moon and star is a symbol of the Islamic faith.

0 — 200 km
0 — 200 miles
(approximate scale)

ALGIERS (ALGER) · Mediterranean Sea

Mostaganem · Chlef · Sétif · Annaba

Oran · Hauts Plateaux · Constantine

Atlas Mountains · Batna

MOROCCO · Béchar

Tindouf · Grand Erg Occidental · Ouargla · TUNISIA

'Erg Iguidi · Grand Erg Oriental · LIBYA

Reggane · I-n-Salah

MAURITANIA · Sahara

MALI · Ahaggar

Mount Tahat 3,003 m (9,852 ft) · Djunet

Tamanrasset

NIGER

- ⬡ 919,595 sq miles (2,381,740 sq km)
- 👥 43 million
- ⭐ Algiers
- 🗣 Arabic, other languages (+4)

Algeria is the **largest country** in Africa and sits between the **Mediterranean Sea** and the **Sahara Desert**. It has **vast deposits** of **oil** and **natural gas** and is among the world's **biggest producers** of **dates**.

Martyrs' Memorial
This massive concrete monument has stood tall over the city of Algiers since 1982. It commemorates Algeria's independence from France in 1962.

Desert fox
The fennec fox lives in the Sahara Desert. This nocturnal hunter uses its large, batlike ears to give off body heat and keep cool in the desert.

Major mosque
The center of Muslim worship in the capital city of Tunis is the Zitouna Mosque, with its 144 ft (44 m) minaret towering over the rooftops of the old part of the city.

Tunisia

Mediterranean Sea

Jebel Chambi 1,544 m (5,065 ft)

Bizerte

El Kef

TUNIS

Nabeul

ALGERIA

Kasserine

Kairouan

Sousse
Monastir

Gafsa

El Jem

Tozeur

Sfax

Chott el Jerid

Gabès

Golfe de Gabès

Medenine

Île de Djerba

Tataouine

Jeffara Plain

Remel el Abiod

Dahar

N

LIBYA

0   50 km

0   50 miles
(approximate scale)

Roman mosaic
Tunisia was part of the Roman Empire and is full of relics, such as this owl mosaic found at El Jem.

Popular sport
Soccer is hugely popular in Tunisia. The boy wearing the striped shirt supports Club Africain, a top league team in Tunis.

⊘ 63,170 sq miles (163,610 sq km)

⊕ 11.7 million

★ Tunis

◐ Arabic, French

Although a **small country** that is largely desert, Tunisia also has **rich farmland** where **cereal crops**, **olive trees**, and **fruits** grow in abundance. Traditional foods and crafts are sold at **colorful city markets** called **souks**.

Libya

0   200 km

0   200 miles
(approximate scale)

TUNISIA

Az Zawiyah

TRIPOLI
(ṬARABULUS)

Nalut

Mediterranean Sea

Mistratah

ALGERIA

Sirte
(Surt)

Gulf of Sirte

Benghazi
(Banghazi)

Tuareg riders
Tuaregs are nomadic people who live in the Sahara Desert. Their traditions and folklore are kept alive, including this camel race through the desert dunes at the Ghat Festival.

Awbari

Waddan

Ajdabiya

Tobruk

Ghat

Birak

Jalu

Al Jaghbub

Idhan Murzuq

NIGER

Great Sand Sea

EGYPT

Pic Bette 2,286 m (7,500 ft)

Al Kufrah

CHAD

Libyan Desert

N

The colors stand for Libya's main regions: Fezzan, Cyrenaica, and Tripolitania.

Early art
In the Tadrart Acacus Mountains, near the city of Ghat, prehistoric rock art features wild animals, camels, and, seen here, human hunters.

⊘ 679,362 sq miles (1,759,540 sq km)

⊕ 6.9 million

★ Tripoli

◐ Arabic, Tuareg

Libya is dominated by the **sands** of the **Sahara Desert**. Early people created fine **rock art** inland some 10,000 years ago, and **ancient Greek** and **Roman ruins** dot the coast. The country is rich in **oil** and **gas**.

Egypt

City of minarets
Built amid ancient cities, Egypt's teeming capital, Cairo, is more than 1,000 years old. Its historic center has spectacular Islamic architecture, showcased in the 14th-century Sultan Hassan Mosque.

On the ball
Egyptian super striker Mohamed Salah is a two-time winner of the African Footballer of the Year Award. He also plays for England's Liverpool Football Club.

Gulf of Sallum

Sidi Barrani

Marsa Matru

Libyan Plateau

Al'Alamay

Qattara Depression

Siwah

Al Bawiti

Great Sand Sea

Qasr al Farafirah

L I B Y A

Libyan Desert

Al Qasr

Gilf Kebir Plateau

The **Libyan Desert** *is a mostly rocky expanse covering two-thirds of Egypt.*

Sweet fruits
Dates have been cultivated and eaten in Egypt since ancient times. More than 15 percent of the world's dates are grown here, making Egypt one of the top producers.

Magnificent treasures
More than 5,000 years ago, a great civilization was growing along the banks of the Nile River. We know about life in ancient Egypt from the extraordinary discoveries of archaeologists, such as this well-preserved coffin for an elderly woman named Nesmutaatneru.

Hieroglyphs are an ancient form of writing in which pictures and symbols represent sounds and ideas.

Sailing on the Nile
Egypt depends on the Nile River for water for farming. For thousands of years, it was also the country's main transportation highway. Today, tourists travel on it in wooden sailboats called feluccas.

Lying in the **northeast corner** of Africa, Egypt is more than **90 percent desert**. Most Egyptians live in the **valley** of the fertile **Nile River**. Thousands of years ago, Egypt was home to one of the world's **first great civilizations**.

- 386,662 sq miles (1,001,450 sq km)
- 104.1 million
- Cairo
- Arabic, English, French, Berber

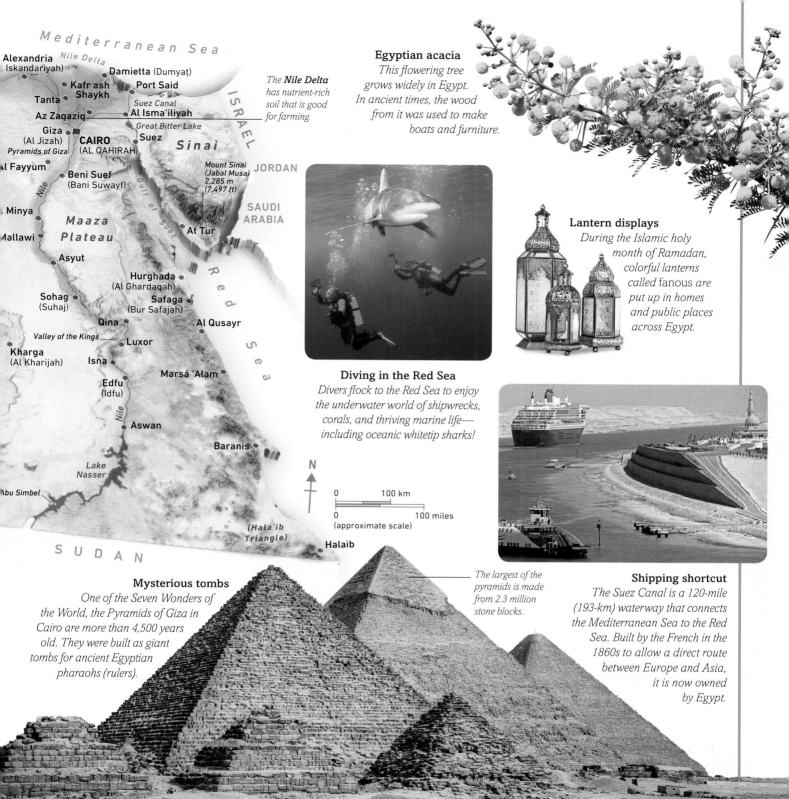

Mediterranean Sea

Alexandria (Iskandariyah)
Nile Delta
Damietta (Dumyaṭ)
Kafr ash Shaykh
Port Said
Tanta
Suez Canal
Az Zaqaziq
Al Isma'iliyah
Giza (Al Jizah)
Great Bitter Lake
CAIRO (AL QAHIRAH)
Suez
Pyramids of Giza
Sinai
Al Fayyum
Beni Suef (Bani Suwayf)
Minya
Maaza Plateau
Mallawi
Asyut
Sohag (Suhaj)
Hurghada (Al Ghardaqah)
Qina
Safaga (Bur Safajah)
Valley of the Kings
Al Quṣayr
Kharga (Al Kharijah)
Luxor
Isna
Marsá 'Alam
Edfu (Idfu)
Aswan
Baranis
Lake Nasser
Abu Simbel
(Halaʿib Triangle)
Halaib
SUDAN

ISRAEL
JORDAN
SAUDI ARABIA
Mount Sinai (Jabal Musa) 2,285 m (7,497 ft)
At Tur
Gulf of Suez
Red Sea

*The **Nile Delta** has nutrient-rich soil that is good for farming.*

N

0 — 100 km
0 — 100 miles
(approximate scale)

Egyptian acacia
This flowering tree grows widely in Egypt. In ancient times, the wood from it was used to make boats and furniture.

Diving in the Red Sea
Divers flock to the Red Sea to enjoy the underwater world of shipwrecks, corals, and thriving marine life— including oceanic whitetip sharks!

Lantern displays
During the Islamic holy month of Ramadan, colorful lanterns called fanous are put up in homes and public places across Egypt.

Mysterious tombs
One of the Seven Wonders of the World, the Pyramids of Giza in Cairo are more than 4,500 years old. They were built as giant tombs for ancient Egyptian pharaohs (rulers).

The largest of the pyramids is made from 2.3 million stone blocks.

Shipping shortcut
The Suez Canal is a 120-mile (193-km) waterway that connects the Mediterranean Sea to the Red Sea. Built by the French in the 1860s to allow a direct route between Europe and Asia, it is now owned by Egypt.

Geography: Egypt consists of vast swaths of **desert**, green **river valleys**, **mountains**, and **Red Sea** and **Mediterranean coastline**.

History: Egypt's **ancient civilization** lasted for around **3,000 years**. From the mid-600s, Egypt was ruled by **Muslim Arabs**.

Culture: Everyday life is largely centered on the **family** and **Muslim traditions**. Egypt also has a thriving **media and arts scene**.

Natural wonders: The **Nile** is the **world's longest river**—it flows over a distance of **more than 4,100 miles (6,600 km)**.

Wildlife: Jackals, fennec foxes, and scorpions are desert dwellers. **Vipers** and **cobras** are sometimes seen in the Nile Valley.

Food and drink: Egyptian cuisine blends **spices**, **lentils**, and **rice** to make a variety of dishes often served with **minced** or **grilled lamb**.

Mali

Dogon *dama*
The Dogon people of Mali create elaborate masks and costumes for the *dama* dance ceremony, which is held to honor deceased village elders.

An ancient Arabic manuscript on astronomy from Timbuktu

Striking, geometric designs often decorate bògòlanfini.

Patterned textiles
Bògòlanfini *is a traditional Malian handwoven cotton fabric. Its bold, colored patterns are created with natural dyes made from river mud and local plants.*

Precious manuscripts
Timbuktu is home to scholarly manuscripts—on subjects such as medicine, art, and religion—that date back to the 13th century.

Erg Chech

ALGERIA

MAURITANIA

S A H A R A

Taoudenni

N

Tessalit

Araouane

Adrar des Ifôghas

Azaouâd

MAURITANIA

Timbuktu · Niger

Hombori Tondo 1,155 m (3,789 ft)

Gao

Kayes · Nioro

SENEGAL

Bafoulabé

Kita

Sokolo

Ménaka

Mopti

Ségou · Djenné

NIGER

BAMAKO

Koutiala

Bani

GUINEA

Bougouni · Sikasso

BURKINA FASO

IVORY COAST

0   200 km
0   200 miles
(approximate scale)

Great Mosque of Djenné
The towering mosque at Djenné creates a spectacular backdrop to a weekly market where traders sell food, fuel, and household goods.

The Great Mosque was constructed in 1907 using mud bricks.

⤢ 478,841 sq miles (1,240,192 sq km)

👥 19.6 million

⭐ Bamako

🗣 Bambara, Fulani, other languages (+3)

Between **dry desert** and **tropical savannah**, Mali is a large, **flat country**. The **Niger River**, which runs through it, is used for **fishing**, **transportation**, and **trade**. Mali's main exports are **gold** and **cotton**.

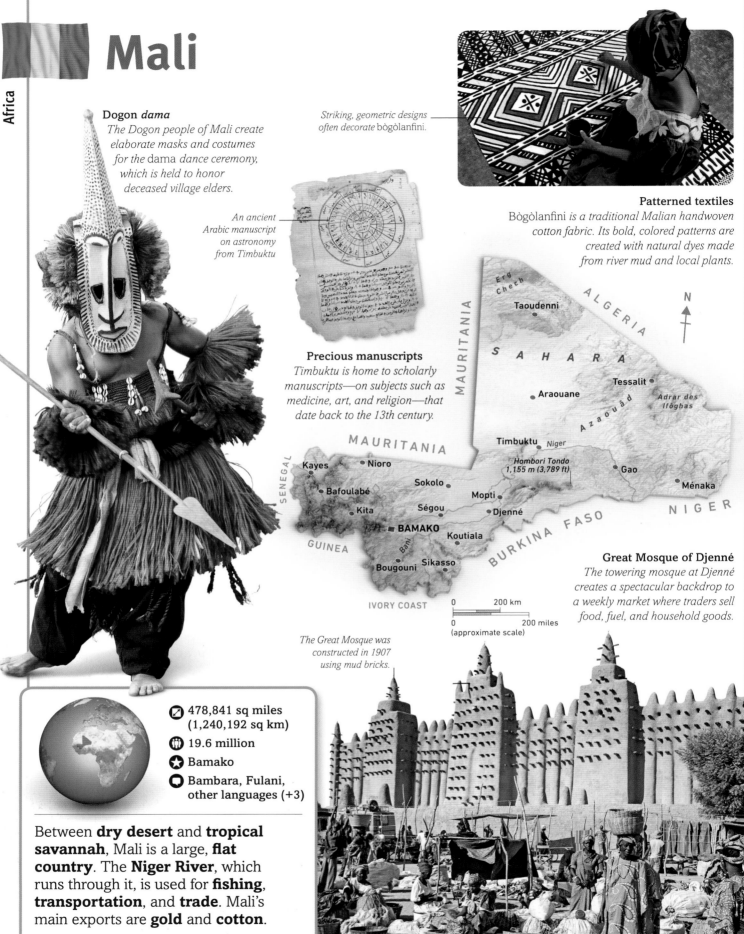

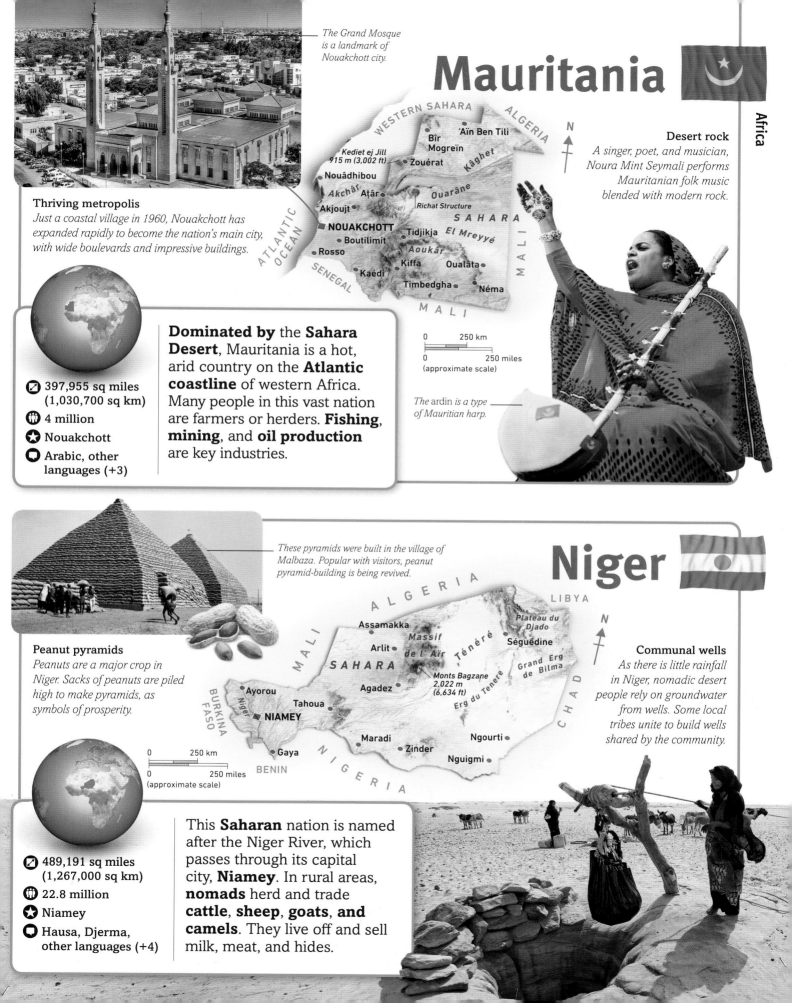

The Grand Mosque is a landmark of Nouakchott city.

Mauritania

Thriving metropolis
Just a coastal village in 1960, Nouakchott has expanded rapidly to become the nation's main city, with wide boulevards and impressive buildings.

Desert rock
A singer, poet, and musician, Noura Mint Seymali performs Mauritanian folk music blended with modern rock.

WESTERN SAHARA
ALGERIA

Kediet ej Jill
915 m (3,002 ft)

Bîr Mogreïn
'Aïn Ben Tili
Kâghet
Zouérat

Nouâdhibou
Akchâr Atâr
Ouarâne
Richat Structure

Akjoujt
S A H A R A

ATLANTIC OCEAN
NOUAKCHOTT
Boutilimit
Tidjikja
El Mreyyé

Rosso
Aoukâr

Kaédi
Kiffa
Oualâta

SENEGAL
Timbedgha
Néma

MALI
MALI

| 0 | 250 km |
| 0 | 250 miles |
(approximate scale)

The ardin is a type of Mauritian harp.

🌍

⚿ **397,955 sq miles
(1,030,700 sq km)**

👥 **4 million**

★ **Nouakchott**

🗨 **Arabic, other
languages (+3)**

Dominated by the **Sahara Desert**, Mauritania is a hot, arid country on the **Atlantic coastline** of western Africa. Many people in this vast nation are farmers or herders. **Fishing, mining**, and **oil production** are key industries.

These pyramids were built in the village of Malbaza. Popular with visitors, peanut pyramid-building is being revived.

Niger

Peanut pyramids
Peanuts are a major crop in Niger. Sacks of peanuts are piled high to make pyramids, as symbols of prosperity.

ALGERIA
LIBYA

MALI
Assamakka
Massif de l'Aïr
Plateau du Djado
Séguédine

Arlit
Ténéré
Grand Erg de Bilma

S A H A R A
Agadez
Monts Bagzane
2,022 m
(6,634 ft)

BURKINA FASO
Ayorou
Niger
Tahoua
Erg du Ténéré

NIAMEY
CHAD

Maradi
Zinder
Ngourti

Gaya
Nguigmi

BENIN
N I G E R I A

| 0 | 250 km |
| 0 | 250 miles |
(approximate scale)

Communal wells
As there is little rainfall in Niger, nomadic desert people rely on groundwater from wells. Some local tribes unite to build wells shared by the community.

🌍

⚿ **489,191 sq miles
(1,267,000 sq km)**

👥 **22.8 million**

★ **Niamey**

🗨 **Hausa, Djerma,
other languages (+4)**

This **Saharan** nation is named after the Niger River, which passes through its capital city, **Niamey**. In rural areas, **nomads** herd and trade **cattle**, **sheep**, **goats**, **and camels**. They live off and sell milk, meat, and hides.

Chad

0   250 km
0   250 miles
(approximate scale)

N

Prehistoric paintings
Ancient rock art, including hundreds of drawings of camels and cattle, is found in the Tibesti Mountains.

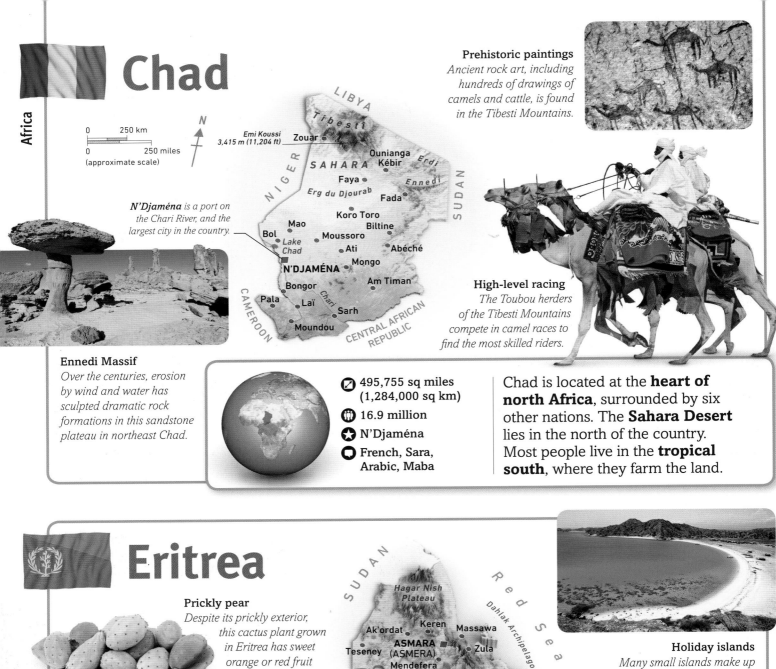

LIBYA

Tibesti

Emi Koussi
3,415 m (11,204 ft)

Zouar

SAHARA

Ounianga Kébir

Erdi

Faya

Ennedi

SUDAN

Fada

N'Djaména is a port on the Chari River, and the largest city in the country.

Koro Toro

NIGER

Erg du Djourab

Mao

Biltine

Bol

Moussoro

Lake Chad

Ati

Abéché

N'DJAMÉNA

Mongo

Bongor

Am Timan

Pala

Laï

Sarh

CAMEROON

Chari

Moundou

CENTRAL AFRICAN REPUBLIC

High-level racing
The Toubou herders of the Tibesti Mountains compete in camel races to find the most skilled riders.

Ennedi Massif
Over the centuries, erosion by wind and water has sculpted dramatic rock formations in this sandstone plateau in northeast Chad.

- 495,755 sq miles (1,284,000 sq km)
- 16.9 million
- N'Djaména
- French, Sara, Arabic, Maba

Chad is located at the **heart of north Africa**, surrounded by six other nations. The **Sahara Desert** lies in the north of the country. Most people live in the **tropical south**, where they farm the land.

Eritrea

Prickly pear
Despite its prickly exterior, this cactus plant grown in Eritrea has sweet orange or red fruit that can be eaten raw.

SUDAN

Hagar Nish Plateau

Red Sea

Dahlak Archipelago

Ak'ordat

Keren

Massawa

ASMARA (ASMERA)

Teseney

Zula

Mendefera

ETHIOPIA

Mount Soira
3,013 m (9,885 ft)

Ïdi

N

0   100 km
0   100 miles
(approximate scale)

Aseb

DJIBOUTI

Holiday islands
Many small islands make up the beautiful Dahlak Archipelago off the coast of Eritrea. Tourist boats and scuba divers visit the clear waters and coral reefs.

- 45,406 sq miles (117,600 sq km)
- 6 million
- Asmara
- Tigrinya, English, other languages (+8)

A mountainous country situated on the **Red Sea** in **northeastern Africa**, Eritrea takes its name from the Greek for "Red Sea." Eritrea gained **independence** from Ethiopia in 1993, though conflict continued until 2018.

Two-towered landmark
Sitting on a hill in the capital, Asmara, is the colorful Enda Mariam Cathedral. Christianity and Islam are the two major religions practiced in Eritrea.

Sudan

Dancing dervishes
Islam is the largest religion in Sudan. Every Friday at Omdurman, near Khartoum, Muslim mystics called dervishes *come together to chant and dance.*

Jabal al 'Uwaynat
1,934m (6,345 ft)

EGYPT

LIBYA

CHAD

Libyan Desert

Wadi Halfa

Nubian Desert

Red Sea

El'Atrun

Dongola

Merowe

Port Sudan

Haiya

Darfur

Omdurman

Ed Damer

KHARTOUM

Kassala

ERITREA

El Geneina

Marrah Hills

El Fasher

Wad Medani

En Nuhud

El Obeid

Gedaref

Nyala

Rabak

White Nile

Blue Nile

ETHIOPIA

El Muglad

Kadugli

Ed Damazin

SOUTH SUDAN

0 — 250 km
0 — 250 miles
(approximate scale)

⊘ 718,723 sq miles
(1,861,484 sq km)

👥 45.6 million

★ Khartoum

◯ Arabic, Nubian, Beja, Fur, English

Sudan has had an unsettled past, and in 2011 it **split into two nations**. Its **population is diverse**, with many different **ethnic groups**. Sudan's capital, **Khartoum**, is the meeting point of the **Blue Nile** and **White Nile** rivers.

Walls of sand
Huge dust storms called haboobs *often sweep through Sudan. Sand carried from the Sahara Desert blows across the land at high speed.*

Sudanese cuisine
Farmers grow a variety of grains, including corn, sorghum, and millet. These are used in popular local dishes.

South Sudan

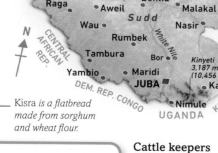

SUDAN

0 — 200 km
0 — 200 miles
(approximate scale)

Raga

Aweil

Melut

Bentiu

Malakal

Wau

Sudd

Nasir

CENTRAL AFRICAN REP.

Rumbek

White Nile

ETHIOPIA

Tambura

Bor

Kinyeti
3,187 m
(10,456 ft)

Yambio

Maridi

JUBA

Kapoeta

DEM. REP. CONGO

Nimule

KENYA

UGANDA

Kisra is a flatbread made from sorghum and wheat flour.

Boma National Park
Among Africa's largest national parks, Boma provides a grassland habitat for antelope, elephants, giraffes, and lions.

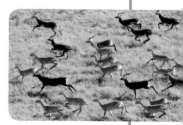

Longhorn cattle are highly valued.

Cattle keepers
The Dinka people in South Sudan lead a traditional herding life.

⊘ 248,777 sq miles
(644,329 sq km)

👥 10.6 million

★ Juba

◯ Arabic, Dinka, other languages (+6)

After a long civil war, South Sudan **voted to become independent** from Sudan **in 2011**. The country has a more African feel than largely Arab Sudan. Its **grassy plains** and **swamps** are **havens for wildlife**.

47

Ethiopia

Bubbling hot spot
A sizzling temperature of 49°C (120°F) is not unheard of in the low-lying Danakil Depression. It has volcanic rocks, a lava lake, and hot green ponds, such as Dallol, that are highly acidic.

Gelada
The Ethiopian Highlands are the home of grass-eating gelada baboons. Males display a red, heart-shaped patch on their chest to attract a mate.

Pastoral people
The Mursi people live as nomads in the Omo River valley. They raise cattle for meat and milk.

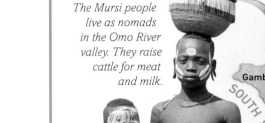

Aksum
Ras Dashen 4,620 m (15,157 ft)
Mek'ele
ERITREA
Red Sea
Danakil Desert
Lake Tana (T'ana Hayk')
Gonder
Weldiya
Tendaho
DJIBOUTI
Gulf of Aden
Bahir Dar
SUDAN
Dese
Awash
Debre Mark'os
Asosa
Debre Birhan
Dire Dawa
Gimbi
ADDIS ABABA (ADIS ABEBA)
Harer
Gambela
Ethiopian Highlands
Nazret
Great Rift Valley
Ogaden
Jima
Hosa'ina
SOUTH SUDAN
Awasa
Goba
Omo
Lake Abaya
Shebeli
Gode
Negele
Yabelo
SOMALIA
KENYA
Moyale
Doolow

0   100 km
0   100 miles
(approximate scale)

Addis Ababa, meaning "new flower," is located in the heart of Ethiopia.

African Union headquarters
The African Union, an organization that promotes cooperation on the continent, has its headquarters in Addis Ababa.

Mesob baskets
Women weave these flat-bottomed baskets in brightly colored patterns. The lidded baskets are used to store food and as tables to eat off.

Ethiopia is a country in the **Horn of Africa**, dramatically split by the **Great Rift Valley** in the Afar region. One of the **oldest cultures** in the world, it is the only part of Africa that was **never colonized**. Ethiopia is where the **coffee plant** came from, and coffee is grown in its mountainous **highlands**. It is the country's main export.

- 426,373 sq miles (1,104,300 sq km)
- 108 million
- Addis Ababa
- Amharic, Tigrinya, other languages (+5)

Saline lake
Salt slabs are extracted from Lake Assal, the world's largest salt reserve. At 508 ft (155 m) below sea level, it is the lowest point in Africa.

Djibouti

Whale sharks
Djibouti's coral reefs are the habitat of whale sharks. Scuba diving with the huge, harmless sharks is a popular tourist attraction.

Camel caravans
Groups of camels are used to transport heavy loads to markets for sale.

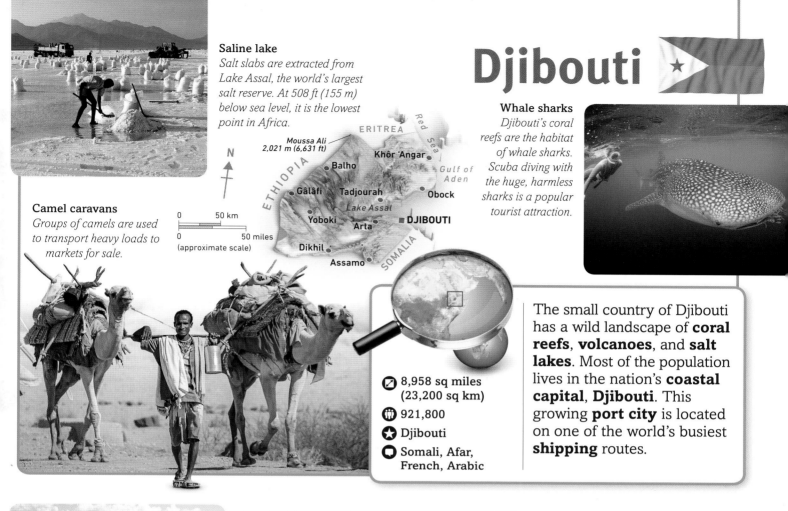

ERITREA
Red Sea
Moussa Ali 2,021 m (6,631 ft)
Khôr 'Angar
Gulf of Aden
Balho
ETHIOPIA
Gâlâfi
Tadjourah
Obock
Lake Assal
Yoboki
Arta
DJIBOUTI
Dikhil
SOMALIA
Assamo

0 — 50 km
0 — 50 miles
(approximate scale)

⤢ 8,958 sq miles (23,200 sq km)
👥 921,800
⭐ Djibouti
💬 Somali, Afar, French, Arabic

The small country of Djibouti has a wild landscape of **coral reefs**, **volcanoes**, and **salt lakes**. Most of the population lives in the nation's **coastal capital, Djibouti**. This growing **port city** is located on one of the world's busiest **shipping** routes.

Trading port
Somalia's capital Mogadishu is a port city on the Indian Ocean. It is one of Africa's most densely populated urban areas.

Somalia

DJIBOUTI
Gulf of Aden
Caluula
Boosaaso
Berbera
Shimbiris 2,407 m (7,897 ft)
Karkaar Mountains
Hurdiyo
Hargeysa
Burco
Raas Xaafuun
SOMALILAND
Garoowe
PUNTLAND
Bandarbeyla
Eyl
ETHIOPIA
Gaalkacyo
Dhuusa Marreeb
Beledweyne
Luuq
Shebeli
Baydhabo
KENYA
MOGADISHU (MUQDISHO)
Jawhar
Juba
Marka
Bu'aale
INDIAN OCEAN
Jamaame
Kismaayo
Buur Gaabo

0 — 200 km
0 — 200 miles
(approximate scale)

Wooden headrest
Somali nomads use headrests for sleeping. These are carved out of wood and painted with intricate patterns.

⤢ 246,200 sq miles (637,657 sq km)
👥 11.8 million
⭐ Mogadishu
💬 Somali, Arabic, English, Italian

Somalia runs along the **eastern coast** of the **Horn of Africa**. The landscape is hot and dry. Some believe this country was once the **fabled Land of Punt**, an ancient kingdom where goods such as **gold**, **myrrh**, and **frankincense** were traded.

Traditional dance
Dhaanto *is a traditional dance performed to local music by groups of Somalis.*

Senegal

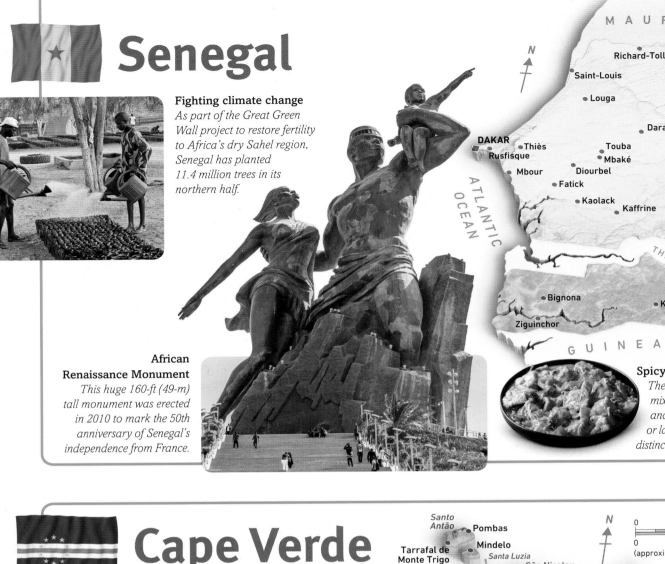

Fighting climate change
As part of the Great Green Wall project to restore fertility to Africa's dry Sahel region, Senegal has planted 11.4 million trees in its northern half.

African Renaissance Monument
This huge 160-ft (49-m) tall monument was erected in 2010 to mark the 50th anniversary of Senegal's independence from France.

MAURITANIA

Richard-Toll • Podor
Saint-Louis •
• Louga
Ferlo De
• Dara
DAKAR • Thiès • Touba • Barkedji • Ranéro
Rufisque • Mbaké
• Mbour • Diourbel
• Fatick
ATLANTIC OCEAN
• Kaolack • Kaffrine
• Koungheul
THE GAMBIA
Tambacounda •
Wassadou •
• Bignona • Kolda
Ziguinchor •
GUINEA - BISSAU

Mboun •

Spicy stew
The traditional mafé stew mixes tomatoes, peppers, and peanuts with beef or lamb to create its distinctive spicy flavor.

Cape Verde

Pico do Fogo
At 9,281 ft (2,829 m) tall, Pico do Fogo is the highest peak in Cape Verde. This active volcano last erupted in 2015.

Santo Antão • Pombas
Tarrafal de Monte Trigo • Mindelo
Santa Luzia
São Vicente
São Nicolau
Tarrafal de São Nicolau • Ribeira Brava
Espargos • *Sal* • Santa Maria
Ilhas do Barlavento
ATLANTIC OCEAN
Boa Vista
Sal Rei •
Ilhas do Sotavento
Maio
São Filipe • Tarrafal • Vila do Maio
Nova Sintra • **PRAIA**
Brava • *Santiago*
Fogo | Pico do Fogo 2,829 m (9,281 ft)

Praia, the largest city, is located on Santiago Island.

0 — 50 km
0 — 50 miles
(approximate scale)

Mindelo
The port city of Mindelo is surrounded by dramatic mountains. It is known for its deep natural harbor, fine beach, and colorful carnivals.

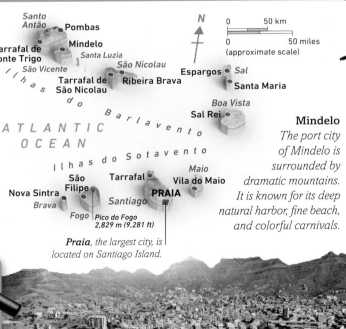

Lying far off the coast of northwestern Africa, Cape (or Cabo) Verde is made up of **10 islands** and many **smaller islets**. Its landscape features **forested hillsides**, **beaches**, and **active volcanoes**. It is also famous for its **unique music**, known as *morna*.

- ⤢ 1,557 sq miles (4,033 sq km)
- 👥 583,000
- ★ Praia
- ◯ Portuguese Creole, Portuguese

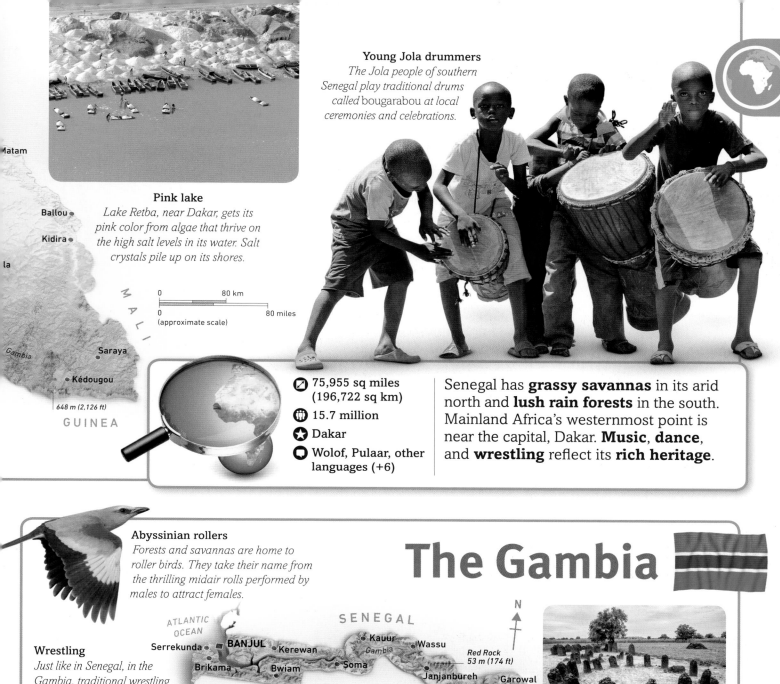

Young Jola drummers
The Jola people of southern Senegal play traditional drums called bougarabou *at local ceremonies and celebrations.*

Pink lake
Lake Retba, near Dakar, gets its pink color from algae that thrive on the high salt levels in its water. Salt crystals pile up on its shores.

Matam

Ballou
Kidira
la

0   80 km
0   80 miles
(approximate scale)

Gambia
Saraya
Kédougou

648 m (2,126 ft)
GUINEA

MALI

⊘ 75,955 sq miles (196,722 sq km)
👥 15.7 million
⭐ Dakar
⬭ Wolof, Pulaar, other languages (+6)

Senegal has **grassy savannas** in its arid north and **lush rain forests** in the south. Mainland Africa's westernmost point is near the capital, Dakar. **Music**, **dance**, and **wrestling** reflect its **rich heritage**.

Abyssinian rollers
Forests and savannas are home to roller birds. They take their name from the thrilling midair rolls performed by males to attract females.

The Gambia

Wrestling
Just like in Senegal, in the Gambia, traditional wrestling is a huge sport as well as a cultural event.

ATLANTIC OCEAN

SENEGAL

N

Serrekunda • **BANJUL** • Kerewan   • Kauur   • Wassu
Brikama •   • Bwiam   *Gambia*   Red Rock
        •   Soma   • Janjanbureh   53 m (174 ft)
SENEGAL   • Garowal
                    Basse Santa Su

0   40 km
0   40 miles
(approximate scale)

Stone Circles of Senegambia
Stone circles dating back to the 3rd century BCE *are spread across the Gambia River region.*

⊘ 4,363 sq miles (11,300 sq km)
👥 2.2 million
⭐ Banjul
⬭ Mandinka, other languages (+5)

A **long**, **narrow** country that follows the **Gambia River**, the Gambia is enclosed by Senegal. The **riverbanks** are home to hundreds of different **bird species** and it has **beautiful beaches** along its tiny **Atlantic coast**.

Sierra Leone

Big butterfly
Found in the Sierra Leonean forests, the African giant swallowtail has a wingspan of up to 9 in (23 cm).

Star of Sierra Leone
Discovered in a mine near Koidu in 1972, this huge diamond weighed 969 carats. It is the fourth-largest gem-quality diamond ever found.

Support for survivors
In 1991–2002, a civil war ravaged Sierra Leone. A young girl who suffered but survived, Mariatu Kamara set up a foundation in 2009 to support fellow victims.

Freetown
The capital and large port city is famous for its nearby beaches.

GUINEA
GUINEA

Kamakwie
Falaba
Kabala
Kambia
Loma Mountains
Kurubonla
Pepel *Rokel* Makeni
Mount Bintumani
1,945 m
(6,381 ft)
FREETOWN
Magburaka
Rotifunk
Koidu
Shenge *Jong* *Sewa* Kailahun
Gbangbatok Bo
Sherbro Island Bonthe Sumbuya *Moa* Kenema
Zimmi
Pujehun
Sulima

ATLANTIC OCEAN
LIBERIA

The Cotton Tree, Freetown
This mighty cotton tree has stood for centuries in the capital of Freetown. It is a protected, peaceful place, with historical and spiritual links.

```
0        50 km
0             50 miles
(approximate scale)
```

Women processing garri *in a factory.*

Making *garri*
A staple food of Sierra Leone is cassava root ground into a type of flour called garri, *which is used in many different ways in cooking.*

Elaborate hairstyle

Stone sculpture
Sierra Leone is rich in masks and other forms of traditional art. This carved stone head is thought to date from the 15th century.

Sierra Leone, the "**Lion Mountains**," takes its name from the dramatic range behind the capital, Freetown. It has some of West Africa's highest **peaks** and stunning **beaches**. The biggest industries are **farming** and **mining**.

- 27,699 sq miles (71,740 sq km)
- 6.6 million
- Freetown
- Mende, Temne, Krio, English

Guinea-Bissau

Cashews
The major export of Guinea-Bissau is cashew nuts, the seeds of the cashew tree.

Cashew seed

*The 88 islands of **Bijagos Archipelago**, home to a rich wildlife, form a protected nature reserve.*

SENEGAL

Cacheu · Farim

Canchungo · Mansôa · Bafatá · Gabú
BISSAU · Rio Gêba

Bolama · Fulacunda · Boe

ATLANTIC OCEAN

Arquipélago dos Bijagós

Buba

Catió

GUINEA

310 m (1,017 ft)

N

0 — 40 km
0 — 40 miles
(approximate scale)

Saltwater hippopotamus
On the island of Bubaque in the Bijagós archipelago, saltwater hippopotamuses keep cool by wading in the sea and swamps.

⊘ **13,948 sq miles (36,125 sq km)**

⊕ **1.9 million**

★ **Bissau**

▭ **Portuguese Creole, Balante, other languages (+3)**

Most of this small West African nation is a **low-lying flood plain**, with tides reaching far inland. Its **estuary landscape** is lush with **mangroves** and **national parks**. Half of the population lives along the coast.

Bissau
A busy port in the vast Geba River estuary, Bissau was founded in 1687. The statue in front of the presidential palace is dedicated to heroes of the independence.

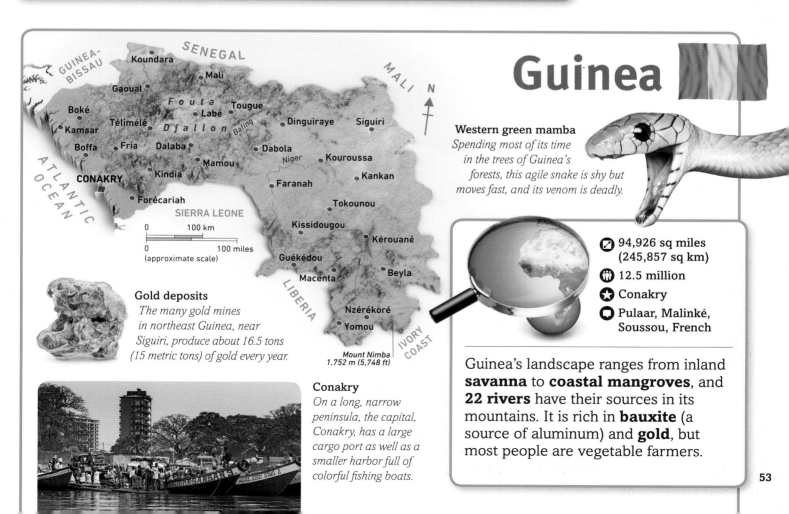

Guinea

GUINEA-BISSAU · SENEGAL · MALI

Koundara

Gaoual · Mali

Boké · *Fouta* · Tougue
Télimélé · Labé

Kamsar · *Djallon* · Dinguiraye · Siguiri
Boffa · Fria · Dalaba · Bafing · Dabola
Mamou · Niger · Kouroussa
Kindia · Kankan
CONAKRY · Faranah
Forécariah · Tokounou

ATLANTIC OCEAN

SIERRA LEONE

Kissidougou · Kérouané

Guékédou · Beyla
Macenta

LIBERIA

Nzérékoré
Yomou

IVORY COAST

Mount Nimba
1,752 m (5,748 ft)

0 — 100 km
0 — 100 miles
(approximate scale)

MALI

N

Western green mamba
Spending most of its time in the trees of Guinea's forests, this agile snake is shy but moves fast, and its venom is deadly.

Gold deposits
The many gold mines in northeast Guinea, near Siguiri, produce about 16.5 tons (15 metric tons) of gold every year.

⊘ **94,926 sq miles (245,857 sq km)**

⊕ **12.5 million**

★ **Conakry**

▭ **Pulaar, Malinké, Soussou, French**

Guinea's landscape ranges from inland **savanna** to **coastal mangroves**, and **22 rivers** have their sources in its mountains. It is rich in **bauxite** (a source of aluminum) and **gold**, but most people are vegetable farmers.

Conakry
On a long, narrow peninsula, the capital, Conakry, has a large cargo port as well as a smaller harbor full of colorful fishing boats.

Ivory Coast

Soccer legend
Twice African Footballer of the Year, the nation's top goal scorer is Didier Drogba. He has used his international profile to highlight critical issues in Ivory Coast and the rest of Africa.

MALI
GUINEA
BURKINA FASO
GHANA
LIBERIA

Tengréla
Odienné
Ferkessédougou
Boundiali
Korhogo
Bouna
Mount Nimba 1,752 m (5,748 ft)
Touba
Katiola
Bondoukou
Monts Nimba
Lac de Kossou
Man
Bouaké
Danané
Daloa
YAMOUSSOUKRO
Gagnoa
Abengourou
Divo
Sassandra
Sassandra
Abidjan
Aboisso
San-Pédro

ATLANTIC OCEAN

Komoé
Bandama

Basilica of Our Lady of Peace
Built in the 1980s in the capital of Yamoussoukro, this huge Catholic basilica is topped by a dome that is 489 ft (149 m) tall.

This West African nation (also known as Côte d'Ivoire) is one of the **world's biggest cocoa exporters**. **Farming**, **fishing**, and **tourism** are the main industries, thanks to vast areas of flat grassland and long, sandy beaches.

- 124,504 sq miles (322,463 sq km)
- 27.5 million
- Yamoussoukro
- Akan, French, Krou, Voltaïque

Liberia

Making *fufu*
Fufu is popular in Liberian, and West African, cuisine. Served with stew, it is made from cassava roots, carefully prepared to form a white, sticky mash.

Pushing soaked cassava through a sieve is a step in one of the many ways to make fufu.

SIERRA LEONE
ATLANTIC OCEAN

Mount Wuteve 1,440 m (4,724 ft)
Voinjama
Kolahun
Konia
Zorzor
Kongo
Bopolu
Saint Paul
Robertsport
Ga
Tubmanburg
Gbarn
Bong Town
Zienzu
Brewerville
MONROVIA
Tap
Harbel
Marshall
Edina
Hartford
Buchanan
Cestos
River Cess
Greenville

Coastal capital
On the Atlantic coast, Monrovia is Liberia's capital and largest city and also a major port. One-third of the total population lives here.

Special spoon
Ceremonial wakemia ladles have been handcrafted for centuries. Carved out of wood in ornate designs, they are made to reward individual generosity.

Burkina Faso

Tour du Faso
Burkina Faso has played host to this 10-day bicycle race since 1987. Covering about 800 miles (1,300 km), it is the African stage of an international cycling competition.

MALI
NIGER

Djibo
Ouahigouya
Dori
Nouna
Tougan
Kaya
Dédougou
Bogandé
OUAGADOUGOU
Bobo-Dioulasso
Koudougou
Fada-Ngourma
Orodara
White Volta
Léo
Pô
Tenkodogo
Diapaga
Banfora
Black Volta
GHANA
TOGO
BENIN
Gaoua
Mount Tenakourou
747 m (2,451 ft)
IVORY COAST

0   100 km
0   100 miles
(approximate scale)

Traditional architecture
Many villages in Burkina Faso feature traditional granaries. They are built on circular wooden bases and have straw-topped roofs.

Flat and surrounded by six countries, Burkina Faso is a **farming** nation. Its landscape is dominated by **savanna** and most people live on the central plateau. Its large, biannual **arts and crafts** fair attracts artists from many African countries.

- 105,869 sq miles (274,200 sq km)
- 20.8 million
- Ouagadougou
- Mossi, other languages (+5)

Joseph Jenkins Roberts
Arriving in Liberia in 1829, this African American merchant became the country's first president in 1848.

Surfing
A growing community of surfers ride the waves off Robertsport, a coastal town considered among the best surf spots in Africa.

Yekepa
Sanniquellie
gleipie
IVORY COAST
Zwedru

Woodland kingfisher
This species of kingfisher is recognized by its blue feathers, bright beak, and fast flight through the forests of Liberia.

Fish Town
asstown
Nyaake
Barclayville
Grand Cess
Harper

- 43,000 sq miles (111,369 sq km)
- 5.1 million
- Monrovia
- Kpelle, Vai, Bassa, other languages (+6)

Getting its name ("freedom") when it was **settled by African Americans** freed from slavery, Liberia has been **independent** since 1848. It elected the **first female president** in Africa, Ellen Johnson Sirleaf (2006–2017).

Ghana

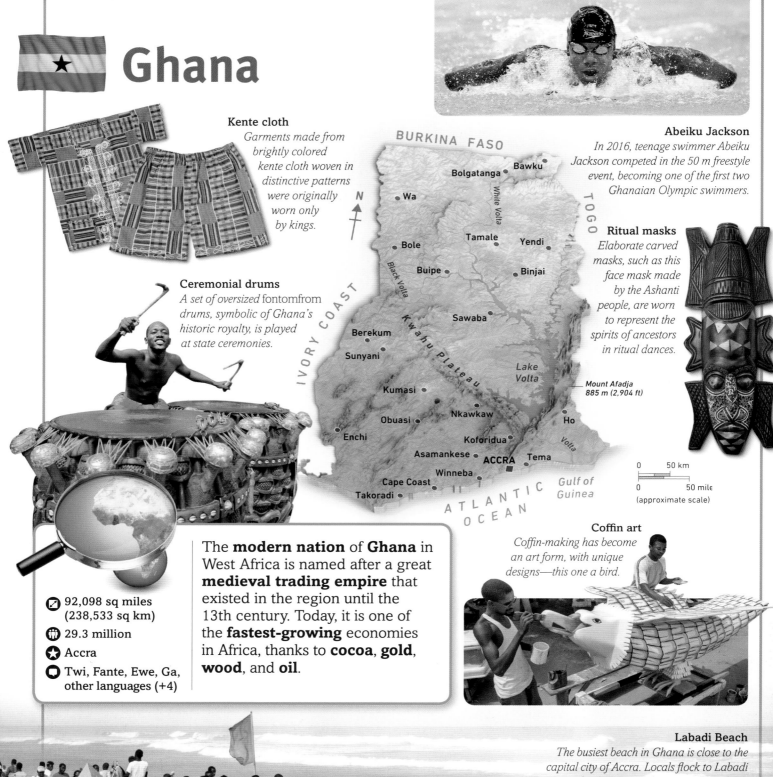

Kente cloth
Garments made from brightly colored kente cloth woven in distinctive patterns were originally worn only by kings.

Abeiku Jackson
In 2016, teenage swimmer Abeiku Jackson competed in the 50 m freestyle event, becoming one of the first two Ghanaian Olympic swimmers.

Ceremonial drums
A set of oversized fontomfrom drums, symbolic of Ghana's historic royalty, is played at state ceremonies.

Ritual masks
Elaborate carved masks, such as this face mask made by the Ashanti people, are worn to represent the spirits of ancestors in ritual dances.

BURKINA FASO

Bolgatanga · Bawku ·
· Wa
Bole · · Tamale · Yendi
Buipe · · Binjai
· Sawaba
Berekum · Kwahu Plateau
Sunyani ·
· Kumasi Lake Volta
Obuasi · · Nkawkaw
Enchi · Koforidua · Ho
Asamankese · ACCRA · Tema
Cape Coast · Winneba
Takoradi ·

White Volta
Black Volta
IVORY COAST
TOGO
Mount Afadja 885 m (2,904 ft)
Volta
ATLANTIC OCEAN
Gulf of Guinea

N

0   50 km
0   50 mile
(approximate scale)

The **modern nation** of **Ghana** in West Africa is named after a great **medieval trading empire** that existed in the region until the 13th century. Today, it is one of the **fastest-growing** economies in Africa, thanks to **cocoa**, **gold**, **wood**, and **oil**.

- 92,098 sq miles (238,533 sq km)
- 29.3 million
- Accra
- Twi, Fante, Ewe, Ga, other languages (+4)

Coffin art
Coffin-making has become an art form, with unique designs—this one a bird.

Labadi Beach
The busiest beach in Ghana is close to the capital city of Accra. Locals flock to Labadi for the spectacular sea and sunshine.

Togo

West African tree viper
Green, scaly skin camouflages this venomous snake in the leafy undergrowth of Togo's forests.

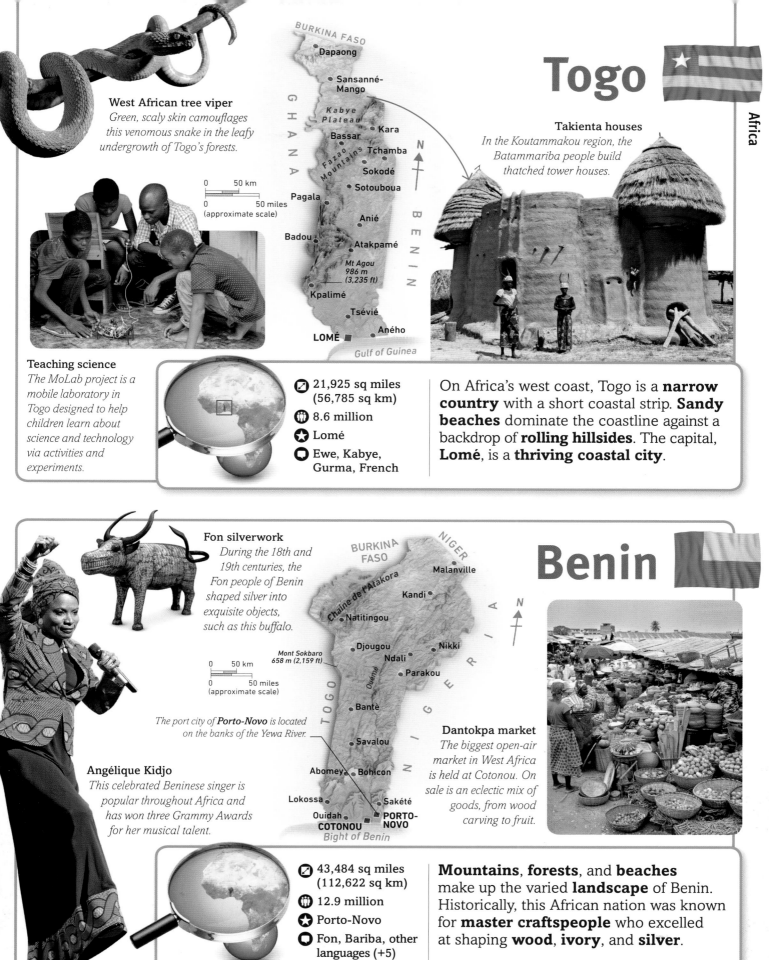

Teaching science
The MoLab project is a mobile laboratory in Togo designed to help children learn about science and technology via activities and experiments.

Map locations: Dapaong, Sansanné-Mango, Kabye Plateau, Kara, Bassar, Tchamba, Fazao Mountains, Sokodé, Sotouboua, Pagala, Anié, Badou, Atakpamé, Mt Agou 986 m (3,235 ft), Kpalimé, Tsévié, Aného, LOMÉ, Gulf of Guinea, GHANA, BURKINA FASO, BENIN

0 50 km
0 50 miles
(approximate scale)

Takienta houses
In the Koutammakou region, the Batammariba people build thatched tower houses.

- 21,925 sq miles (56,785 sq km)
- 8.6 million
- Lomé
- Ewe, Kabye, Gurma, French

On Africa's west coast, Togo is a **narrow country** with a short coastal strip. **Sandy beaches** dominate the coastline against a backdrop of **rolling hillsides**. The capital, **Lomé**, is a **thriving coastal city**.

Benin

Fon silverwork
During the 18th and 19th centuries, the Fon people of Benin shaped silver into exquisite objects, such as this buffalo.

Angélique Kidjo
This celebrated Beninese singer is popular throughout Africa and has won three Grammy Awards for her musical talent.

Map locations: BURKINA FASO, NIGER, Malanville, Chaîne de l'Atakora, Kandi, Natitingou, Djougou, Nikki, Mont Sokbaro 658 m (2,159 ft), Ndali, Ouémé, Parakou, Bantè, Savalou, Abomey, Bohicon, Lokossa, Sakété, Ouidah, PORTO-NOVO, COTONOU, Bight of Benin, TOGO, NIGERIA

0 50 km
0 50 miles
(approximate scale)

The port city of Porto-Novo is located on the banks of the Yewa River.

Dantokpa market
The biggest open-air market in West Africa is held at Cotonou. On sale is an eclectic mix of goods, from wood carving to fruit.

- 43,484 sq miles (112,622 sq km)
- 12.9 million
- Porto-Novo
- Fon, Bariba, other languages (+5)

Mountains, **forests**, and **beaches** make up the varied **landscape** of Benin. Historically, this African nation was known for **master craftspeople** who excelled at shaping **wood**, **ivory**, and **silver**.

Nigeria

Benin bronzes

The historic Kingdom of Benin, in what is now Nigeria, was known for its skilled metalworkers. More than 1,000 bronze plaques and sculptures once decorated the royal palace in Benin City.

Made from an alloy of brass and bronze, this ornate plaque depicts the oba, or king, with his attendants.

Four-horned chameleon

Native to Nigeria and neighboring Cameroon, this chameleon can be recognized by the four prominent horns on its snout. Its striking green skin allows it to effortlessly blend in with forest foliage.

Digital media

Nigeria has hundreds of newspapers, TV networks, and radio stations, but new media, accessed via laptops and cell phones, are taking over, especially in the cities.

Abuja is the purpose-built capital city in the center of Nigeria.

Hakeem Olajuwon

Nigerian-born basketball star Hakeem Olajuwon played in the US National Basketball Association (NBA) from 1984 to 2002 and secured his place in the prestigious Naismith Memorial Basketball Hall of Fame.

Nollywood

Nicknamed "Nollywood," the prolific Nigerian movie industry produces more than 1,500 movies every year, including the 2018 drama Lionheart.

NIGER

Sokoto
Birnin Kebbi
Katsina
Gusau
Koko
Zar
Yelwa
Kaduna
Kainji Reservoir
Kontagora
BENIN
Minna
Shaki
Jebba
Bida
ABUJA
Ilorin
Keff
Iseyin
Ogbomosho
La
Oyo
Imeko
Oshogbo
Lokoja
Ibadan
Iwo
Ado Ekiti
Makuro
Ife
Akure
Ikare
Udi Hills
Abeokuta
Ondo
Owo
Idah
Oturk
Ijebu-Ode
Lagos
Nsukka
Benin City
Agbor
Enugu
Bight of Benin
Sapele
Onitsha
Awka
Orlu
Ikom
Warri
Umuahia
Owerri
Yenagoa
Aba
Uyo
Port Harcourt
Calabar
Opobo
Mouths of the Niger
Gulf of Guinea
ATLANTIC OCEAN

⊘ 356,669 sq miles (923,768 sq km)

👥 214 million

★ Abuja

⬤ Hausa, Yoruba, English, Ibo

Nigeria has the **largest population** and **richest economy** of any African nation. The country's **oil industry**, centered around Port Harcourt in the **Niger Delta**, contributes to its wealth. Half of the population live in **urban areas**. Lagos, Africa's **biggest city**, sits on the coast, while the smaller capital, Abuja, was built inland in the 1980s.

Megacity

Known for business, industry, and shipping, Lagos is also a vibrant cultural hub with many universities. Set around a lagoon, it sprawls across several islands and has two enormous cargo ports.

Jollof rice

Traditional West African jollof rice is a tasty one-pot dish made of cooked meat, rice, tomatoes, onions, peppers, and spices. Jollof is often sold by vendors in marketplaces.

Palm oil

Oil extracted from the fruit of the African oil palm tree is used for cooking in many parts of Africa. Nigeria ranks among the world's largest palm oil producers.

Horses, along with their riders, are dressed in regal decorations as they parade through the streets.

Map labels

Nguru • Hadejia • Damasak • Hadejia • Dutse • Jamaare • Potiskum • Maiduguri • Ngala • Bauchi • Gongola • Gombe • Biu • Kumo • Gombi • Mubi • Numan • Mandara Mountains • Jalingo • Yola • Wukari • Benue • Shebshi Mountains • Chappal Waddi 2,419 m (7,936 ft) • Gotel Mountains • Jos Plateau • ano • CHAD • CAMEROON

75 km
75 miles
(approximate scale)

Nigerian beats

From the legendary Fela Kuti to today's Afrobeats stars, such as Burna Boy (right), Nigerian music is big worldwide.

Durbar festival

Celebrated in northern Nigerian cities such as Kano, this annual Islamic festival marks the end of the holy month of Ramadan and is known for its colorful parades of horse riders.

Geography: Nigeria's varied mix of landscapes range from **drier savanna** to **tropical forests** and **swampy river deltas**.

History: Ancient African **empires** were established here thousands of years ago. Nigeria gained **independence** in 1960.

Culture: More than **250 ethnic groups**, speaking **hundreds of languages**, keep traditional culture alive. **Art**, **literature**, and **music** thrive.

Natural wonders: These include the vast **Niger River**, **Ogbunike Caves**, tumbling waterfalls, the **Ikogosi Springs**, and wildlife parks.

Equatorial Guinea

A silk-cotton tree is featured on the national flag.

Pico Basilé
3,011 m
(9,879 ft)
■ MALABO
● Luba
Isla de Bioco

Gulf of Guinea

Bight of Biafra

CAMEROON

0   50 km
0   50 miles
(approximate scale)

N

On the volcano's edge
The port city of Malabo, built on the rim of a volcano on Bioko Island, exports cocoa, wood, and coffee from its deep harbor.

Social baboon
The world's largest baboon species, mandrills live in big hordes in the rain forests of this region, foraging for fruit and insects on the ground.

Bata ●
Mbini ●
RÍO MUNI
Niefang ●
CIUDAD DE LA PAZ
(under construction)
Evinayong ●
Ebebiyin ●
Río Uolo
Mongomo ●

● Corisco

G A B O N

Africa Cup qualifier
Soccer is a popular sport in Equatorial Guinea. The national soccer team has twice qualified for the Africa Cup of Nations.

Five islands and the mainland territory of **Río Muni** make up Equatorial Guinea. An **oil boom** has fueled the building of a **new capital**, Ciudad de la Paz, in the **rain forest**.

⊘ 10,831 sq miles (28,051 sq km)
👥 836,000
★ Malabo
🗣 Spanish, Fang, Bubi, French

São Tomé and Príncipe

Chocolate islands
Chocolate makers have set up cooperatives to grow cocoa on the islands, feeding a global appetite for high-quality, fairly traded chocolate.

Cocoa pods

0   50 km
0   50 miles
(approximate scale)

N

ATLANTIC OCEAN

● Santo António
Príncipe

Gulf of Guinea

Pico de São Tomé
2,024 m (6,640 ft)
Neves ●
São Tomé ■ SÃO TOMÉ
● Ribeira Afonso
Porto Alegre ●

Pico Cão Grande
The needle-shaped Pico Cão Grande, meaning "Great Dog Peak," is a landmark on São Tomé Island. This towering volcanic rock stands 1,266 ft (386 m) tall.

⊘ 372 sq miles (964 sq km)
👥 211,000
★ São Tomé
🗣 Portuguese Creole, Portuguese

The two **mountainous islands** of São Tomé and Príncipe and their **islets** lie off the west coast of Africa. Their **jungled slopes** throng with **endemic birds**, such as the giant sunbird, and **tree frogs**. São Tomé, the **bigger island**, is home to the **capital**.

Cameroon

Ekom-Nkam waterfalls
The twin Waterfalls of Ekom-Nkam cascade 260 ft (80 m) down in the heart of Cameroon's lush rain forest near Nkongsamba.

Gourd rattle
This local instrument, known as a sekere, produces a sound similar to a rattle.

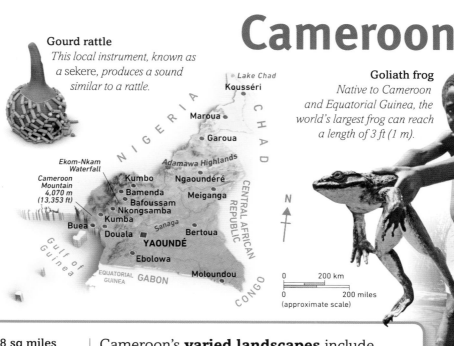

Goliath frog
Native to Cameroon and Equatorial Guinea, the world's largest frog can reach a length of 3 ft (1 m).

Lake Chad
Kousséri
Maroua
Garoua
NIGERIA
CHAD
Adamawa Highlands
Ekom-Nkam Waterfall
Cameroon Mountain 4,070 m (13,353 ft)
Kumbo
Bamenda
Bafoussam
Nkongsamba
Kumba
Buea
Douala
Sanaga
Ngaoundéré
Meiganga
CENTRAL AFRICAN REPUBLIC
Bertoua
YAOUNDÉ
Ebolowa
Gulf of Guinea
EQUATORIAL GUINEA
GABON
Moloundou
CONGO
N

0   200 km
0   200 miles
(approximate scale)

🌐 183,568 sq miles (475,440 sq km)
👥 27.8 million
⭐ Yaoundé
⬤ Bamileke, Fang, other languages (+3)

Cameroon's **varied landscapes** include **volcanic mountains**, **tropical rain forests**, and **desert**. Called the **"hinge" of Africa** for its location between West and Central Africa, the country is home to a **diverse culture**.

Gabon

Guardian figures
The Kota people of Gabon crafted ornate guardian figures, known as mbulu-ngulus, to watch over their ancestral remains.

This figure's legs are coated in brass.

CAMEROON
N
EQUATORIAL GUINEA
Oyem
Mont Bengoué 1,070 m (3,510 ft)
Mitzic
Mékambo
LIBREVILLE
Makokou
Port-Gentil
Ogooué
Lambaréné
Massif du Chaillu
Okondja
Koulamoutou
Francceville
Mouila
Ngounié
Gamba
Tchibanga
ATLANTIC OCEAN
CONGO

0   100 km
0   100 miles
(approximate scale)

Mont-Bouët market
The huge Mont-Bouët market in Libreville sells everything from fruit and vegetables to fabric printed in traditional styles.

Protecting wildlife
The Loango National Park south of Omboué provides sanctuary to many animals, including the African slender-snouted crocodile.

🌐 103,346 sq miles (267,667 sq km)
👥 2.2 million
⭐ Libreville
⬤ Fang, French, Punu, Sira, Nzebi, Mpongwe

A **forested country** on the **west coast** of Africa, Gabon is committed to preserving the natural environment. **One-tenth** of the **land** is **protected** for its flora and fauna.

Central African Republic

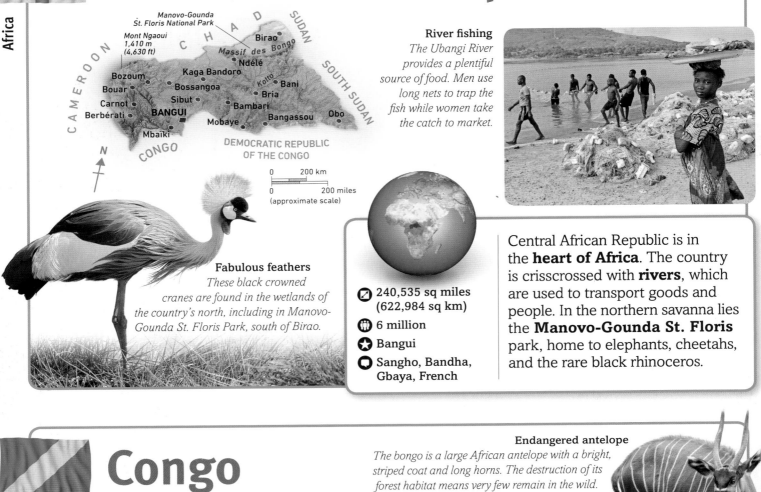

Manovo-Gounda
St. Floris National Park

Mont Ngaoui
1,410 m
(4,630 ft)

C H A D

SUDAN

SOUTH SUDAN

CAMEROON

Birao

Massif des
Bongo

Ndélé

Kaga Bandoro

Bozoum

Bossangoa
Kotto
Bani

Bouar

Carnot
Sibut
Bria

Berbérati
Bambari

BANGUI
Bangassou
Obo

Mobaye

Mbaïki

CONGO

DEMOCRATIC REPUBLIC
OF THE CONGO

0   200 km
0   200 miles
(approximate scale)

River fishing
The Ubangi River provides a plentiful source of food. Men use long nets to trap the fish while women take the catch to market.

Fabulous feathers
These black crowned cranes are found in the wetlands of the country's north, including in Manovo-Gounda St. Floris Park, south of Birao.

⬿ **240,535 sq miles**
(622,984 sq km)

🌐 **6 million**

★ **Bangui**

▭ **Sangho, Bandha,**
Gbaya, French

Central African Republic is in the **heart of Africa**. The country is crisscrossed with **rivers**, which are used to transport goods and people. In the northern savanna lies the **Manovo-Gounda St. Floris** park, home to elephants, cheetahs, and the rare black rhinoceros.

Congo

Endangered antelope
The bongo is a large African antelope with a bright, striped coat and long horns. The destruction of its forest habitat means very few remain in the wild.

Unique sport
Nzango is a high-energy sport combining gymnastics with dance, in which two teams compete. It evolved from a playground game.

Mont Nabemba
1,020 m
(3,346 ft)

CENTRAL AFRICAN
REPUBLIC

CAMEROON

Bétou

Impfondo

Sembé
Ouésso

Makoua
Ubangi

DEMOCRATIC REPUBLIC
OF THE CONGO

G A B O N

Ewo

Owando
Congo

Mpama

Gamboma

Mossendjo
Djambala
Ngo

Dolisie
Sibiti
Plateaux
Batéké

Pointe-Noire
Nkayi

BRAZZAVILLE

Kinkala

ATLANTIC
OCEAN

ANGOLA
(CABINDA)

0   150 km
0   150 miles
(approximate scale)

⬿ **132,047 sq miles**
(342,000 sq km)

🌐 **5.3 million**

★ **Brazzaville**

▭ **Kongo, Teke,**
Lingala, French

About two-thirds of this central African country is covered in **dense rain forest**. Most people live in towns and cities by rivers. The capital, **Brazzaville**, is just across the **Congo River** from **Kinshasa**, capital of neighboring Democratic Republic of the Congo.

Democratic Republic of the Congo

Simple but sturdy
In some parts of the country, young people earn their livelihood delivering goods using a reliable handmade vehicle called a chukudu.

This inexpensive two-wheeler is made from wood and recycled materials.

Musical metropolis
Home to more than 11 million people and growing rapidly, Kinshasa is the cradle of Congolese rumba dance music.

Mount Nyiragongo
This active volcano in the Great Rift Valley last erupted in 2002. A lake of lava has formed inside the volcano's crater.

Sociable apes
Found only in the lush rain forests along the Congo River, these bonobo apes live in peaceful communities of 30–100 individuals.

Ornate drum
A tradition of the Vili people, who live across Central Africa, is to sculpt these unique drums, mounted on top of intricately carved figures.

The human figurine supporting the drum is sitting on a leopard.

Ingenious fishermen
Near Kisangani the Wagenya people catch fish in sievelike baskets attached to poles suspended over the Congo River rapids.

- 905,355 sq miles (2,344,858 sq km)
- 101.8 million
- Kinshasa
- Kiswahili, Tshiluba, other languages (+3)

Previously called Zaire, the Democratic Republic of the Congo is the **second-largest country** in Africa. It straddles the **equator** so at the same time that it is **spring in the north** of the country, it is **fall in the south**.

Map

CENTRAL AFRICAN REPUBLIC

SOUTH SUDAN

Gemena

Uele

Buta

Isiro

Bumba

Congo

Lake Albert

Mbandaka

Congo Basin

Kisangani

Mount Stanley 5,109 m (16,762 ft)

Butembo

UGANDA

Lac Ntombe

Ikela

Lake Edward

Congo

Lac Mai-Ndombe

Mount Nyiragongo 3,470 m (11,385 ft)

RWANDA

Bandundu

Lukenie

Lodja

Kindu

Bukavu

BURUNDI

KINSHASA

Mangai

Ilebo

Kasongo

Matadi

Kikwit

Kananga

Kabinda

Kalemie

TANZANIA

Tshikapa

Mbuji-Mayi

Gandajika

Mwene-Ditu

Manono

Lake Tanganyika

Kamina

Lake Mweru

ATLANTIC OCEAN

ANGOLA

Kolwezi

Likasi

Lubumbashi

ZAMBIA

Mitumba Range

Great Rift Valley

0   200 km
0   200 miles
(approximate scale)

Burundi

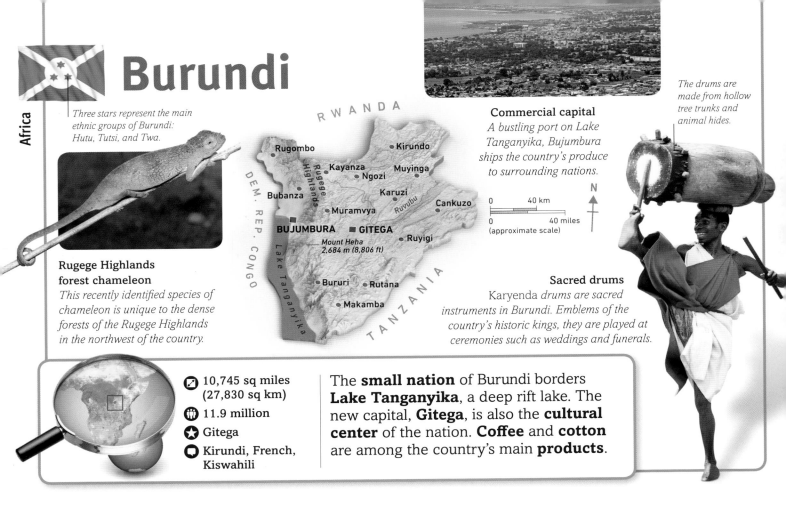

Three stars represent the main ethnic groups of Burundi: Hutu, Tutsi, and Twa.

Rugege Highlands forest chameleon
This recently identified species of chameleon is unique to the dense forests of the Rugege Highlands in the northwest of the country.

Commercial capital
A bustling port on Lake Tanganyika, Bujumbura ships the country's produce to surrounding nations.

The drums are made from hollow tree trunks and animal hides.

Sacred drums
Karyenda *drums are sacred instruments in Burundi. Emblems of the country's historic kings, they are played at ceremonies such as weddings and funerals.*

- ⬈ 10,745 sq miles (27,830 sq km)
- 👥 11.9 million
- ⭐ Gitega
- 🔾 Kirundi, French, Kiswahili

The **small nation** of Burundi borders **Lake Tanganyika**, a deep rift lake. The new capital, **Gitega**, is also the **cultural center** of the nation. **Coffee** and **cotton** are among the country's main **products**.

King's Palace
This beehive-shaped, thatched building is a reconstruction of the Rwandan king's traditional residence in Nyanza near Nyabisindu, where the royal court settled in 1899.

Rwanda

The sun represents the enlightenment of Rwanda's people.

Women working in coffee bean collectives share in the profits of the group.

Kigali *extends over several hills and valleys.*

- ⬈ 10,169 sq miles (26,338 sq km)
- 👥 12.7 million
- ⭐ Kigali
- 🔾 Kinyarwanda, French, Kiswahili, English

Rwanda's hilly **terrain** includes the volcanic **Virunga Mountains**. **Lush rain forests** carpet the slopes, the habitat of many **primate species**, including **chimpanzees**, **golden monkeys**, and rare **mountain gorillas**.

Powerful women
Women in Rwanda hold more power than women in any other country in the world, with 62 percent of seats in the parliament. In 2020, the nation ranked sixth in the world for overall equality between women and men.

Uganda

On the shores of Lake Victoria
Kampala, meaning "hill of the impala," has spread over several hills on the shores of Lake Victoria. It is one of Africa's fastest-growing cities.

Mountain gorilla
The country's rain forests are home to more than 450 rare mountain gorillas. Most live in Bwindi Impenetrable National Park in the southwest.

Rwenzori Mountains
Astride the border of Uganda and the Democratic Republic of the Congo, this area of snowcapped peaks and glaciers is known as the Mountains of the Moon.

Climate protest
Vanessa Nakate is a Ugandan activist bringing to the attention of the world the dangers of rising temperatures and drought on agriculture and food supply in Africa.

SOUTH SUDAN

0   100 km
0   100 miles
(approximate scale)

DEMOCRATIC REPUBLIC OF THE CONGO

KENYA

Moyo
Koboko
Arua
Albert Nile
Kitgum
Kaabong
Kotido
Gulu
Pakwach
Lira
Moroto
Amudat
Masindi
Lake Kyoga
Hoima
Soroti
Lake Albert
Nakasongola
Kapchorwa
Rwenzori Mountains
Fort Portal
Mbale
Margherita Peak 5,109 m (16,762 ft)
Mubende
Bombo
Kaliro
Victoria Nile
Kasese
Iganga
Tororo
Ntusi
KAMPALA
Jinja
Lake Edward
Entebbe
Bwindi Impenetrable National Park
Masaka
Bukakata
Mbarara
Rukungiri
Lake Victoria
Kisoro
Kabale
N
RWANDA
TANZANIA

Lake Victoria
This lake is shared by Uganda, Tanzania, and Kenya. Its waters teem with fish such as the Nile perch.

- 93,065 sq miles (241,038 sq km)
- 43.3 million
- Kampala
- Luganda, Nkole, Chiga, Lango, Acholi, others languages (+3)

Uganda lies between **Lake Albert** and **Lake Edward** to the north, and **Lake Victoria**—Africa's **largest freshwater lake**—to the south. **Mt. Stanley** in the **Rwenzori range** is Africa's **third-highest** mountain.

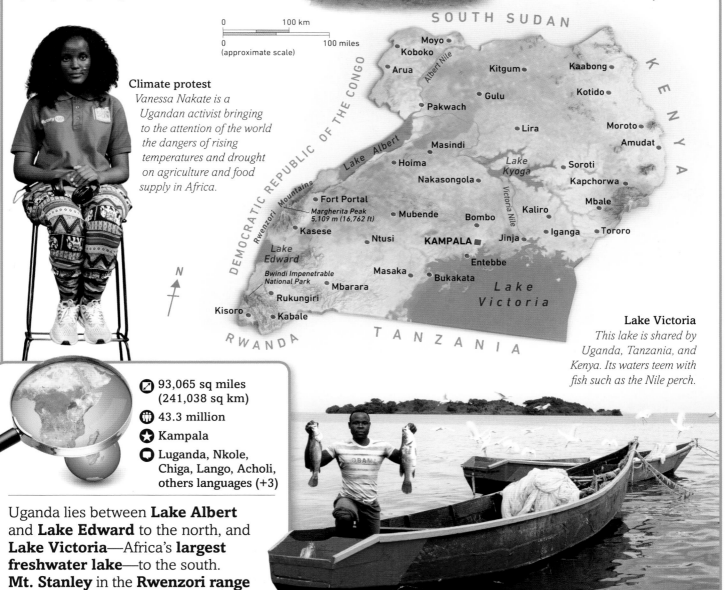

Tanzania

Dar es Salaam
Overlooking the Indian Ocean, Dar es Salaam is the largest city and port of Tanzania. Its name means "Abode of Peace" in Arabic.

Black-capped social weaver
Shrubland in East Africa is home to these gregarious birds. They live in colonies, building nests that hang from the branches of acacia trees.

Tanzanite
The striking blue gemstone called tanzanite is very rare and can be mined only in the Mirerani hills near Arusha.

Maasai people
Around a million Maasai people live across Tanzania and Kenya. These nomadic hunters and cattle herders wear distinctive shuka *blankets and jewelry.*

UGANDA
RWANDA
Bukoba
Lake Victoria
KENYA
Biharamulo
Musoma
BURUNDI
Mwanza
Serengeti Plain
Bariadi
Kibondo
Shinyanga
Kigoma
Nzega
Lake Eyasi
Arusha
Moshi
Kilimanjaro 5,895 m (19,341 ft)
Lake Tanganyika
Tabora
Singida
Babati
Shama
Masai Steppe
Mpanda
DEM. REP. CONGO
Kipili
Lake Rukwa
DODOMA
Tanga
Pemba
Sumbawanga
Great Ruaha
Great Rift Valley
Zanzibar
Morogoro
Zanzibar
ZAMBIA
Iringa
Rubeho Mountains
Dar es Salaam
Rufiji
Mafia
Mbeya
Sao Hill
Mohoro
MALAWI
Njombe
Kilwa Kivinje
Livingstone Mountains
Rufiji
INDIAN OCEAN
Songea
Lindi
Tunduru
Masasi
Mtwara
MOZAMBIQUE

0   100 km
0   100 miles
(approximate scale)

N

Spice island
Zanzibar was a longtime center for Indian, Persian, and Arab trade with the African continent. It still exports spices, such as cloves, from its harbor.

⊘ 365,755 sq miles (947,300 sq km)

👥 58.6 million

★ Dodoma

💬 Kiswahili, Sukuma, Chagga, others (+6)

Mount Kilimanjaro
At 19,341 ft (5,895 m), this dormant volcano is the highest peak in Africa.

Tanzania is a land of **high mountains**, **lush coastal plains**, **savanna**, and the **Zanzibar archipelago**. The **Serengeti National Park** is known for its herds of **migratory zebras** and **wildebeest**, while the volcanic crater of **Ngorongoro Park** is home to **rhinos** and **elephants**.

Kenya

Flamingos of Lake Bogoria
Lesser flamingos flock to this Great Rift Valley lake near Nakuru to feed on brine shrimp and blue-green algae in the very salty waters. This food gives these birds their pink coloring.

Olympian runner
Kenyan athletes have often gained victory in distance running. David Rudisha has won two Olympic gold medals and holds a world record in the 800 m race.

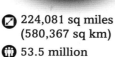

***Kiondo* baskets**
Kikuyu, Kamba, and Taita people weave decorative bags from sisal fibers. Known as kiondos, *these are used to carry market goods and store supplies.*

Most Samburu girls wear bead necklaces.

Map labels:
SOUTH SUDAN
Ilemi Triangle (administered by Kenya)
ETHIOPIA
Lokitaung
Lake Turkana (Lake Rudolf)
Lodwar
Chalbi Desert
Mandera
Awara Plain
Marsabit
UGANDA
Wajir
Bungoma
Eldoret
Maralal
Kirinyaga 5,200 m (17,061 ft)
Woyamdero Plain
Kisumu
Lake Victoria
Nakuru
Nyeri
Meru
Tana
SOMALIA
Migori
Maasai Mara
Thika
NAIROBI
Garissa
TANZANIA
Ngangerabeli Plain
Garsen
Voi
Malindi
Mombasa
INDIAN OCEAN

N

0   100 km
0   100 miles
(approximate scale)

Geothermal power station
Kenya was the first country in Africa to build geothermal power stations. In the Great Rift Valley, these use energy stored inside Earth to generate power.

Samburu people
In northern Kenya, the Samburu live as they always have, by raising cattle, moving around to find grazing, and building mud and grass huts for shelter.

Maasai Mara lions
Hundreds of lions live in prides in the Maasai Mara National Reserve, west of Nairobi. They live alongside buffalo, many species of antelope, and other big cats.

Famous for its **wildlife**, Kenya sees the annual **migration** of millions of **animals** across the **Maasai Mara**, and the **Great Rift Valley** lakes attract flocks of **birds**. The capital, **Nairobi**, is a thriving **modern city**, and the port, **Mombasa**, is one of Africa's most **multicultural** cities.

- 224,081 sq miles (580,367 sq km)
- 53.5 million
- Nairobi
- Kiswahili, English, Kikuyu, other languages (+3)

Angola

Luanda
Angola's largest city sits on the Atlantic coastline. This thriving port city is the trading center of the country.

Palácio de Ferro
Designed by French architect Gustave Eiffel, this building was originally constructed in Paris before being dismantled and rebuilt in Luanda in 1902. Its name means "Iron Palace."

Chokwe art
The Chokwe people of northeastern Angola, Congo, and Zambia are renowned for their ornately carved figurines, drums, and masks.

N

CABINDA
(part of Angola)

Cabinda

M'Banza Congo

N'Zeto

Ambriz

Uíge

Caxito

Camabatela

LUANDA

N'Dalatando

Dondo

Malanje

Gabela

Sumbe

Cuanza

Cacolo

Mount Moco
2,620 m (8,600 ft)

Lobito

Benguela

Camacupa

Luena

Cubal

Kuito

Bié Plateau

Huambo

Caconda

Lóvua

Chitato

Lucapa

Saurimo

Zambezi

Lungué-Bungo

Cazombo

Z A M B I A

Cangamba

ATLANTIC OCEAN

Namibe

Lubango

Cubango

Menongue

Tombua

Huíla Plateau

Cuito Caunavale

Cuando

Chiume

Xangongo

Cubango

Cuito

N'Giva

N A M I B I A

Luiana

DEM. REP. CONGO

Cuango

The bird has a bright red crest.

Red-crested turaco
Found only in the tropical forests of northern Angola, this colorful bird has a distinctive, shrill song.

0   150 km
0   150 miles
(approximate scale)

Temminck's ground pangolin
Pangolins are the world's only scaly mammals. This species is found throughout southern Africa.

Angolan Carnival
The country's annual carnival marks the end of the period before Lent. Dancers and musicians perform in parades watched by crowds.

⬈ 481,354 sq miles (1,246,700 sq km)

👥 32.5 million

★ Luanda

🗨 Portuguese, other languages (+3)

Angola is a large country rich in **natural resources**, including oil, minerals, and fertile farmland. Set back by many years of civil war, it is now one of the **fastest-growing economies** in Africa.

Zambia

Rally racing
The Zambia International Motor Rally is a high-speed racing event that takes place every year. The tough course starts in Lusaka and heads north into the desert.

Bat migration
Toward the end of each year, more than 10 million fruit bats descend on Kasanka National Park in northern Zambia. They migrate from forests in the Democratic Repbulic of Congo to feast on the park's plentiful fruit trees.

Batonga baskets
The Batonga people live in farming villages around Lake Kariba. Women weave traditional baskets from palm leaves.

Palm leaves are boiled to make them soft for weaving.

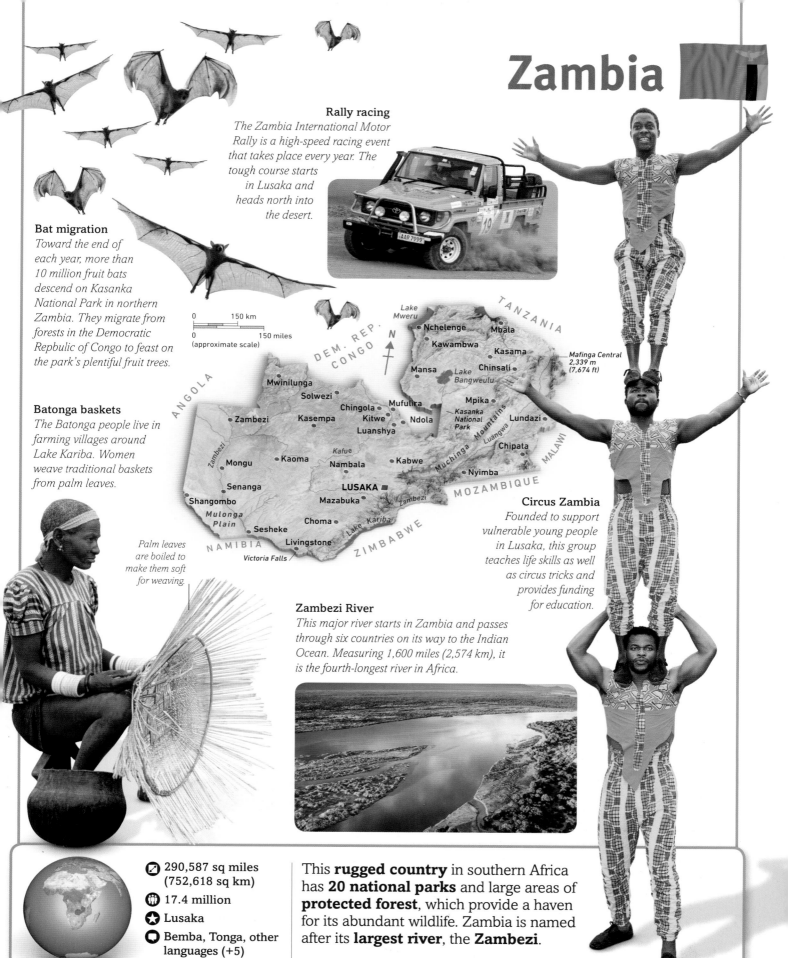

0   150 km
0   150 miles
(approximate scale)

Lake Mweru
TANZANIA
Nchelenge
Mbala
Kawambwa
Kasama
DEM. REP. CONGO
Mansa
Chinsali
Mafinga Central 2,339 m (7,674 ft)
Lake Bangweulu
Mwinilunga
Mpika
ANGOLA
Solwezi
Kasanka National Park
Chingola
Mufulira
Lundazi
Zambezi
Kasempa
Kitwe
Ndola
Muchinga Mountains
Luangwa
Chipata
Luanshya
MALAWI
Kafue
Kaoma
Nambala
Kabwe
Mongu
Nyimba
Senanga
LUSAKA
MOZAMBIQUE
Shangombo
Mazabuka
Zambezi
Mulonga Plain
Choma
Sesheke
Lake Kariba
ZIMBABWE
NAMIBIA
Livingstone
Victoria Falls

Circus Zambia
Founded to support vulnerable young people in Lusaka, this group teaches life skills as well as circus tricks and provides funding for education.

Zambezi River
This major river starts in Zambia and passes through six countries on its way to the Indian Ocean. Measuring 1,600 miles (2,574 km), it is the fourth-longest river in Africa.

- 290,587 sq miles (752,618 sq km)
- 17.4 million
- Lusaka
- Bemba, Tonga, other languages (+5)

This **rugged country** in southern Africa has **20 national parks** and large areas of **protected forest**, which provide a haven for its abundant wildlife. Zambia is named after its **largest river**, the **Zambezi**.

Namibia

Cheetah
With a population of more than 1,400 wild cheetahs, Namibia has the largest number of any country. The Cheetah Conservation Fund at Otjiwarongo protects these rare animals.

Dune 7
Huge sand dunes run across the Namib Desert. The highest is Dune 7, measuring 1,256 ft (383 m) tall.

ANGOLA

Olifa
Opuwo
Oshikango
Oshakati
Ongandjera
Ovamboland
Rundu
ZAMBIA
Caprivi Strip
Katima Mulilo
Etosha Pan
BOTSWANA
Tsumeb
Otavi
Grootfontein
Tsumkwe
Brandberg 2,573 m (8,442 ft)
Otjiwarongo

0   150 km
0   150 miles
(approximate scale)

N

Traditional odelela fabric has red, pink, and black stripes.

Wlotzkasbaken
Karibib
WINDHOEK
Windhoek, meaning "windy corner," is Namibia's largest city.
Swakopmund
Walvis Bay
Gobabis

Rehoboth

Kalahari Desert

Deadvlei
Marinetal
Nossob

Namaqualand

Lüderitz
Aus
Keetmanshoop

Ovambo people
The largest ethnic group in Namibia, the Ovambo make up more than half of the country's population.

Great Karas Mountains
Rosh Pinah
Karasburg
Ariamsvlei
Oranjemund

SOUTH AFRICA

Herero dolls
Women of the Herero ethnic group make traditional dolls by hand, dressing them in decorative outfits that mimic their own colorful dress.

*The **Namib Desert** stretches for 1,200 miles (1,900 km) along the coastal plain.*

⊘ 318,261 sq miles (824,292 sq km)

👥 2.6 million

★ Windhoek

⬭ Ovambo, Kavango, English, Bergdama, German, Afrikaans

Namibia is situated on the **southwest coast** of Africa. This **vast country** of **deserts**, **mountains**, and **grasslands** is almost entirely **arid**, meaning it is so dry that few plants can grow. It was one of the first countries to **protect** its **environment** by law.

Deadvlei
Silhouettes of long-dead trees create a dramatic skyline against the red sands in Deadvlei, which means "dead marsh." This is a white clay pan near Sossusvlei in the center of the country's dunes.

Mopane worms

The large caterpillar of the emperor moth is a delicacy eaten in Zimbabwe, either sun-dried or fried in a tasty sauce.

Zimbabwe

Flame lily

This vibrant red and yellow flower looks like flames. It is a protected species and the national flower of Zimbabwe.

Map labels:
ZAMBIA
MOZAMBIQUE
BOTSWANA
Lake Kariba
Kariba
Mvurwi Range
Binga
Chinhoyi
Bindura
Victoria Falls
HARARE
Hwange
Kadoma
Chitungwiza
Lupane
Mount Nyangani 2,592 m (8,504 ft)
Kwekwe
Gweru
Mutare
Plumtree
Bulawayo
Masvingo
Matobo Hills
Zvishavane
Gwanda
Umzingwani
Chiredzi
Beitbridge
SOUTH AFRICA

0   100 km
0   100 miles
(approximate scale)

- 150,872 sq miles (390,757 sq km)
- 14.5 million
- Harare
- Shona, isiNdebele, English

This **landlocked country** has been at the heart of **trading empires** such as medieval **Great Zimbabwe** since the 11th century. It is known for the **stunning scenery** and **wildlife** of its **ridge** and **river valleys**.

Victoria Falls

These are among the world's largest waterfalls, extending over 5,604 ft (1,708 m) along the Zambezi River.

Lake Malawi

One of the largest lakes in Africa, Lake Malawi is home to more than 850 different species of colorful cichlid fish.

Malawi

Map labels:
TANZANIA
Chitipa
Karonga
ZAMBIA
Great Rift Valley
Euthini
Mzuzu
Mzimba
MOZAMBIQUE
Lake Malawi
Kasungu
Nkhotakota
Mchinji
Salima
LILONGWE
Dedza
Mangochi
Ntcheu
Lake Malombe
Liwonde
Mount Mulanje 3,002 m (9,849 ft)
Zomba
Blantyre
Mulanje
MOZAMBIQUE
Chiromo
Nsanje

0   100 km
0   100 miles
(approximate scale)

The national flag features a rising sun to symbolize the new dawn of freedom in Africa.

- 45,747 sq miles (118,484 sq km)
- 21.2 million
- Lilongwe
- Chewa, Lomwe, Yao, Ngoni, English

The **Great Rift Valley**, where the rock that makes up Africa divides, cuts through this **long**, **narrow** country. Formed in the rift, **Lake Malawi**, also known as Lake Nyasa, is one of Africa's **Great Lakes**. It is 360 miles (580 km) long and 47 miles (75 km) wide.

Vibrant wraps

Many women in southern Africa traditionally wear the chitenge, *a vivid, patterned fabric worn as a sarong or a headdress. It is also fashioned into skirts, blouses, and dresses.*

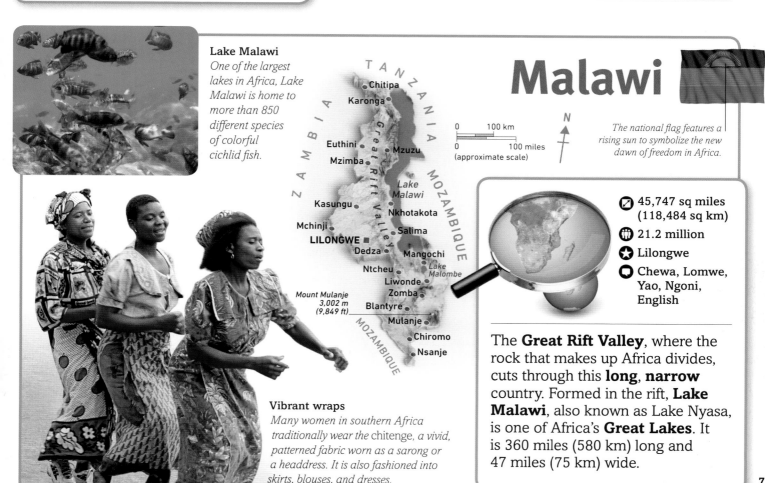

Botswana

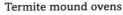

Termite mound ovens
Abandoned yet sturdy termite mounds can be used as outdoor ovens for cooking bread and meat, since they are excellent at retaining heat.

A hole is made on one side to allow excess smoke to escape.

Okavango River
The Okavango is 1,050 miles (1,700 km) long and flows into the Kalahari Desert, forming a huge inland delta of marshland and floodplains. Here live some of the most endangered animals, such as rhinos and lions.

Kalahari Desert
Kalahari sands spread across 84 percent of Botswana. This desert is the second largest in Africa, after the Sahara.

Meerkat mob
Found only in parts of Southern Africa, these small members of the mongoose family live in large colonies across Botswana's plains.

Map labels:
ZAMBIA
NAMIBIA
ZIMBABWE
Shakwe
Kasane
Okavango
Okavango Delta
Tsau
Maun
Nata
Ntwetwe Pan
Sowa Pan
Ghanzi
Mopipi
Francistown
Mamuno
Serowe
Palapye
K a l a h a r i
Mahalapye
Limpopo
Lehututu
D e s e r t
Molepolole
Mochudi
GABORONE
Werda
Kanye
Otse Hill 1,491 m (4,892 ft)
Tsabong
Lobatse
SOUTH AFRICA

N

0   100 km
0   100 miles
(approximate scale)

Capital city
The largest city in Botswana, Gaborone is also the center of government. As well as many cultural sites, the city has a game reserve within its limits.

San hunters use arrows dipped in a poison made from beetle larvae.

San people
For 20,000 years, these indigenous people have led a nomadic lifestyle in the Kalahari Desert, where they use their hunting, fishing, and foraging skills to survive.

- 224,607 sq miles (581,730 sq km)
- 2.3 million
- Gaborone
- Setswana, English, other languages (+4)

Botswana is sometimes called the "**Gem of Africa**" due to its many diamond deposits. A large part of the country is **desert**, but it also has a lush river delta, **plains**, and **plateaus**, all home to a diverse range of **wildlife**.

Mozambique

Maputo Railway Station
The classically designed building is notable for its grand style. Built in the 20th century, it has a large dome, striking green exteriors, and ornate pillars.

Mangrove conservation
Saltwater-loving mangrove trees form an important swamp ecosystem. Many are found near the capital, Maputo, and Mozambique has committed to conserving these habitats.

Peri-peri chiles
Small but spicy, these peppers are farmed in Mozambique. They are mixed with garlic and other ingredients to make the popular peri-peri sauce.

Gorongosa National Park balances wildlife conservation with the needs of local people.

Wild warthogs
This large pig species roams the grasslands of the Gorongosa National Park, along with a wide variety of other wildlife.

N

TANZANIA
ZAMBIA
MALAWI
ZIMBABWE
SOUTH AFRICA
ESWATINI

Lake Nyasa
Lichinga Plateau
Negomane
Mocímboa da Praia
Lichinga
Mitande
Marrupa
Pemba
Maúa
Rio Lúrio
Mutuali
Nacala
Cassacatiza
Marávia Highlands
Ulonguè
Nampula
Lake Cahora Bassa
Zobuè
Tete
Milange
Angoche
Mocuba
Changara
Macossa
Vila de Senna
Quelimane
Zambezi
Manica
Chinde
Chimoio
Beira
Monte Binga 2,440 m (8,005 ft)
Rio Save
Massangena
Vilankulo
Mapai
Tesenane
Inhambane
Mabalane
Panda
Macia
Quissico
Xai-Xai
MAPUTO
Matola
Manhoca
Limpopo

Mozambique Channel

0   125 km
0   125 miles
(approximate scale)

Star athlete
Mozambican sprinter Maria Mutola is a three-time world champion in the 800 m race and has taken part in six Olympic Games.

Pristine coastline
Mozambique's 1,550-mile (2,500 km) long coastline features coral reefs, pure white sand beaches, and tropical islands.

⊘ 308,642 sq miles (799,380 sq km)

👥 30 million

★ Maputo

🗣 Portuguese, other languages (+10)

With vast stretches of **beautiful coastline**, Mozambique is famed for its beaches as well as its **fertile countryside** and rich **mineral resources**. The **Zambezi River** runs through the middle of the country.

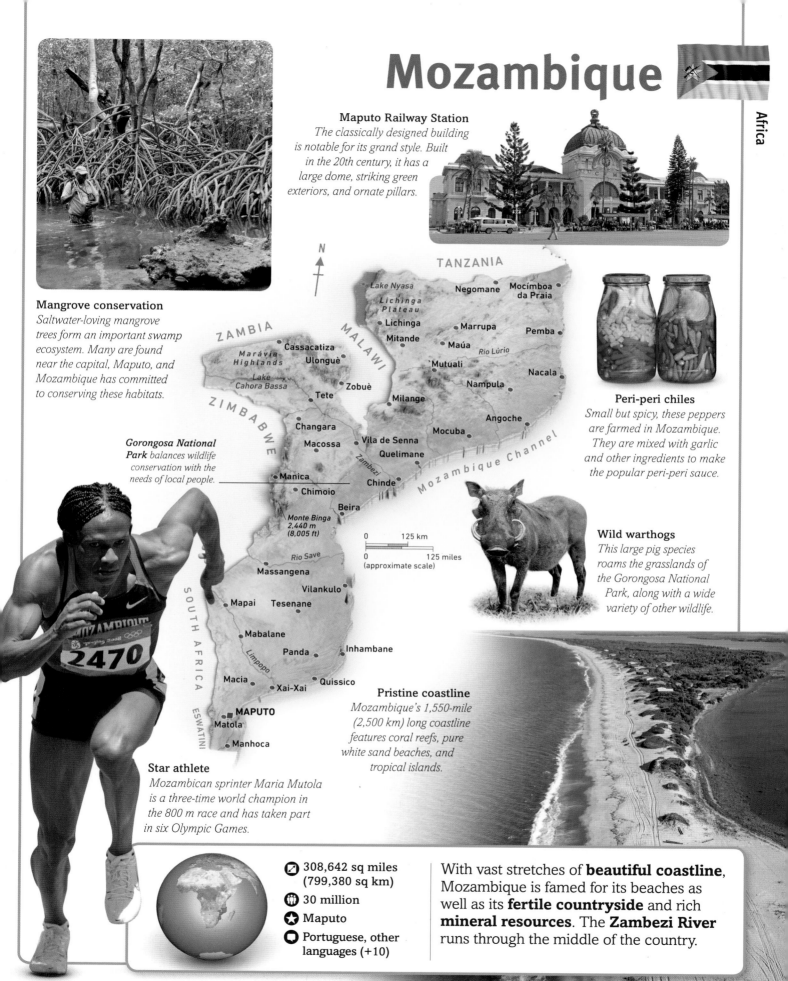

South Africa

The Cullinan Heritage diamond weighs about 507 carats.

Digging for diamonds
The country is one of the leading producers of gem-quality diamonds, which are excavated in seven major mines.

Father of the nation
Revolutionary, statesman, and Nobel Peace prize winner Nelson Mandela (1918–2013) is an icon of modern, democratic South Africa. He was known as Madiba, meaning "father of the nation."

0   100 km
0   100 miles
(approximate scale)

NAMIBIA

Alexander Bay

Upington

Springbok

Prieska

Northern Karoo

ATLANTIC OCEAN

Vanhynsdorp

Carnarvon

St. Helena Bay

Beaufort West

Saldanha

Great Karo

Paarl   Worcester

CAPE TOWN

Stellenbosch   Swellendam   George

Cape of Good Hope

Mosselbaai

Cape Agulhas

Ndebele people
Traditionally skilled at many crafts, the Ndebele people produce colorful and patterned beadwork, mats, and dolls.

Cosmopolitan city
First inhabited thousands of years ago, Cape Town with its natural harbor has long attracted seafarers. Today, the city is a thriving mix of cultures.

Table Mountain looms over the city. Its flat top can be climbed on foot or reached by cable car.

At the southern tip of the African continent, **South Africa** is known today for its **diverse culture**—a "**rainbow nation**" with **11 official languages**. It is **one of the richest African nations** and the only country in the world to have **three capitals: Pretoria** for administration, **Cape Town** for lawmaking, and **Bloemfontein** for justice.

- 470,693 sq miles (1,219,090 sq km)
- 56.5 million
- Pretoria, Cape Town, and Bloemfontein
- English, isiZulu, isiXhosa, Afrikaans, other languages (+7)

Johannesburg is the largest and most modern city.

Map labels:

ZIMBABWE

BOTSWANA

Musina (Messina)

Thohoyandou

Louis Trichardt (Makhado)

Polokwane (Pietersburg)

Mokopane (Potgieterstrus)

Modimolle (Nylstroom)

Mashishing (Lydenburg)

Mmabatho

Rustenburg

PRETORIA

Middelburg

MOZAMBIQUE

Mbombela (Nelspruit)

Johannesburg

Benoni

Highveld

Soweto

Springs

Potchefstroom

Vereeniging

Bethal

ESWATINI

Vryburg

Klerksdorp

Bloemhof

Standerton

Welkom

Kroonstad

Volksrust

Vryheid

Mkuze

Bethlehem

Mafadi 3,450 m (11,320 ft)

Kimberley

Brandfort

Ladysmith

Ulundi

BLOEMFONTEIN

LESOTHO

Richards Bay

De Aar

Caledon

Pietermaritzburg

Colesberg

Aliwal North

Kokstad

Durban

Middelburg

Drakensberg

Cradock

Queenstown

Mthatha

aaff-Reinet

Mdantsane

INDIAN OCEAN

East London

itenhage

Port Alfred

Port Elizabeth

aap Plateau

Vaal

N

Kruger National Park
Giraffes, elephants, lions, leopards, rhinos, and buffalos are among the animals that roam the country's largest national park.

King Protea
This tropical flowering plant native to South Africa is the national flower.

Xhosa people
The Xhosa people are the second-largest ethnic group. Historically linked with the Cape Town area, they live in all parts of South Africa.

Traditionally, married women wear an embroidered apron.

A boy from a Zulu cultural village dresses up for a show.

Zulu people
The largest ethnic group is the Zulu people. Traditionally, male warriors wore animal fur and feathers.

The Springboks
The South African rugby union team won the 2019 Rugby World Cup—their third win since 1995, when "one team, one country" symbolized national unity.

Geography: South Africa is dominated by a **high plateau**, fringed by **grasslands**, **deserts**, and narrow **coastal plains**.

History: The system of racial segregation known as **apartheid** ended in 1994, when **Nelson Mandela** became the first **black president**.

Culture: The **vibrant cultural mix** fuses many traditions in **literature** and the **music** of artists such as singer **Miriam Makeba**.

Natural wonders: The dramatic **Drakensberg Mountains** contrast with the lush **Garden Route coastline** west of Port Elizabeth.

Wildlife: South Africa is home to a rich variety of wildlife, including more than **200 mammal species** and **800 bird species**.

75

Eswatini

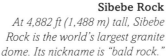

Sibebe Rock
At 4,882 ft (1,488 m) tall, Sibebe Rock is the world's largest granite dome. Its nickname is "bald rock."

Swazi Cultural Village
In this living museum near Lobamba, the traditional Swazi way of life is on display in huts containing local artifacts. Village people introduce visitors to their customs.

Emlembe
1,862 m (6,109 ft)

Piggs Peak
Mhlume
MBABANE
Simunye
Bhunya
LOBAMBA
Siteki
Mankayane
Manzini
Siphofaneni
Sicunusa
Hlathikulu
Big Bend
Hluti
Lavumisa

SOUTH AFRICA
MOZAMBIQUE
SOUTH AFRICA

0   50 km
0   50 miles
(approximate scale)

Manzini market
The best-known market in Eswatini is held weekly in Manzini. Local sellers trade handicrafts such as painted fabrics, wooden sculptures, woven baskets, and pottery.

- 🗺 6,704 sq miles (17,364 sq km)
- 👥 1.1 million
- ★ Mbabane, Lobamba
- 💬 English, siSwati, isiZulu, Xitsonga

Eswatini was known as **Swaziland** until the **king** renamed it in **2018**. One of Africa's **smallest countries**, it has **two capitals**: Mbabane and **Lobamba**, home to the parliament and **royal family**. Its **reserves** are known for **big mammals** and **birds**.

Lesotho

Horseback rider
Many mountain villages can be reached only on horseback. Riders often wear a conical Basotho hat woven from reeds.

Spiral aloe
The spiny leaves of this succulent plant grow in a spiral-shaped pattern. It is native to the Drakensberg Mountains.

0   50 km
0   50 miles
(approximate scale)

SOUTH AFRICA

Butha Buthe
Hlotse
Teyateyaneng
Lejone
MASERU
Mokhotlong
Thaba-Tseka
Thabana Ntlenyana
3,482 m (11,424 ft)
Mafeteng
Mohale's Hoek
Patlong
Qacha's Nek
Orange River
Quthing
SOUTH AFRICA

Drakensberg

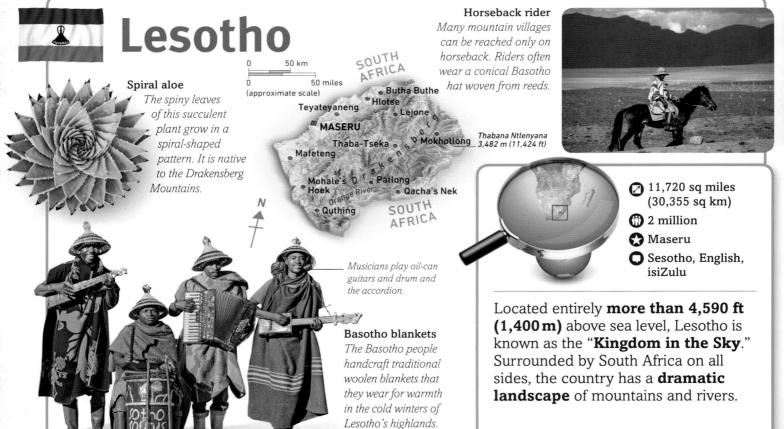

Musicians play oil-can guitars and drum and the accordion.

Basotho blankets
The Basotho people handcraft traditional woolen blankets that they wear for warmth in the cold winters of Lesotho's highlands.

- 🗺 11,720 sq miles (30,355 sq km)
- 👥 2 million
- ★ Maseru
- 💬 Sesotho, English, isiZulu

Located entirely **more than 4,590 ft (1,400 m)** above sea level, Lesotho is known as the "**Kingdom in the Sky**." Surrounded by South Africa on all sides, the country has a **dramatic landscape** of mountains and rivers.

Madagascar

Panther chameleon

Comet moth

The pods are the fruit of the vanilla orchid.

Vanilla pods
More than two-thirds of the global supply of vanilla is produced in Madagascar.

Madagascan wildlife
Wildlife found only on the island includes about 40 species of lemur, about half of the world's chameleons, and a large moth called the comet moth.

Ring-tailed lemur

Antsirañana

Maromokotro 2,876 m (9,436 ft)

Ambanja

Analalava

Antsohihy

Sambava

Antalaha

Mahájanga

Maroantsetra

Marovoay

Ambalabongo Canyon

Besalampy

Betsiboka

Maintirano

Fenoarivo Atsinanana

Ambatondrazaka

Tsiroanomandidy

ANTANANARIVO

Toamasina

Mania

Betafo

Morondava

Makay

Ambositra

Mangoky

Mananjary

Morombe

Fianarantsoa

Ihosy

Manakara

Toliara

Onilahy

Farafangana

Vangaindrano

Amboasary

Tôlañaro

Mozambique Channel

INDIAN OCEAN

0 — 100 km
0 — 100 miles
(approximate scale)

Solar energy
Power supplies are limited on the island, but year-round sunshine means solar power plants can harness the abundant sunlight to generate renewable energy.

Colorful *lambas*
The Sakalava people are one of many Malagasy ethnic groups. Traditionally, men and women wear a wraparound cloth called a lamba.

Grandidier's baobab tree
The trunk of this rare tree can be as wide as 10 ft (3 m). Humans and animals depend on baobab trees for water, food, and shelter.

Situated off Africa's southeast coast, Madagascar is the world's **fifth-largest island**. First settled around 500 CE, its **ethnically diverse** people came from Asia and Africa. Its **isolation** and **rain forest habitats** have allowed unique **flora** and **fauna** to evolve.

- 226,658 sq miles (587,041 sq km)
- 27 million
- Antananarivo
- Malagasy, French, English

Seychelles

Coco de mer
Nicknamed the "double coconut," the fruit of the coco de mer palm grows only in the Seychelles. The islanders eat this rare nut, or gift it to one another, but never sell it.

The seed of the coco de mer palm weighs up to 38.8 lb (17.6 kg).

Dazzling sands
Regularly named one of the world's most breathtaking beaches, Anse Source d'Argent has swaying palms, rocky boulders, soft sands, and clear, shallow waters.

```
0          200 km
0          200 miles
(approximate scale)
```

Meat-eating plant
The only species of its kind that grows in the Seychelles, Perville's pitcher plant is carnivorous. Its leaves form a deadly trap for insects that fall inside.

Mauritius

- ⊘ 788 sq miles (2,040 sq km)
- 👥 1.4 million
- ★ Port Louis
- 💬 French Creole, others (+6)

The **picturesque island** of Mauritius in the **Indian Ocean** has more than 105 miles (170 km) of **spectacular coastline**. Volcanic **mountains** blanketed in **rain forest** rise up steeply in the center.

Award-winning architecture
Designed by the Mauritian architect Jean-Francois Koenig, the Mauritius Commercial Bank building in Port Louis has won awards for its unique design.

INDIAN OCEAN
INDIAN OCEAN

Flat Island
Round Island
Gunner's Quoin
Triolet
Ile d'Ambre
Goodlands
PORT LOUIS
Rose Hill
Centre de Flacq
Quatre Bornes
Bel Air
Tamarin
Curepipe
Ile aux Cerfs
Rose Belle
Piton de la Petite Rivière Noire 828 m (2,717 ft)
Mahebourg
Chemin Grenier

```
0          10 km
0          10 miles
(approximate scale)
```

Underwater waterfall
Sand in shallow waters near the Le Morne peninsula is carried along by currents and dropped back down to the sea bed, creating an effect like a waterfall beneath the waves.

Rodrigues
Port Mathurin
Île aux Cocos
Mont Lubin
Petite Butte

```
0          8 km
0          8 miles
(approximate scale)
```
INDIAN OCEAN

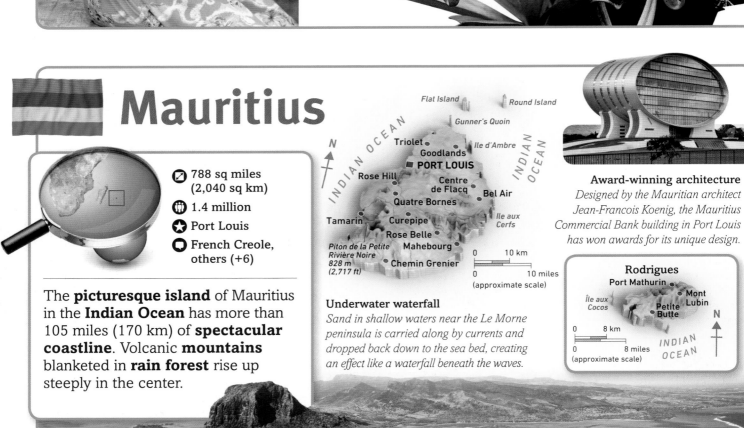

Seychelles blue pigeon
Found in the dense forests on many of the country's islands, this pretty pigeon feeds on tropical fruits.

Capital of the islands
The capital city of Victoria on Mahé Island has leafy palms and a mix of architectural styles, including the Victoria Clock Tower, which was built in 1903.

Aldabra Atoll is a group of four large coral islands on the outer edges of the Seychelles.

Inner Islands
Île aux Vaches
Île Denis
Praslin
Silhouette
Mahé
Frégate
Île Desroches
Poivre Atoll
Île Platte

Amirante Islands
Alphonse Group
Coëtivy

Outer Islands
Aldabra Atoll
Grande Terre
ssomption
Cosmolédo Atoll
Astove
St. Pierre
Providence Atoll
Farquhar Group
FarquharAtoll
ldabra Group

INDIAN OCEAN

N

Aldabra giant tortoise
The Aldabra Atoll is home to this rare tortoise. It can weigh up to 550 lb (250 kg) and live for 150 years.

Mahé Island
North Island
Aride
Grand Anse
Baie Ste Anne
Silhouette Island
Praslin
La Digue
Morne Seychellois 905 m (2,969 ft)
Mahé
VICTORIA
Bel Ombre
Fregate
Anse Boileau
Anse Royale
0   20 km
0   20 miles
(approximate scale)
N

- 176 sq miles (455 sq km)
- 96,000
- Victoria
- French Creole, English, French

An archipelago of 115 granite and coral **islands** off Africa's east coast, the Seychelles were settled in the 18th century. The continent's **smallest nation**, it has a diverse population and is known for its **beaches** and **reefs**.

Sweet fragrance
The scented yellow flowers of the ylang-ylang tree grow all year round in the Comoros islands. They are used to make perfumes and essential oils.

Mitsamiouli
Mount Karthala 2,361 m (7,746 ft)
Mbéni
MORONI
Grande Comore (Ngazidja)
Moroni is located on Grande Comore, the largest of the Comoros islands.
Mitsoudjé
Dembéni
Foumbouni

0   25 km
0   25 miles
(approximate scale)

INDIAN OCEAN
N

Mohéli (Mwali)
Miringoni
Fomboni
Nioumachoua
Mozambique Channel

Anjouan (Nzwani)
Sima
Moutsamoudou
Domoni
Moya
Mramani

Comoros

Grande Mosquée de Moroni
Muslims gather for daily prayers at this 19th-century mosque. Many Comorans are of Arab or Persian descent.

Decorative clothes
Comoran women traditionally wear dresses called shiromani. *These colorful, patterned fabrics are worn draped over the body, together with head scarves.*

A paste of sandalwood and coral, called msinzano, *is used to decorate the face.*

- 863 sq miles (2,235 sq km)
- 846,300
- Moroni
- Arabic, Comorian, French

The **three volcanic islands** of **Comoros** in the Indian Ocean are known as the "**perfumed islands**" because of the abundant **fragrant tropical plants**. The trade in **spices** such as **vanilla** and **cloves** has brought **people from many continents** to settle in Comoros.

EUROPE

Barents Sea

Norwegian Sea

ICELAND

Faroe Islands
(to Denmark)

Shetland Islands

NORWAY

Scandinavia

SWEDEN

FINLAND

Gulf of Bothnia

Lake Vaner

Gotland

Baltic Sea

Outer Hebrides

Orkney Islands

North Sea

DENMARK

A
T
L
A
N
T
I
C

O
C
E
A
N

IRELAND

UNITED
KINGDOM

THE NETHERLANDS

GERMANY

CZECHIA
(CZECH REPUBL

Rhine

BELGIUM

LUXEMBOURG

LIECHTENSTEIN

AUSTRI

Seine

SWITZERLAND

A L P S

SLOVEN

Channel Islands

FRANCE

SAN
MARINO

N

Massif Central

Bay of Biscay

Ape

ITALY

ANDORRA

MONACO

0   300 km

0   300 miles

(approximate scale)

Pyrenees

Corsica

VATICAN
CITY

SPAIN

Sardinia

PORTUGAL

Iberian

Majorca

Minorca

Tagus

Ibiza

Peninsula

Balearic Islands

AFRICA

Gibraltar
(to UK)

*Novaya
Zemlya*

*Kola
ninsula*

ASIA

U r a l   M o u n t a i n s

*Lake
Onega*

*Lake
Ladoga*

N o r t h   E u r o p e a n   P l a i n

RUSSIA

*Central
Russian
Upland*

Volga Uplands

Volga

Caspian Sea

STONIA

LATVIA

THUANIA

ﾠiningrad
Russia)

BELARUS

Dnieper

UKRAINE

El'brus
5,642 m (18,510 ft)

C a u c a s u s

POLAND

Carpathian Mountains

MOLDOVA

SLOVAKIA

Black Sea

HUNGARY

ROMANIA

Danube

iatic   *Sea*

nes

CROATIA

**BOSNIA
& HERZEGOVINA**

SERBIA

BULGARIA

TURKEY

ASIA

MONTENEGRO

KOSOVO

**NORTH
MACEDONIA**

rrhenian
Sea

ALBANIA

GREECE

*Ionian
Sea*

Crete

Sicily

MALTA

M e d i t e r r a n e a n   S e a

United Kingdom

The flag of the UK is known as the "Union Jack."

Giant's Causeway
These spectacular hexagonal basalt columns on the coast of Northern Ireland were formed from volcanic lava 50 million years ago.

Basalt columns are said to look like stepping stones for giants.

0   100 km
0   100 miles
(approximate scale)

Medieval strongholds
The UK has many castles—the fortresses of ancient monarchs and nobles. The well-preserved 13th-century Harlech Castle (left) is one of many in Wales.

Caribbean carnival
London is a multicultural city, and its annual Notting Hill Carnival is a celebration of Caribbean culture. Millions flock to enjoy the live music, dancing, and colorful parades.

Cream tea
An afternoon tea of scones, homemade jam, clotted cream, and a cup of hot tea is a national treat.

Channel Islands
Guernsey, Jersey, and other islands in the English Channel are self-governing.

English Channel
St Anne
Alderney
Guernsey
Herm
St Peter Port   Sark
N
FRANCE
St John
St Mary   Jersey
St Helier

0   20 km
0   20 miles
(approximate scale)

Isle of Lewis
St Kilda
Outer Hebrides
Inner Hebrides
Isle of Skye
North West Highland
Inverness
Loch Ness
Ben Nevis 1,345 m (4,413 ft)
Fort William
Grampian Mountains
SCOT
Per
Stirling
Glasgow
Edinb
Ayr
Dumfries
Carlis
Derry/ Londonderry
NORTHERN IRELAND
Omagh
Lisburn   Lough Neagh   Belfast
IRELAND
Isle of Man
Douglas
Lake District
Irish Sea
Mount Snowdon 1,085 m (3,560 ft)
Blackpool
Anglesey
Liverpool
Caernarfon
Che
Aberystwyth
Cambrian Mountains
Seve
Fishguard
WALES
Glouces
Swansea
Cardiff
Newpo
Bristol Channel
Bristol
B
Barnstaple
Exeter
Bournemou
Plymouth
Torquay
Celtic Sea
Isles of Scilly
Penzance
Falmouth
Land's End
English

Off the **northwest coast of Europe** lies the United Kingdom, or UK, which consists of four small countries—**England**, **Scotland**, **Wales**, and **Northern Ireland**. This island nation is steeped in history. The UK is famous for its **royal family**, **theater**, **modern music**, and **red buses**.

⬡ 94,058 sq miles (243,610 sq km)
👥 66 million
★ London
🗨 English, other languages (+3)

Shetland Islands

Lerwick

Orkney Islands

Kirkwall

Wick

ray Firth

N

Peterhead

Aberdeen

D

Jundee

North Sea

Newcastle upon Tyne

Sunderland

Middlesborough

Swale

Scarborough

York

Bradford

Leeds

nchester

Sheffield

ke

Trent

Nottingham

The Wash

NGLAND

rmingham

Leicester

ventry

Peterborough

Northampton

Norwich

Milton Keynes

Cambridge

xford

Luton

Ipswich

eading

LONDON

Chelmsford

Thames

Southend-on-Sea

Guildford

uthampton

Maidstone

Canterbury

Portsmouth

Dover

Brighton

Isle of Wight

Hastings

Strait of Dover

FRANCE

C h a n n e l

Rugged landscape
The UK countryside consists of green rolling hills, moors, and rocky coastline. Scotland is known for its rugged mountains and unspoiled wilderness, such as that on the Isle of Skye (above).

High-pitched pipes
Playing bagpipes in traditional dress is a custom in Scotland and Ireland. Bagpipes were once played on battlefields to scare enemy troops.

Sherlock Holmes
Scottish writer Arthur Conan Doyle (1859–1930) created the famous fictional detective Sherlock Holmes, hero of The Hound of the Baskervilles *novel.*

THE HOUND OF THE BASKERVILLES

CONAN DOYLE

Angel of the North
Standing 65 ft (20 m) tall, this landmark steel sculpture by British artist Antony Gormley has dominated the skyline in northeast England since 1998.

Super city
The Thames River flows through London, one of the oldest major cities in the world and now a buzzing metropolis with nearly 9 million people.

The Shard is a 95-story skyscraper with panoramic views.

Geography: The highest **mountains** lie in Scotland and Wales, while the **Pennines** are known as the **spine of England**.

History: The UK was one of the **first nations** to grow its economy as a result of the **Industrial Revolution** in the 19th century.

Culture: Cricket, **rugby**, and **soccer** were first played in the UK. British **literature**, **music**, and **theater** are popular worldwide.

Natural wonders: These include the **Lake District** in England, **Loch Ness** in Scotland, and **Mount Snowdon** in Wales.

Ireland

The bodhrán is a type of Irish drum.

Folk instruments
Folk music is embedded in Irish tradition. The main instrument is the violin, also known as a fiddle.

Fiddle

Low whistle

Tin whistle

Recorder

Blackthorn
Native to Ireland, this prickly, hardy shrub grows white flowers in spring and black berries in fall.

Trinity College
Founded in 1592, this world-famous university in Dublin has educated many celebrated Irish writers, including Bram Stoker and Oscar Wilde.

*The capital **Dublin** is also Ireland's largest city and home to about one-third of the population.*

Step-dancing
Performed since the 19th century, this traditional Irish dance form involves a straight body and fast foot movements.

Gaelic football
In this action-packed Irish team sport, players can kick, catch, or throw the ball.

Skellig Islands
Off the southwest coast of Ireland are two rocky islets providing a safe haven for seabirds such as gannets and puffins.

N

Letterkenny
Donegal
Northern Ireland (UK)
Glenamoy
Achill Island
Sligo
Monaghan
Clare Island
Westport
Dundalk
Connemara
Roscommon
Lough Ree
Drogheda
Lough Carrib
Galway
Shannon
Irish Sea
Aran Islands
DUBLIN
Lough Derg
Wicklow Mountains
Galway Bay
Shannon
Barrow
Wicklow
Limerick
Kilkenny
Suir
Tralee
Dingle Bay
Killarney
Wexford
Waterford
Cork
Carrauntoohil 1,038 m (3,406 ft)
Celtic Sea

ATLANTIC OCEAN

0   50 km
0   50 miles
(approximate scale)

⊘ 27,132 sq miles (70,273 sq km)
👥 5.2 million
★ Dublin
◯ English, Irish

Once part of the United Kingdom, **southern Ireland**, where most people are Roman Catholic, **became independent** in **1921**. **Northern Ireland**, where people are mainly **Protestant**, remains **part of the UK**.

Ice caves
Vatnajökull is among the largest glaciers in Europe. In summer, channels of melting water flow under the surface of the glacier, cutting through the ice, creating enormous caverns.

Iceland

Puffins of the Atlantic
Native to the Atlantic Ocean, puffins are strong swimmers that live at sea but head for breeding colonies on land every spring. Their colorful beaks have earned them their nickname of "sea parrots."

Hallgrímskirkja
The unusually shaped Hallgrímskirkja is the tallest church in Iceland and was completed in 1986. It stands 243 ft (74 m) tall, and the view from the top of the spire gives a spectacular view of Reykjavik.

Map labels

Denmark Strait
Ísafjarðardjúp
Ísafjörður

N

Greenland Sea

Skagafjörður
Siglufjörður
Eyjafjörður
Öxarfjörður
Þistilfjörður

Húnaflói
Sauðárkrókur
Húsavík

Breiðafjörður
Akureyri
Vopnafjörður

Stykkishólmur
Jökulsá á Fjöllum

*More than 90 percent of Icelanders live in **Reykjavík**.*

Borgarnes
Langjökull Glacier
Hofsjökull Glacier
Egilsstaðir
Reyðarfjörður

Faxaflói
Hvítá
Þjórsá

REYKJAVÍK

Keflavík

Vatnajökull Glacier
Hvannadalshnúkur
2,110 m (6,923 ft)

Selfoss
Höfn

ATLANTIC OCEAN

Mýrdalsjökull Glacier
Kirkjubæjarklaustur

Vestmannaeyjar

0   50 km
0   50 miles
(approximate scale)

⬦ 39,769 sq miles (103,000 sq km)

👥 350,730

★ Reykjavík

🗩 Icelandic

A **remote island** in the northern Atlantic Ocean, Iceland lies just south of the Arctic Circle. It is known as the **land of "fire and ice"** because of its many **active volcanoes**, **lava fields**, **geysers**, and **hot-water springs**.

Icelandic horses
Viking settlers brought these horses to Iceland during the 9th and 10th centuries. Small and stocky in size, the breed is hardy and tough and capable of crossing any terrain.

Aurora Borealis
Also called the Northern Lights, this incredible light display is often visible on clear nights in Iceland. The natural phenomenon is caused by solar winds hitting oxygen and nitrogen atoms high up in Earth's atmosphere.

Norway

Fjord view
Standing about 2,300 ft (700 m) above Lake Ringedalsvatnet, the cliff edge of Trolltunga offers a breathtaking view of the surrounding fjords.

0   100 km
0   100 miles
(approximate scale)

Hammerfest
Vadsø
Alta
Varangerfjorden
Tromsø   Finnmarksvidda   FINLAND   Kirkenes
Finnsnes   RUSSIA
Andfjorden
Harstad
Lofoten   Narvik
Svolvær
Vestfjorden
Bodø
N
Svartisen
Mo i Rana
Sandnessjøen

Norwegian Sea

On the hunt
In Norway's forests, solitary wolverines hunt down large prey, including moose and goats.

Rørvik
Frohavet   Namsos
Steinkjer

Troll warning!
Mythical trolls are considered lucky in Norway. They can be seen on signs but are mostly found as souvenirs!

Kristiansund   Trondheim
Molde
Ålesund
Dovrefjell
Galdhøpiggen
2,469 m (8,100 ft)
Florø   Jotunheimen
Hermansverk
Lillehammer
Bergen
Hamar
Hardangervidda
Trolltunga
1,100 m (3,600 ft)
Haugesund
OSLO   Lillestrøm
Boknafjorden   Drammen
Sandnes   Stavanger
Skien   Tønsberg
Egersund
North Sea
Arendal
Kristiansand
Oslofjorden
Skagerrak

SWEDEN
Glåma

Sámi people
Thousands of indigenous Sámi people live in northern Norway, where they herd reindeer, fish, and farm the land.

Heddal Stave Church
In medieval times, many churches constructed of timber walls on wooden corner posts, known as staves, were built in Norway. Only 28 survive today. The church at Heddal is the largest.

Cross-country skiing
Snow covers much of Norway in winter, and cross-country skiing is popular for exercise, sport, and to get around.

- 125,021 sq miles (323,802 sq km)
- 5.5 million
- Oslo
- Norwegian, Sámi

The dramatic landscape of Norway is a wilderness of **icy glaciers** and **deep fjords** (sea channels surrounded by cliffs). **Two-thirds** of the **Norwegian landscape** is covered by **rugged mountains**. About **50,000 tiny islands** lie off its long, craggy coastline.

Denmark

Traditional Faroese houses
Turf roofs are a familiar sight on the volcanic Faroe Islands (see p.181) in the North Atlantic Ocean, about 900 miles (1,500 km) from Copenhagen.

Turf roofs keep the houses warm and protect them from the wet weather.

Fun in the city
Founded in 1843, Tivoli Gardens in Copenhagen is the second-oldest amusement park in the world. Here, visitors enjoy rides and games.

Danish design
A clean, simple style of architecture and furniture design developed in Denmark in the 20th century. A classic example of this is the iconic Egg Chair by the Danish designer Arne Jacobsen.

Viking drinking horn
The Viking Danes were part of the seafaring people who lived in Scandinavia in the Middle Ages. They used animal horns to make drinking cups (above) and musical instruments.

Cozy way of life
The Danish word hygge describes a cozy mood when family or friends gather together to share food and drink in a comfortable setting.

Danish sandwich
A traditional Danish open sandwich, called Smørrebrød, is rye bread layered with meat or fish and other toppings.

Øresund Bridge
Sweden and Denmark are linked across the Øresund Strait. The Øresund Bridge carries cars and trains from the Swedish city of Malmö to an artificial island, which has a tunnel leading to Copenhagen in Denmark.

Map labels

Skagen
Hjørring · Frederikshavn
Hanstholm · Læsø
Aalborg
Hurup · Kattegat
Skive · Viborg
Ringkøbing · Jutland (Jylland) · Randers · Anholt
Silkeborg
Aarhus
Møllehøj 171 m (561 ft)
Skjern · Samsø · Helsingør
Vejle · Endelave
Esbjerg · Kalundborg
Kolding · COPENHAGEN (KØBENHAVN)
Rømø · Odense · Fyn · Sjælland
Skærbæk · Svendborg · Næstved
Tønder · Ærø · Langeland · Møn · Bornholm · Rønne
Kiel Bay · Lolland · Saksøbing
GERMANY · Falster

North Sea
Skagerrak
SWEDEN
The Sound
Great Belt
Baltic Sea

N

0 — 50 km
0 — 50 miles
(approximate scale)

- ◿ 16,639 sq miles (43,094 sq km)
- 5.9 million
- ★ Copenhagen
- Danish

Denmark is the **southernmost Scandinavian country**, made up of the **flat landscape** of the **Jutland Peninsula** and more than **400 islands**. Statistical studies often show that the **Danish people** are **among the happiest in the world**.

Sweden

Medieval Stockholm
Sweden's capital city is built across 14 islands. On one of them lies the medieval Old Town, known for its cobbled streets and colorful buildings.

Alfred Nobel was a 19th-century Swedish inventor, chemist, and engineer.

Nobel Prize
First awarded in 1901, the annual Nobel Prize recognizes major achievements in chemistry, physics, medicine, lterature, and peace.

Dala horses
Since the 17th century, these decorative wooden horses have been handcrafted and sold throughout Sweden.

Icehotel
In 1989, the world's first hotel made entirely of ice was built near Kiruna in northern Sweden.

Kebnekaise
2,097 m (6,880 ft)

0   150 km
0   150 miles
(approximate scale)

Kiruna
Lapland
Pajala
Gäddede
Arvidsjaur
Luleå
Vilhelmina
Skellefteå
Östersund
Örnsköldsvik
Umeå
Sundsvall
Transtrand
Bollnäs
Borlänge Falun
Karlstad Gävle
Trollhättan Vänern Örebro Västerås
Gothenburg Mariestad Uppsala
(Göteborg) Borås **STOCKHOLM**
Jönköping Vättern Norrköping
Linköping Nyköping
Halmstad
Helsingborg Växjö Gotland
Kristianstad Visby
Malmö Kalmar
Karlskrona Öland

NORWAY
FINLAND
Kölen
Skagerrak
DENMARK
Baltic Sea
Gulf of Bothnia
Ljungan
Kalixälven
Byskeälven

Climate activism
In 2018, at age 15, Greta Thunberg found world recognition when she stopped going to school and sat outside the Swedish Parliament, calling for action on climate change.

Reindeer
Thick, furry coats for warmth and strong hoofs to dig out food make reindeer well suited to the country's cold mountains, where they number in the thousands in herds kept by the indigenous Sámi people.

Kräftskiva
For this traditional Swedish summer celebration, friends and family gather to feast on crayfish, often wearing themed paper hats.

SKOLSTREJK FÖR KLIMATET

⤢ 173,860 sq miles (450,295 sq km)

👥 10.2 million

★ Stockholm

◯ Swedish, other languages (+5)

The **natural landscape** of this Scandinavian country in **northern Europe** changes from the **icy peaks** of **mountains** such as the Kebnekaise, past **rolling hills** and **freshwater streams**, to **thousands of islands** off its Baltic Sea coastline.

Finland

Telecom giant
In the 1990s, the Finnish company Nokia became a global telecommunications pioneer, selling millions of its Nokia cell phones.

Jean Sibelius was honored on a set of postage stamps.

JEAN SIBELIUS
5 mk
LXXX 8·XII·45
SUOMI·FINLAND

National icon
Through musical pieces such as Finlandia, *the 20th-century Finnish composer Jean Sibelius helped his country discover its national identity.*

Glass decor
Finland is known for its art and design—in particular for furniture, lighting, fabrics, and glassware, such as these glass birds.

The Australian Grand Prix trophy is lifted by winner Kimi Räikkönen in 2007.

Grand Prix champ
The Formula One driver Kimi Räikkönen has won 21 Grand Prix races.

Dog sledding
In winter, the Finnish countryside is perfect for dog sledding. This fun activity is enjoyed by young and old alike. In the past, dogs were used to transport goods or people across the snow.

Map labels

NORWAY
SWEDEN
Halti 1,365 m (4,478 ft)
Inarijärvi
Lapland
Maanselkä
RUSSIA

Lapland in the north is the legendary home of Father Christmas.

Sodankylä
Kemijärvi
Salla
Rovaniemi
Kemi
Hailuoto
Oulu (Uleåborg)
Kokkola (Karleby)
Oulujärvi
Kajaani (Kajana)
Vaasa (Vasa)
Iisalmi
Seinäjoki
Lieksa
Gulf of Bothnia
Suomenselkä
Kuopio
Pori (Björneborg)
Joensuu
Jyväskylä
Åland Islands (Ahvenanmaa)
Tampere (Tammerfors)
Mikkeli (Sankt Michel)
Hämeenlinna (Tavastehus)
Savonlinna
Lahti (Lahtis)
Mariehamn (Maarianhamina)
Turku (Åbo)
Kouvola
HELSINKI (HELSINGFORS)
Baltic Sea
Gulf of Finland

Helsinki lies on a peninsula.

N

0   125 km
0   125 miles
(approximate scale)

Finnish summer
After a dark winter, families enjoy long, sunny summer days by spending time at lakeside cottages.

The musher, or driver of the sled, controls the dogs by using spoken commands.

130,558 sq miles (338,145 sq km)
5.8 million
Helsinki
Finnish, Swedish, Sámi

Finland lies on the **eastern edge of Scandinavia,** on the border with Russia. With **three-quarters** of the **land** covered in **forests,** it is the **most densely forested country** in Europe. There are also about **188,000 lakes.**

Estonia

Siberian flying squirrel
Despite its name, this small species of squirrel leaps rather than flies through the Estonian forests to escape predators.

Kõpu Lighthouse
The oldest lighthouse in the Baltic States is Kõpu on the Estonian island of Hiiumaa. It has guided the way for ships since 1531.

Tallinn is the country's largest and most populated city.

Gulf of Finland

Paldiski
TALLINN
Kunda
Kohtla-Järve
Tapa
Rakvere
Narva

Kärdla
Vormsi
Hiiumaa
Haapsalu
Rapla
Paide
Põltsamaa

Muhu
Virtsu
Mustvee
Lake Peipus

Saarema
Pärnu
RUSSIA

Kuressaare
Pärnu
Viljandi
Tartu
Emajõgi
Võrtsjärv

Kihnu
Kilingi-Nõmme

Ruhnu
Gulf of Riga
LATVIA
Räpina
Valka
Võru

BALTIC SEA

Delivery robots
Estonian engineers in Tallinn have designed self-driving robots to deliver packages, shopping, or food.

Estonian Song Festival
Every five years, this festival in Tallinn showcases a group of 25,000 singers and dancers for an audience of nearly 100,000.

0 — 50 km
0 — 50 miles
(approximate scale)

Suur Munamägi
318 m (1,043 ft)

Dancers in traditional clothing perform at the festival.

Old Town in Tallinn
The capital of Tallinn has an Old Town known for its medieval architecture, including St. Olaf's Church, which is believed to have been built around the 13th century.

Estonia is the **smallest** of the three states on the **Baltic Sea**. It has many **lakes** and **forests** and is made up of more than **1,500 islands**. Estonia is one of the world's **most digitally connected** countries, with almost all services **available online**.

- 17,463 sq miles (45,228 sq km)
- 1.2 million
- Tallinn
- Estonian, Russian

Lithuania

White storks
The national bird of Lithuania is the white stork. There are more than 22,000 stork nests across the country.

LATVIA

Baltic Sea

Courland Spit

Plungė

Klaipėda

Žemaičių Aukštumas

Tauragė

Šiauliai

Panevėžys

RUSSIA (Kaliningrad)

Jurbarkas

Dubysa

Nevėžis

Šventoji

Utena

Ukmergė

Kaunas

Neris

POLAND

Marijampolė

Alytus

VILNIUS

Druskininkai

Neman

Aukštojas Hill 294 m (964 ft)

N

BELARUS

0 — 50 km
0 — 50 miles
(approximate scale)

Saint Jonas's Festival
On June 24, Lithuanians celebrate this midsummer festival by singing, dancing, and wearing flower wreaths.

Trakai Island Castle
The picturesque castle sits on an island in Lake Galvė, attached to the lakeshore by two bridges.

Lithuania is the **largest** of the **Baltic states**. It was the last country in Europe to adopt Christianity. Like Estonia and Latvia, it **gained independence** from Russia in **1991**.

- ⤢ 25,212 sq miles (65,300 sq km)
- 👥 2.7 million
- ★ Vilnius
- ⬡ Lithuanian, Russian

Latvia

Irbe Strait

Cape Kolka

Ventspils

Talsi

Gulf of Riga

Valka

ESTONIA

Venta Rapid

Kuldīga

Venta

Jūrmala

RIGA

Valmiera

Alūksne

Gauja

Vidzemes Augstiene

Liepāja

Saldus

Ogre

Gaiziņkalns 312 m (1,024 ft)

RUSSIA

Jelgava

Lubāns

LITHUANIA

Bauska

Lielupe

Alzkraukle

Western Dvina

Rēzekne

Ludza

N

Daugavpils

BELARUS

0 — 50 km
0 — 50 miles
(approximate scale)

According to one legend, the flag is the blood-soaked sheet of a Latvian soldier.

Vibrant Riga
At the heart of the capital city of Riga is a medieval Old Town, known for its striking architecture and bustling markets.

Latvian symbol
Latvia's national flower is the daisy, which grows wild in summer and is featured in floral displays and bouquets.

Latvia is known for its **forests**, **beaches**, and the **Venta Rapid**—the widest waterfall in Europe. The city of **Ventspils** in the country's northwest is one of the **busiest ports** on the **Baltic Sea**.

- ⤢ 24,938 sq miles (64,589 sq km)
- 👥 1.9 million
- ★ Riga
- ⬡ Latvian, Russian

Poland

European bison
Although European bison were hunted to the point of extinction in 1921, herds have successfully been reintroduced to Poland, especially in Białowieża Forest.

White-tailed eagle
Poland's national bird is the white-tailed eagle. This large sea eagle is depicted on the national coat of arms wearing a crown.

Corpus Christi
The small town of Łowicz comes alive on this public holiday as priests parade with crosses, flower girls throw petals, and families come together to share feasts.

Warsaw reborn
Poland's capital was badly damaged in World War II, but the historic old town was reconstructed and a bustling modern city has grown up alongside.

Szczecin

Pomerani

Noteć

Gorzów
Wielkopolski

Warta

Poznań

GERMANY

Zielona
Góra

N o r t

Oder (Odra)

Legnica

Wrocław

S u d e t e

S i l e s i a

Wałbrzych

Opo

CZECHIA

Wroclaw is a city on the banks of the Oder River.

N

0		50 km
0		50 miles

(approximate scale)

The Mermaid
This statue of a mermaid is an iconic symbol of the capital. Legend goes that a syrenka, or a mermaid, swam up the Wisła River to Warsaw and became captivated by the city.

A large country in **Central Europe**, Poland is surrounded by seven other nations and the Baltic Sea. The **north** and **central** regions of the country are characterized by a **vast plain**, while to the **south** the **Carpathian Mountains** mark the border with Slovakia. Poland's **main industries** are **farming**, **manufacturing**, **mining**, and **shipbuilding**.

- 120,728 sq miles (312,685 sq km)
- 38.3 million
- Warsaw
- Polish

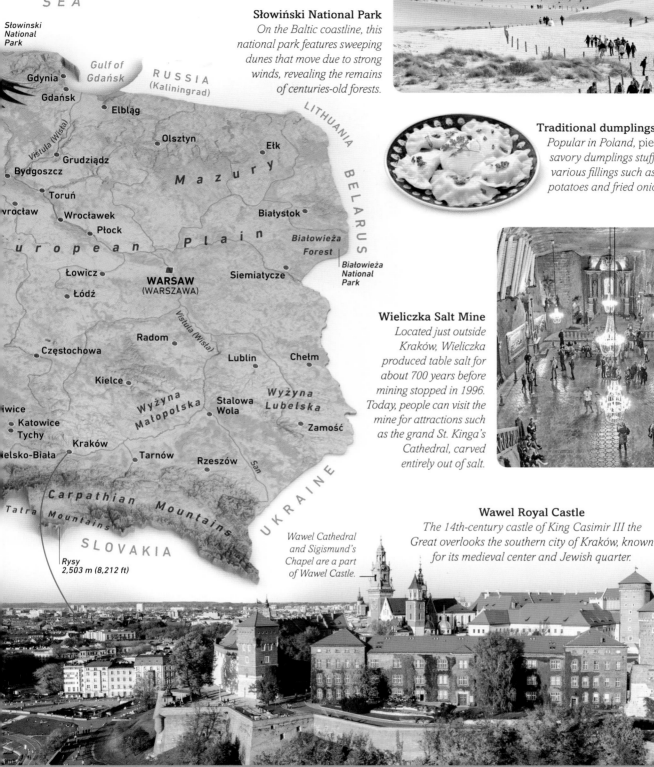

Słowiński National Park

Gulf of Gdańsk

RUSSIA (Kaliningrad)

Gdynia

Gdańsk

Elbląg

Olsztyn

Ełk

Vistula (Wisła)

Grudziądz

Bydgoszcz

Toruń

LITHUANIA

BELARUS

M a z u r y

Wrocławek

vrocław

Białystok

Płock

Białowieża Forest

u r o p e a n P l a i n

Łowicz

Siemiatycze

Białowieża National Park

WARSAW (WARSZAWA)

Łódź

Vistula (Wisła)

Radom

Lublin

Chełm

Częstochowa

Kielce

Wyżyna Małopolska

Stalowa Wola

Wyżyna Lubelska

iwice

Katowice

Tychy

Kraków

Zamość

ielsko-Biała

Tarnów

Rzeszów

San

UKRAINE

Carpathian Mountains

Tatra Mountains

SLOVAKIA

Rysy 2,503 m (8,212 ft)

Słowiński National Park
On the Baltic coastline, this national park features sweeping dunes that move due to strong winds, revealing the remains of centuries-old forests.

Traditional dumplings
Popular in Poland, pierogi are savory dumplings stuffed with various fillings such as boiled potatoes and fried onions.

Wieliczka Salt Mine
Located just outside Kraków, Wieliczka produced table salt for about 700 years before mining stopped in 1996. Today, people can visit the mine for attractions such as the grand St. Kinga's Cathedral, carved entirely out of salt.

Wawel Royal Castle
The 14th-century castle of King Casimir III the Great overlooks the southern city of Kraków, known for its medieval center and Jewish quarter.

Wawel Cathedral and Sigismund's Chapel are a part of Wawel Castle.

Geography: Poland enjoys a **rich landscape** of **forests**, **mountains**, **lakes**, **rivers**, and **beaches**.

History: After World War II, Poland was allied to communist Russia. It became an **independent republic** in **1989**.

Culture: Traditions based on **local folklore** and the festivals of the **Roman Catholic Church** are part of everyday life.

Natural wonders: The country is home to the vast **Białowieża forest** and **National Park**, one of the **largest** and **oldest** forests in Europe.

Wildlife: While **bears** are rare, **wolves**, **bison**, **wild boar**, **elk**, and **foxes** can all be found here. Birds include **white storks** and **eagles**.

Food and drink: Dumplings, **stews**, and **sausages** are all popular Polish dishes, often served with **sauerkraut** (pickled cabbage).

Germany

Beethoven

The 18th-century German composer Ludwig van Beethoven is remembered for many great musical works. Other famous German composers include J. S. Bach and J. Brahms.

Black Forest

With evergreen trees and beautiful lakes, the Black Forest is popular with tourists. It got its name from the dense conifers that appear almost black from afar.

Soccer fans

The most popular sport in Germany is soccer. The national team has won the World Cup four times.

Neuschwanstein Castle

In the 19th century, King Ludwig II of Bavaria commissioned a castle near Munich in honor of composer Richard Wagner. The result was Neuschwanstein, a fairy-tale castle with towers and turrets.

Neuschwanstein Castle was the inspiration for the Sleeping Beauty Castle at Disneyland.

Europe's **fourth-largest country** is located in the northwest of the continent. Germany has the **largest economy** in **Europe**, thanks to a **thriving industry,** exporting cars, electronics, machinery, and other goods and services. The **picturesque German landscape** ranges from forests and mountains to rivers and valleys.

- 137,846 sq miles (357,022 sq km)
- 80.2 million
- Berlin
- German, Turkish

NETHERLANDS

Bremerhave

Oldenburg

Bren

Osnabr

Münster

Bielefeld

Duisburg • Essen

Dortmund Paderbo

Düsseldorf • Wuppertal

Cologne (Köln) • Leverkusen

Aachen

Bonn

BELGIUM

Rheinisches Schiefergebirge

Eifel

Giess

Koblenz

LUXEMBOURG

Taunus

Frankfur am Main

Trier

Wiesbaden

Hunsrück

Mainz • Offenbach

Darmstadt

Kaiserlautern • Mannheim

Saarbrücken

Heidelber

FRANCE

Rhine (Rhein)

Karlsruhe

Stuttg

Tübingen

Schwäbische A

Freiburg im Breisgau

Black Forest (Schwarzwald)

Konstanz

Lake Constan

SWITZERLAND

Wind power
More than 30,000 turbines are installed in wind farms across Germany, with plans for more.

Beautiful Berlin
The capital has a turbulent past, divided by the Berlin Wall from 1961 to 1989. Today this exciting city is known for galleries, museums, restaurants, and the Berlin opera.

Berlin was built in the 13th century and is now Germany's largest city.

German folk tales
Brothers Jacob and Wilhelm Grimm published Grimms' Fairy Tales *in the 18th century. This classic collection of folk tales includes* Snow White, Sleeping Beauty, *and* Hansel and Gretel.

Car production
Germany is a global leader in luxury car production with famous makers, including Volkswagen, BMW, Audi, Porsche, and Mercedes-Benz.

The accordion is a traditional instrument popular in Germany.

Oktoberfest
Millions of people flock to this annual folk festival in Munich. Oktoberfest celebrates Bavarian history over two weeks with plentiful food, beer, music, and parades.

MARK
Flensburg
Kiel
Lübeck
Hamburg
Rostock
Schwerin
Neubrandenburg
Baltic Sea
Hanover (Hannover)
Wolfsburg
Brandenburg
Braunschweig
Magdeburg
Potsdam
BERLIN
Frankfurt an der Oder
Harz
Göttingen
Halle
Dessau-Roßlau
Cottbus
sel
Erfurt
Jena
Gera
Leipzig
Dresden
Görlitz
Chemnitz
Zwickau
Thüringer Wald
Ore Mountains (Erzgebirge)
Coburg
Main
Bayreuth
rzburg
Bamberg
Erlangen
Fürth
Nuremberg (Nürnberg)
Fränkische Alb
Regensburg
Bohemian Forest
Bavarian Forest
Danube
Ingolstadt
Augsburg
Passau
Munich (München)
pten
Bavarian Alps
Rosenheim
AUSTRIA
Zugspitze 2,962 m (9,718 ft)
Elbe
POLAND
CZECHIA (CZECH REPUBLIC)

0   50 km
0   50 miles
(approximate scale)
N

Geography: The **flatlands** of the north lead to the North Sea, while in the center and south are **highlands**, **forests**, and **rivers**.

History: Germany was divided into **East** and **West** Germany after **World War II**. The two countries **reunited** in 1989.

Culture: Known as "the land of poets and thinkers," Germany is recognized for **art**, **philosophy**, and **literature**.

Natural wonders: Among Germany's most scenic spots are **Urach Waterfall** in Swabian Alb and **Lake Königssee** in Bavaria.

Wildlife: Wildcats and **ibex** roam in the nature reserves in the south, while the north coast teems with **fish** and **sea birds**.

Food and drink: Best known for **sausages** and specialty baked **breads,** the country also produces fine **wines** and **beers**.

The Netherlands

Great masters
The 17th-century Dutch painter Rembrandt van Rijn is one of the country's great masters. His works include many self-portraits, painted throughout his life.

Top team
The Dutch women's field hockey team is the most successful in history with eight World Cup wins.

Dutch tulips
The Netherlands has been the center of the world's cut flower market for centuries.

The capital and largest city is Amsterdam, but the parliament sits in The Hague.

Anne Frank
The famous Jewish diarist Anne Frank hid with her family in an Amsterdam building during World War II.

North Sea

West Frisian Islands (Waddeneilanden)

Waddenzee

GERMANY

Leeuwarden
Groningen
Den Helder
Heerenveen
Assen
Hoorn
Emmen
Alkmaar
Zaanstad
IJsselmeer
Haarlem
Zwolle
AMSTERDAM
Leiden
Amersfoort
Apeldoorn
THE HAGUE
('S-GRAVENHAGE)
Zoetermeer
Utrecht
Enschede
Neder-Rijn
IJssel
Rotterdam
Arnhem
Dordrecht
Waal
Nijmegen
Oosterhout
's-Hertogenbosch
Middelburg
Roosendaal
Breda
Tilburg
Eindhoven

B E L G I U M

Meuse

Maastricht

Vaalserberg
322 m (1,056 ft)

0   20 km
0   20 miles
(approximate scale)

N

- 16,039 sq miles (41,543 sq km)
- 17.3 million
- Amsterdam and The Hague
- Dutch, Frisian

Picturesque waterways
Amsterdam's canals were once used to trade goods in the city, but now boats use these waterways to carry tourists.

Almost half of the **low-lying** Netherlands has been **reclaimed from the sea**, creating farmland for cultivating flowers and raising cattle. This **flat landscape** is known for its **canals**.

Belgium

NATO
Based in Brussels, the North Atlantic Treaty Organization (NATO) is a military alliance between 29 countries from Europe and North America.

Antwerp is the world's diamond center where diamonds are cut and traded.

Belgian chocolates
Belgium is the world's leading exporter of chocolates such as pralines and truffles.

N

0   20 km
0   20 miles
(approximate scale)

Map labels
North Sea
Ostend (Oostende)
Bruges (Brugge)
Flanders
Ghent (Gent)
Kortrijk
Scheldt
Schaerbeek
Leuven
Hasselt
Genk
NETHERLANDS
Antwerp (Antwerpen)
BRUSSELS (BRUSSEL/ BRUXELLES)
Wavre
Wallonia
Mons
Charleroi
Namur
Meuse
Liège
Verviers
Botrange 694 m (2,277 ft)
Fagne
Famenne
Ardennes
LUXEMBOURG
GERMANY
FRANCE
Neufchâteau
Arlon

Tintin
Comic books by the Belgian cartoonist Hergé featuring the adventures of Tintin have sold more than 200 million copies since 1930.

Walking tall
In the past, locals had to walk on stilts due to floods, but now stilt walkers parade through cities just for fun.

Atomium
Standing 335 ft (102 m) tall, the Atomium is an iconic landmark and museum in Brussels. The nine spheres symbolize an iron crystal's atoms, magnified 165 billion times.

- ⌀ 11,786 sq miles (30,528 sq km)
- 👥 11.72 million
- ★ Brussels
- 💬 Dutch, French, German

While much of Belgium is **flat**, to the south it is **rocky** and **forested**. It is one of the world's most **densely populated countries** and is visited by millions of tourists for its **canals** and **chocolate**.

France

Café culture
In French, café means "coffee." While this Paris café is known for the artists and thinkers who met to discuss their ideas, most people simply drink and watch the world go by.

Edgar Degas
This bronze sculpture is by the 19th-century French artist Edgar Degas. He is famous for realistic studies of ballet dancers, including pastels and paintings.

Paris lies on the Seine River in northern France.

UNITED KINGDOM

English Channel

Calais

le Havre

Amie
Beau

Caen • Rouen

Brest • St-Brieuc

PARIS

Quimper

Alencon

Versailles

Rennes

Lorient

le Mans

Orléans

Loire

St-Nazaire

Angers

Nantes

Tours

Bourges

ATLANTIC OCEAN

Bay of Biscay

Niort • Poitiers

la Rochelle

Limoges

Clermon
Ferra

Brive-la-
Gaillarde

Bordeaux

Garonne

Lot

Mas
Cent

Agen

At the end of each stage, the rider with the fastest overall time since the race began gets to wear a yellow jersey.

Biarritz

Toulouse

Tarbes

Béziers

Pyrenees

SPAIN

Perpigna

ANDORRA

N

0 ——— 100 km
0 ——— 100 miles
(approximate scale)

Tour de France
This grueling annual bicycle race was first held in 1903. It is made up of 21 stages over three weeks and covers 2,200 miles (3,500 km).

Château de Chambord
Built in the 16th century as a royal hunting lodge, this château, near Orléans, has more than 400 rooms. Châteaux such as this are the historic residences of France's nobility.

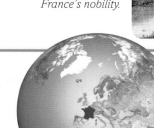

France is the **largest nation** in western Europe. The mainland is known as "the **Hexagon**," while its **island of Corsica** was the birthplace of **Napoleon**, a famous leader. The capital, **Paris**, welcomes **20 million visitors** every year.

- 248,573 sq miles (643,801 sq km)
- 67.8 million
- Paris
- French, other languages (+5)

Parkour

Loose-fitting clothes allow the participant to jump and move freely.

The sport of parkour was founded in the Paris suburbs in the 1980s. It is a way of moving freely over urban terrain by running, jumping, and climbing.

Côte d'Azur

Beautiful resort towns such as Cannes, Nice, and Saint-Tropez are located along the part of the country's Mediterranean coast known as the Côte d'Azur.

Sweet treats

French pastries and sweets—such as croissants, éclairs, and macarons—are known throughout the world.

Macarons are almond meringues sandwiched with buttercream or jam.

Eiffel Tower

Designed by the engineer Gustave Eiffel, the Eiffel Tower was built in Paris in 1889. It stands 1,063 ft (324 m) tall and was the world's tallest building until 1931.

Fashion capital

Paris has long been known as the fashion capital of the world. It is home to many of the big design houses, including Chanel, founded by Coco Chanel (right) in 1920.

Sunflower farming

Sunflowers are grown across southern France. Their heads are harvested for the seeds, which are pressed for oil.

French perfume industry

France has been known for perfume since the perfumers of Grasse, near Nice, first extracted fragrance from flowers.

Geography: The country is bounded by the mountains of the **Pyrenees** and **Alps** and has **Atlantic** and **Mediterranean** coasts.

History: France was **ruled by kings** until the **French Revolution** of 1789, when the **monarchy** was **overthrown**. The country first became a **republic** in 1792.

Culture: A **leader** in **art**, **literature**, **film**, and **philosophy**, France has world-famous **museums**, such as the **Louvre** in Paris.

Food and drink: Celebrated for its **cuisine** and **fine wines**, the country is famous for its variety of **regional cheeses**.

Map labels

BELGIUM
St-Quentin
Charleville-Mézières
LUXEMBOURG
GERMANY
Reims
Metz
Nancy
Strasbourg
Vosges
Auxerre
Mulhouse
Belfort
Dijon
Besançon
Côte d'Or
Saône
Mont Blanc 4,808 m (15,774 ft)
SWITZERLAND
Thonon-les-Bains
Lyon
Annecy
St-Étienne
Grenoble
ALPS
ITALY
Rhône
Avignon
Montpellier
Aix-en-Provence
Nice
MONACO
Marseille
Toulon
Côte d'Azur
Gulf of Lion
MEDITERRANEAN SEA
Ligurian Sea
Bastia
Corsica (Corse)
Ajaccio

Spain

Moorish Palace
The Alhambra is a magnificent fortified palace in the city of Granada. It was built by the Moors, Muslim settlers from North Africa who occupied parts of Spain until 1491.

Canary Islands
Lying off the coast of northwestern Africa, this Spanish archipelago is made up of seven volcanic islands.

| 0 | 100 km |
| 0 | 100 miles |
(approximate scale)

Santa Cruz de la Palma
La Palma
La Gomera
El Hierro
Tenerife
Teide 3,718 m (12,198 ft)
Santa Cruz de Tenerife
Las Palmas
Gran Canaria
Lanzarote
Arrecife
Puerto del Rosario
Fuerteventura

ATLANTIC OCEAN

Fiery flamenco
The flamenco dance originated in Andalusia, southern Spain. It features intricate arm movements, rhythmic footwork, claps, and often castanets.

Seafood platter
First made in Valencia, paella is now popular throughout Spain. It contains rice, seafood, and vegetables and is usually cooked in a wide, shallow pan over an open fire.

| 0 | 100 km |
| 0 | 100 miles |
(approximate scale)

La Sagrada Família
This unique church in Barcelona was designed by the architect Antoni Gaudí. Its construction began in 1882, and it is still being built!

PORTUGAL

A Coruña
Santiago de Compostela
Vigo
Ourense
Cordillera Cantábrica
Ponferrada
León
Oviedo
Gijón
Xixón
Palen
Valladolid
Zamora
Duero
Salamanca
Ciudad-Rodrigo
Sistema
Coria
Sierra de Gredos
Tagus
Cáceres
To
Mérida
Badajoz
Ciudad
Castuera
Zafra
Puertollano
Pozoblanco
Sierra Morena
Cortegana
Guadalquivir
Lir
Córdoba
Jaé
Huelva
Seville (Sevilla)
Olvera
Grana
Gulf of Cádiz
Cádiz
Málaga
Sierr
Marbella
Costa del S
Algeciras
Strait of Gibraltar
Ceuta
MOROCCO

Spain is separated from the rest of Europe by the **Pyrenees Mountains** to the north. In the south, Spain is **just 8 miles (13 km)** from **Morocco**, across the **Strait of Gibraltar**. In between range **17 regions**, each with its own character. **Madrid**, Europe's **highest capital city** at **2,200 ft (670 m)**, sits right in the center of the country. The **Spanish Balearic Islands** lie in the **Mediterranean Sea**, and the **Canary Islands** are found far to the south, in the **Atlantic Ocean**.

Tennis champion
The Spanish tennis legend Rafael Nadal has won 19 Grand Slam singles titles.

Cathedrals beach
Erosion by wind and sea has sculpted dramatic rock formations resembling cathedral arches at this beach to the west of Gijón in northwestern Spain.

Bay of Biscay

antander • Bilbao • Donostia/San Sebastián • Vitoria-Gasteiz urgos • Pamplona/Iruña • Logroño anda de Duero • Soria • Huesca • Zaragoza • Girona • Lleida (Lérida) • Terrassa • Mataró • Barcelona • Alcañiz • Tarragona • Vinaròs

Sistema Ibérico • Ebro • FRANCE • PYRENEES • ANDORRA • Costa Brava

rra do darrama • entral • Guadalajara • **MADRID** • etafe • Tagus • Cuenca • Mota del Cuervo • Manzanares • Albacete • Júcar • Segura • Castellón de la Plana/Castelló de la Plana • Costa del Azahar

Gulf of Valencia

Balearic Islands

• Pollença • Minorca (Menorca) • Palma • Majorca (Mallorca)

Ibiza • Ibiza

Ibiza is the third-largest of the Balearic Islands, famous for its beaches and nightlife.

Alcoy/Alcoi • Benidorm • Alicante/Alacant • Elda • Elche/Elx • Hellín • Costa Blanca • temas Béticos • Murcia • Lorca • Cartagena • Mulhacén 3,479 m (11,413 ft) • evada • Almería

Mediterranean Sea

Las Fallas
In this annual festival in Valencia, people remember Saint Joseph—the patron saint of carpenters—with parades, music, and fireworks. Each neighborhood builds a sculpture called a falla, *filled with firecrackers, which is eventually burned.*

The fallas are made of cardboard and papier-mâché.

Olive oil
Spain produces about half of the world's olive oil—more than any other country.

Wild cats
Iberian lynx live in the mountains of southern Spain. Once on the brink of extinction, conservation projects have saved this solitary cat.

⊘ 195,124 sq miles (505,370 sq km)

⊕ 50 million

★ Madrid

◯ Spanish, Catalan, Galician, Basque

Geography: A **mountainous** country with a **central plain**, Spain is **wet and green** in the **north** and **hot and dry** in the **south**.

History: Spain was divided by **civil war** from **1936–1939** and then ruled by a **dictator** until **1975**, when the **monarchy** and **democracy** were **restored**.

Culture: All over Spain, communities celebrate **local festivals**, or *fiestas*, throughout the year. **Easter** is marked by **Holy Week**.

Food and drink: Spain has a rich cuisine of **seafood** and **meat dishes**, but it is also popular to eat a range of **small plates**, known as *tapas*.

Portugal

Lisbon's trams
Bright yellow trams, known as remodelados, date back to the 1930s and still carry passengers around Lisbon's busy, and often hilly, streets.

Madeira Flower Festival
Every spring, the Flower Festival takes place on the Portuguese island of Madeira. People wear flowers and decorate floral floats in parades through the city of Funchal.

Cristiano Ronaldo
This Portuguese striker from Madeira is one of the best-known soccer players in the world. He has won four European Golden Shoes and the coveted Ballon d'Or five times.

Record-breaking waves
Some of the biggest waves in the world break onto the beaches at Nazaré, on the coast west of Leiria. The annual surfing competitions held here are the ultimate test for surfers.

The waves can be as tall as 80 ft (24 m)—the record for the tallest wave ever surfed, in 2018.

N

Lisbon is the westernmost capital in mainland Europe.

SPAIN

Viana do Castelo · Ponte da B
Póvoa de Varzim · Braga
Vila do Conde · Guimarã
Matosinhos
· Porto · Vila Re
Vila Nova de Gaia
Ovar · Lamego
· São João da Ma
· Aveiro · Albergaria-a-Vel
Ílhavo · Viset
Rio Mondego
Alto da Torre 1,993 m (6,539 ft)
Figueira da Foz · Coimbra · Covill
Serra da Estr
· Leiria
Nazaré · Castelo Branco
· Entroncamento · Tomar
Peniche · Caldas da Rainha · Abrantes
Tagus *Tagus*
Torres Vedras · Santarém
Portalegre
· Coruche · Avis
Sintra · **LISBON** (LISBOA) *Sorraia*
Cascais
Almada · Barreiro · Vendas Novas
Setúbal · Estremoz · Elvas
Serra d'Ossa
Baía de Setúbal *Rio Sado* · Alcácer do Sal · Évora · Redondo
· Grândola · Portel *Guadiana*
· Sines
· Beja · Barranco
Aljustrel · Serpa
ATLANTIC OCEAN
· Odemira · Ourique
Serra de Monchique · Mértola
· Almodôvar
Lagos · SPAIN
· Portimão · Ayamonte
Cabo de São Vicente Tavira ·
· Faro *Gulf of Cadiz*

Lying alongside Spain in the **Iberian Peninsula** in Europe, Portugal has a long, windswept **Atlantic coastline**. In the **15th** and **16th centuries**, **explorers** set out from here to discover the **unknown lands** to the west, passing **Cabo de São Vicente**, Europe's southwesternmost point. More than 600 miles (1,000 km) away, in the Atlantic Ocean, lie the **Portuguese islands** of **Madeira** and the **Azores**.

- 35,556 sq miles (92,090 sq km)
- 10.3 million
- Lisbon
- Portuguese

Chaves
Bragança
Mirandela
Douro
Guarda

SPAIN

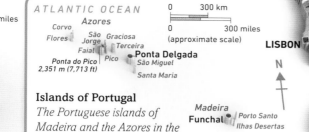

Islands of Portugal
The Portuguese islands of Madeira and the Azores in the Atlantic Ocean are volcanic in origin.

ATLANTIC OCEAN
Azores
Corvo
Flores
São Jorge   Graciosa
Faial   Terceira
Pico
Ponta do Pico   **Ponta Delgada**
2,351 m (7,713 ft)   São Miguel
Santa Maria

0   300 km
0   300 miles
(approximate scale)

LISBON
PORTUGAL
N

Madeira
Funchal   Porto Santo
Ilhas Desertas

Decorative tiles
Glazed ceramic tiles known as azulejos are often used to decorate buildings. Most are blue, and some depict scenes from Portuguese history, such as on this wall at Porto's São Bento Railway Station.

Casa da Música
The unique Casa da Música concert hall opened in the city of Porto in 2005. It can hold an audience of about 1,300 people.

The building has sharply angled concrete walls.

Prince Henry the Navigator helped launch Portugal's "Age of Discovery."

Portuguese rooster
According to local legend, roosters are considered lucky. Painted figurines of roosters are sold as souvenirs.

Monument to the Discoveries
This famous monument on the seafront in Lisbon honors key figures from Portugal's "Age of Discovery," a period starting in the 15th century when explorers, mapmakers, and scientists voyaged over oceans to find unknown lands.

Palácio da Pena
This brightly colored royal castle sits on a hill overlooking the town of Sintra, to the west of Lisbon.

Geography: Portugal has more than **500 miles (850 km)** of **coastline**. It is **rocky** in the **north**, with most **farmland** in the **south**.

History: Once a **global empire**, the **monarchy** was deposed in a **revolution** in **1910**, and Portugal became a **republic**.

Culture: Portuguese traditions include **fado music**—melancholy songs accompanied by guitars—and **popular festivals**.

Natural wonders: The **Grutas de Mira de Aire caves** near Leiria and **Madeira's laurel forests** stand out for their beauty.

Wildlife: Iberian wolves and **lynx** roam the mountains, and **wild boars** and **deer** the countryside. **Dolphins** swim the Atlantic waters.

Food and drink: Portugal is famous for its **sweet custard tarts** and **seafood dishes**, such as **salt cod** and **grilled sardines**.

Malta

Maltese filigree
In the ancient art of filigree, artisans weave delicate jewelry from fine gold and silver threads.

The eight-pointed cross is a common symbol in Maltese filigree.

Painted boats
Colorful Maltese fishing boats called luzzus *can be seen in the popular fishing village of Marsaxlokk.*

Blue Lagoon
Between Kemmuna and Kemmunett islet is a bay with clear, turquoise waters that is popular with swimmers and snorkelers.

Map labels:
Gozo, Mediterranean Sea, Malta Channel, Mediterranean Sea
Xagħra, Victoria, Nadur, Mgarr, Comino (Kemmuna), Blue Lagoon Bay, Mellieħa, Buġibba, Mosta, Malta, Rabat, Hamrun, Sliema, VALLETTA, Paola, Zabbar, Ta' Dmejrek 253 m (830 ft), Marsaxlokk, Zurrieq, Birzebbuġa, Filfla

0   5 km
0   5 miles
(approximate scale)

- ⊘ **122 sq miles** (316 sq km)
- 👥 **457,300**
- ★ Valletta
- ◯ Maltese, English

The **islands** of **Malta, Gozo,** and **Kemmuna,** together with **smaller islets,** form the country of Malta. Over the course of its history, this **archipelago** has attracted **foreign powers** such as the **Phoenicians, Romans,** and **British.**

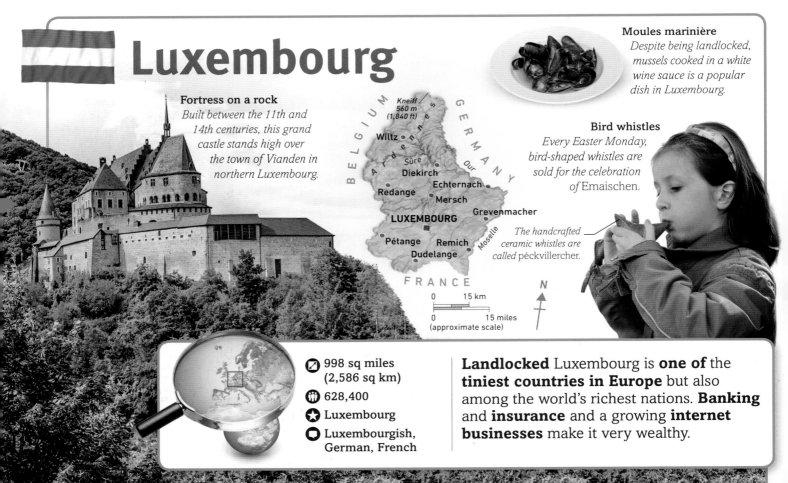

Luxembourg

Moules marinière
Despite being landlocked, mussels cooked in a white wine sauce is a popular dish in Luxembourg.

Fortress on a rock
Built between the 11th and 14th centuries, this grand castle stands high over the town of Vianden in northern Luxembourg.

Bird whistles
Every Easter Monday, bird-shaped whistles are sold for the celebration of Emaischen.

The handcrafted ceramic whistles are called péckvillercher.

Map labels:
BELGIUM, GERMANY, Kneiff 560 m (1,840 ft), Wiltz, Ardennes, Sûre, Our, Diekirch, Echternach, Redange, Mersch, Grevenmacher, LUXEMBOURG, Moselle, Pétange, Remich, Dudelange, FRANCE

0   15 km
0   15 miles
(approximate scale)

- ⊘ **998 sq miles** (2,586 sq km)
- 👥 **628,400**
- ★ Luxembourg
- ◯ Luxembourgish, German, French

Landlocked Luxembourg is **one of** the **tiniest countries in Europe** but also among the world's richest nations. **Banking** and **insurance** and a growing **internet businesses** make it very wealthy.

Andorra

The circular tower was added in the 12th century.

Ancient church
Situated outside the capital is Santa Coloma d'Andorra, one of the oldest churches in the country. It dates back to the 8th century.

Coma Pedrosa 2,943 m (9,656 ft)

FRANCE

Arcalis

El Tarter

Arinsal

Canillo

El Pas de la Casa

ANDORRA LA VELLA

Encamp

Pyrenees

Andorra la Vella is located 3,356 ft (1,023 m) above sea level.

Santa Coloma d'Andorra

Sant Julià de Lòria

Valira

SPAIN

N

0   7 km
0   7 miles
(approximate scale)

Forest dweller
The mountain forests are home to European pine martens. They hunt small mammals and birds.

Madriu-Perafita-Claror Valley
This stunning, steep-sided valley cut by a glacier, not far from La Vella, makes up almost 10 percent of the country.

⚐ 180 sq miles
(468 sq km)

👥 77,000

★ Andorra la Vella

🗩 Spanish, Catalan, French, Portuguese

High in the
Pyrenees Mountains
between France and Spain
lies the small nation of
Andorra. Many tourists visit
the country for **trekking**
and **skiing** and the
ancient churches.

Monaco Grand Prix
Every year, the streets of Monaco are closed so Grand Prix races can be held, such as Formula 1 and the GP2 race shown here.

Monaco

0   700 metres
0   700 yards
(approximate scale)

Gleaming coast
Monaco's best-known neighborhood is Monte Carlo. Casinos and lavish hotels sit alongside a spectacular harbor.

Grand Prix circuit

FRANCE

Lycée de l'Annonciade

La Condamine

Musée National

Larvotto

Palais Princier

Monte Carlo

Casino

Centre de Congrès

Port of Monaco

Fontvieille

Mediterranean Sea

N

⚐ 0.7 sq miles
(2 sq km)

👥 39,000

★ Monaco

🗩 French, English, Monégasque, Italian

The world's **second-smallest**
country lies on the **Riviera**—
the **Mediterranean coastline** in
southeastern France. Many of the
wealthiest people in the world live
here, since residents pay no income tax.

Italy

Pizza
This famous flatbread baked with tomato, mozzarella cheese, and other savory toppings originated in Naples in the 18th century.

*Italy's second-largest city, **Milan** is a center of fashion, design, and industry.*

Ruins of Pompeii
In 79 CE, the volcano of Vesuvius, near modern-day Naples, erupted, covering the city of Pompeii in ash. A visit to the site today is like traveling back to ancient Rome.

Vespa scooter
Italy's iconic motor scooter is popular with young people navigating the busy traffic in cities such as Rome.

The Colosseum
The largest amphitheater in the Roman Empire was the Colosseum. This dramatic location for bloody battles between gladiators still stands today in Rome.

Michelangelo
This sculpture of Moses was made by the Italian Renaissance artist Michelangelo in 1504.

Spectacled salamander
Found only in southern Italy, this amphibian displays its red tummy to warn potential attackers.

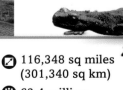

The **boot-shaped** country of Italy stretches 500 miles (800 km) into the **Mediterranean Sea**, with a coastline of 4,600 miles (7,500 km). Its **great cities**, such as **Rome**, **Florence**, and **Milan**, are world-famous centers of **historic art** and **architecture**.

- 116,348 sq miles (301,340 sq km)
- 62.4 million
- Rome
- Italian, other languages (+4)

Map labels:
AUSTRIA · SLOVENIA · SWITZERLAND · FRANCE · ALPS · Apennines
Mont Blanc 4,807 m (15,771 ft) · Aosta · Como · Bergamo · Novara · Milan (Milano) · Bolzano · Trento · Udine · Treviso · Verona · Venice (Venezia) · Ferrara · Parma · Modena · Bologna · Ravenna · SAN MARINO · Ancona · Turin (Torino) · Asti · Genoa (Genova) · Po · Pisa · Florence (Firenze) · Arezzo · Livorno · Siena · Perugia · L'Aquila · Ligurian Sea · Tiber (Tevere) · Civitavecchia · Vatican City · ROME (ROMA) · Olbia · Sassari · Sardinia (Sardegna) · Cagliari

0 50 km
0 50 miles
(approximate scale)

N

Italian vineyards
Vineyards grow over the 20 regions of Italy, and the wine produced from their grapes is one of the country's major exports.

City of islands and waterways
The city of Venice was established on 118 islands in a lagoon in northern Italy. Gondolas and motorboats ferry people up and down the canals of the city.

Leonardo da Vinci
The Italian artist Leonardo da Vinci was also a scientist and inventor, who drew this design for a flying machine in the 15th century.

Adriatic Sea
escara

Foggia
Campobassa
Barletta
Bari
Brindisi
Caserta
Benevento
Taranto
Lecce
Potenza
Salerno
Naples (Napoli)
Capri
Gulf of Taranto

Tyrrhenian Sea

Crotone
Catanzaro
Vibo Valentia
Aeolian Islands
Messina
Reggio di Calabria
Palermo
Ionian Sea
Catania
Mount Etna 3,326 m (10,912 ft)
arsala
Sicily (Sicilia)
Siracusa
Ragusa

Mediterranean Sea

MALTA

The tambourine is a vital part of this dance.

Tarantella
A folk dance for couples, the tarantella has fast, lively steps. According to legend, this dance started out as a cure for hysteria brought on by a tarantula spider's bite.

Parmigiano-Reggiano
Known for its nutty taste, this hard cheese is grated over many pasta and rice dishes to add flavor.

Italian Grand Prix
This Formula 1 race has been held since 1921 on a racetrack near Monza, north of Milan. With 20 victories, Scuderia Ferrari is the most successful team on this circuit.

Leaning Tower of Pisa
Measuring 183 ft (55.9 m) on its highest side, this iconic tower began to lean as soon as construction started in 1173.

Geography: The Italian **peninsula** extends from the **mountains** of the **Alps** in the **north** to the **island of Sicily** in the **south**.

History: Once the **heart** of the **Roman Empire**, Italy **fragmented** into **medieval city-states** and **kingdoms** before **unification** as a country in **1861**.

Culture: Celebrated for its **ancient** and **Renaissance art** and **architecture**, Italy was also the **birthplace** of **opera** and is now **famous** for its **movies** and **fashion**.

Food and drink: Italy's **healthy diet** is known for its **pasta, tomatoes, olive oil**, and **fish** but has many **regional variations** based on **local produce**.

Vatican City

This part of the ceiling shows God creating Adam, the first man.

Vatican Gardens
More than half of Vatican City is made up of gardens with many statues, fountains, and grottoes.

0 — 150 metres
0 — 150 yards
(approximate scale)

Swiss Guard
Since the 16th century, armed guards in traditional uniform have protected the pope and Vatican City.

Sistine Chapel
The Sistine Chapel was built in the Vatican Palace during the 15th century. The ceiling features vast wall paintings by the Italian artist Michelangelo.

Halberds are ceremonial weapons carried by the Swiss Guards.

Main Entrance

ITALY

Belvedere Palace

Pigna Courtyard

Vatican Museums

Vatican Central Post Office

Belvedere Courtyard

Vatican

Gardens

Sistine Chapel

Apostolic Palace

N

Heliport

Vatican Hill

Government Palace

Vatican Railway Station

St Peter's Basilica

St Peter's Square

ITALY

Pope Francis
Born in Argentina in 1936, Pope Francis is the current head of the Catholic Church.

Coins from the Vatican
The country adopted the euro as currency in 2000 but produces its own euro coins, some of which show the Pope.

St. Peter's Square
Up to 300,000 people are able to gather in St. Peter's Square to listen to the pope speak. It takes its name from Saint Peter, who Catholics consider the first pope.

St. Peter's Basilica is the largest church in the world.

⊘ 0.17 sq miles (0.44 sq km)
⊕ 1,000
★ None
◯ Italian, Latin

Located within the Italian capital of Rome is Vatican City, the **smallest country** on Earth. This tiny city-state is **home** to the **Pope**, the **head** of the **Roman Catholic Church**.

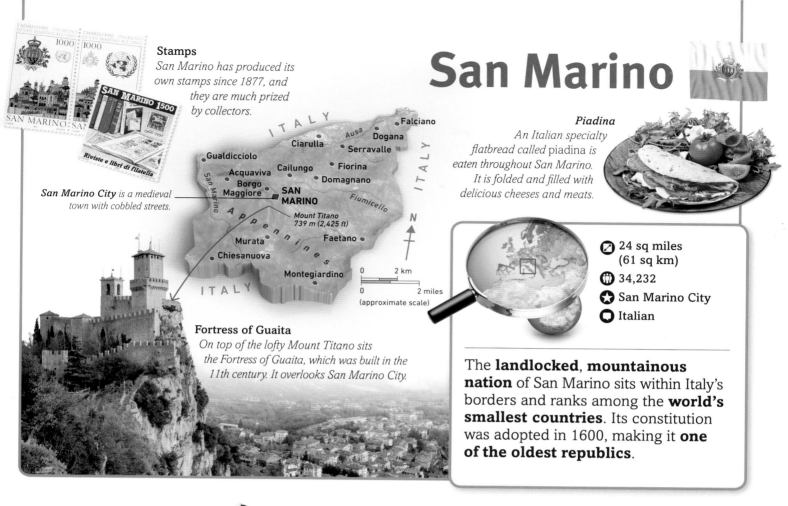

San Marino

Stamps
San Marino has produced its own stamps since 1877, and they are much prized by collectors.

San Marino City is a medieval town with cobbled streets.

Map labels
ITALY
Falciano
Ausa
Dogana
Ciarulla
Serravalle
Gualdicciolo
Cailungo
Fiorina
ITALY
Acquaviva
Domagnano
Borgo
Maggiore
SAN
MARINO
San Marino
Fiumicello
Appennines
Mount Titano
739 m (2,425 ft)
Murata
Faetano
Chiesanuova
Montegiardino
ITALY

0   2 km
0   2 miles
(approximate scale)

N

Piadina
An Italian specialty flatbread called piadina is eaten throughout San Marino. It is folded and filled with delicious cheeses and meats.

Fortress of Guaita
On top of the lofty Mount Titano sits the Fortress of Guaita, which was built in the 11th century. It overlooks San Marino City.

- 24 sq miles (61 sq km)
- 34,232
- San Marino City
- Italian

The **landlocked, mountainous nation** of San Marino sits within Italy's borders and ranks among the **world's smallest countries**. Its constitution was adopted in 1600, making it **one of the oldest republics**.

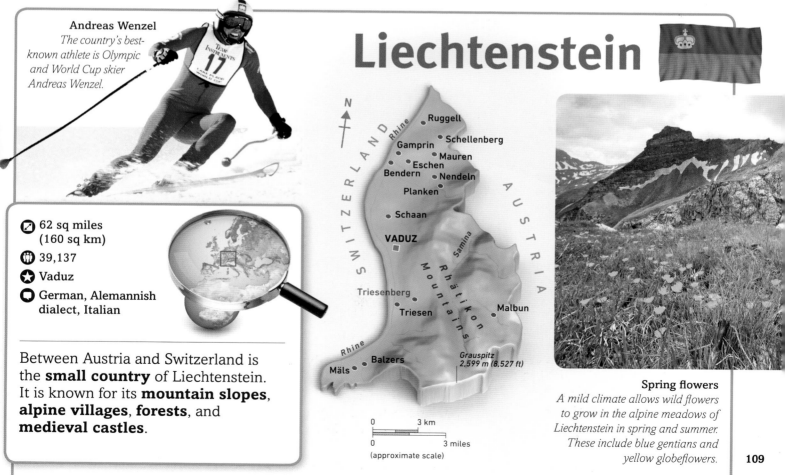

Andreas Wenzel
The country's best-known athlete is Olympic and World Cup skier Andreas Wenzel.

Liechtenstein

Map labels
N
SWITZERLAND
Rhine
Ruggell
Schellenberg
Gamprin
Mauren
Eschen
Bendern
Nendeln
Planken
Schaan
VADUZ
Samina
AUSTRIA
Rhätikon Mountains
Triesenberg
Triesen
Malbun
Rhine
Balzers
Mäls
Grauspitz
2,599 m (8,527 ft)

0   3 km
0   3 miles
(approximate scale)

- 62 sq miles (160 sq km)
- 39,137
- Vaduz
- German, Alemannish dialect, Italian

Between Austria and Switzerland is the **small country** of Liechtenstein. It is known for its **mountain slopes, alpine villages, forests**, and **medieval castles**.

Spring flowers
A mild climate allows wild flowers to grow in the alpine meadows of Liechtenstein in spring and summer. These include blue gentians and yellow globeflowers.

Switzerland

Alpine ibex
The rocky slopes of the Swiss Alps are home to the Alpine ibex. These wild goats have padded hooves that make them expert climbers.

Matterhorn
The pyramid-shaped peak of the Matterhorn rises 14,692 ft (4,478 m) high. It is the most recognizable mountain in the Alps.

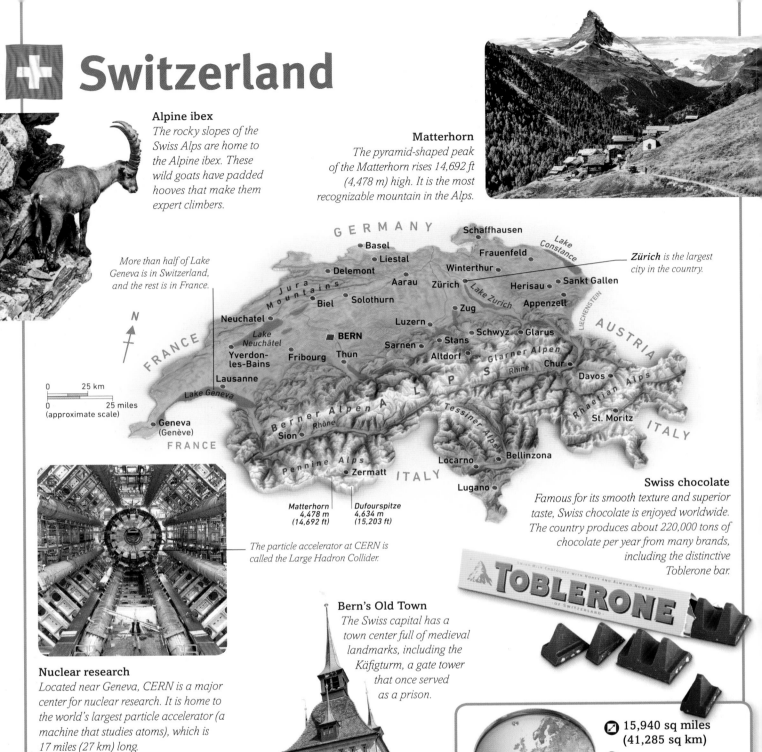

More than half of Lake Geneva is in Switzerland, and the rest is in France.

Zürich is the largest city in the country.

GERMANY

Schaffhausen
Basel
Liestal
Delemont
Frauenfeld
Winterthur
Aarau
Zürich
Herisau
Sankt Gallen
Biel
Solothurn
Zug
Appenzell
Neuchatel
Lake Neuchâtel
Luzern
Schwyz
Glarus
Yverdon-les-Bains
Fribourg
Thun
Sarnen
Stans
Altdorf
Lausanne
BERN
Chur
Davos
Lake Geneva
Sion
Rhône
Locarno
Bellinzona
St. Moritz
Geneva (Genève)
Zermatt
Lugano

Jura Mountains
Berner Alpen
Pennine Alps
Tessiner Alps
Glarner Alpen
Rhaetian Alps
Rhine
ALPS

FRANCE
LIECHTENSTEIN
AUSTRIA
ITALY

N

0 25 km
0 25 miles
(approximate scale)

Matterhorn 4,478 m (14,692 ft)
Dufourspitze 4,634 m (15,203 ft)

The particle accelerator at CERN is called the Large Hadron Collider.

Nuclear research
Located near Geneva, CERN is a major center for nuclear research. It is home to the world's largest particle accelerator (a machine that studies atoms), which is 17 miles (27 km) long.

Bern's Old Town
The Swiss capital has a town center full of medieval landmarks, including the Käfigturm, a gate tower that once served as a prison.

Swiss chocolate
Famous for its smooth texture and superior taste, Swiss chocolate is enjoyed worldwide. The country produces about 220,000 tons of chocolate per year from many brands, including the distinctive Toblerone bar.

TOBLERONE

- 15,940 sq miles (41,285 sq km)
- 8.4 million
- Bern
- German, Swiss-German, French, other languages (+2)

Nestled in **the Alps** and bordered by the **Jura range** to the northwest, this country is famous for its **ski resorts** but also for **watches** and **chocolates** and as a **center for banking**.

Slovenia

Ski jumping
This sport is very popular in the Alpine valleys of northwestern Slovenia. Many ski jumpers from this country have set world records at the Winter Olympics.

Skis are spread in a V-formation, to achieve the longest possible jump.

Tasty treat
A traditional treat in Slovenia is potica. *This rolled dough filled with walnut paste is eaten during Easter and other festivals.*

Lake Bled
Visitors flock to this glacial lake to the southeast of Jesenice. At its center lies an island with a beautiful church, while a medieval castle overlooks its waters from a nearby hill.

Map labels:
AUSTRIA
HUNGARY
ITALY
CROATIA
Triglav 2,864 m (9,396 ft)
Julian Alps
Jesenice
Bovec
Tolmin
Kranj
Velenje
Ravne na Koroškem
Murska Sobota
Maribor
Ptuj
Rogaška Slatina
Save (Sava)
Trbovlje
Nova Gorica
Idrija
LJUBLJANA
Karst
Sežana
Postojna
Škocjan Caves
Novo Mesto
Krško
Gulf of Trieste
Koper
Ilirska Bistrica
Črnomelj

0 — 25km
0 — 25 miles
(approximate scale)

Carniolan honey bee
Beekeeping is an important Slovenian tradition. The native Carniolan honeybee is highly prized by beekeepers.

Sacred symbol
The linden leaf is an important symbol of Slovenia. In the past, linden trees were planted to mark where village councils gathered for discussions.

Ana Desetnica Festival
Circus performers, musicians, and dancers perform in this annual street theater festival in the capital city of Ljubljana.

Slovenia is **one of the greenest countries** in Europe, with more than half of its area covered in **forests**. The snow-covered **Julian Alps** in the north has the country's highest peak, **Mount Triglav**, which is a **national symbol**.

- 7,827 sq miles (20,273 sq km)
- 2.1 million
- Ljubljana
- Slovenian

Lipizzaner horses
For more than 400 years, the famous Lipizzaner horses have been bred at the Lipica stud farm in the southwest of Slovenia. These beautiful gray horses are trained to perform at equestrian shows.

Austria

The Austrian flag has been used since 1230 and is among the world's oldest flags.

Alpine skiing
Austria has about 400 ski resorts. Kitzbühel is home to the famous downhill race on the Hahnenkamm mountain.

Kunst Haus Wien
In the 20th century, the Austrian-born artist and architect Friedensreich Hundertwasser designed several unique buildings, including this museum in Vienna that holds exhibitions of his and other artists' works.

Wolfgang Amadeus Mozart
This 18th-century Austrian musician composed his first work at the age of 5. He had written more than 620 pieces of classical music by the time he died at the age of 35.

Vienna sits on the banks of the Danube River.

Map labels:
CZECHIA
SLOVAKIA
Schrems
Laa an der Thaya
Krems an der Donau
Danube (Donau)
Linz
Wels
Steyr
Sankt Pölten
VIENNA (WIEN)
Baden
Wiener Neustadt
Eisenstadt
Salzburg
LIECH.
Bregenz
Dornbirn
GERMANY
Inn
Innsbruck
Kitzbühel
Kaprun
Liezen
Niedere Tauern
Enns
Kapfenberg
Leoben
Fischbacher Alpen
HUNGARY
Kappl
Ischgl
A L P S
Hohe Tauern
Sölden
Ötztaler Alpen
SWITZERLAND
Grossglockner 3,798 m (12,461 ft)
Lienz
Gurktaler Alpen
Graz
Mur
Feldkirchen
Wolfsberg
Villach
Klagenfurt
ITALY
SLOVENIA
N

Dancing horses
More than 450 years old, the Spanish Riding School in Vienna is the oldest riding academy in the world. It trains horses to perform acrobatic movements, such as this forward jump called the curvet.

Scale:
0   50 km
0   50 miles
(approximate scale)

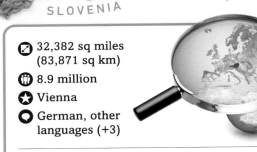

- 32,382 sq miles (83,871 sq km)
- 8.9 million
- Vienna
- German, other languages (+3)

Almost **two-thirds** of Austria is mountainous, with the **dramatic peaks**, **glaciers**, and **sloping meadows** of the **Alps** dominating the landscape. But the country is also known for its **palaces**, **art**, and **classical music**.

Mountain lakes
Many lakes lie between the peaks of the Austrian Alps, carved out of the landscape by glaciers. The beautiful Vorderer Gosausee near Salzburg lies at a height of 3,061 ft (933 m) above sea level.

Sports star

Czechia has produced many great tennis players. Petra Kvitová has won 27 singles titles, including two Wimbledon Championships.

Czechia

Astronomical Clock

This medieval clock has struck the time in Prague since 1410. It is an astronomical clock, which means it not only marks the hours but also the movements of the sun, moon, and stars.

0   50 km
0   50 miles
(approximate scale)

N

GERMANY

Ore Mountains
(Krušné Hory)

Sněžka
1,603 m
(5,259 ft)

Cheb

Karlovy Vary

Ústí nad
Labem

Liberec

Krkonoše

Sudeten

POLAND

Kladno

Mladá
Boleslav

PRAGUE
(PRAHA)

Hradec
Králové

Plzeň

Elbe

Pardubice

Vltava

Českomorayeská
Vrchovina

Dolní Morava

Jeseník

Ostrava

Bohemian Forest

Písek

Tábor

Jihlava

Olomouc

Jindřichův
Hradec

Brno

Zlín

White Carpathians
(Bílé Karpaty)

Český
Krumlov

České
Budějovice

Znojmo

Dyje

Morava

AUSTRIA

SLOVAKIA

Winding walkway

The Sky Walk is a wooden walkway in the mountain resort of Dolní Morava. Reaching a height of 180 ft (55 m) above the ground, it offers majestic views of the Morava Valley.

Officially known as the Czech Republic, **Czechia** lies in the **heart of Europe** and is known for its **castles**, **medieval towns**, and several **spa sites**. **Prague**, the capital, is known as the "**City of 100 Spires**" for its many churches and towers.

- 30,450 sq miles (78,867 sq km)
- 10.7 million
- Prague
- Czech, other languages (+7)

Glassmaking

Czechia is renowned for the quality of its glassmaking, a tradition that dates back to the 13th century. These vases (left) are from the 19th century.

Charles Bridge

This famous bridge over the Vltava River in Prague is lined with statues. It connects the Old Town with the busy Malá Strana district (seen here).

Slovakia

Painted houses

Traditional log houses in the village of Čičmany in northern Slovakia have been preserved for their unusual geometric decorations. The patterns were originally painted in mud and lime by local women.

Towering peaks

The Tatra Mountains mark Slovakia's border with Poland. The sharp peaks and lakes are the habitat of lynx, chamois (alpine goats), marmots, and eagles.

Easter eggs

Decorating eggs is an Easter tradition in Slovakia. They can be dyed or hand-painted like the ones here.

The fujara is held upright while played.

Map labels

0   50 km
0   50 miles
(approximate scale)

CZECHIA

Žilina
Kysucké Beskydy
Dubnica nad Váhom
Martin
Trenčín
Čičmany
Prievidza
Senica
Partizánske
Banská Bystrica
Trnava
Váh
Zvolen
Nitra
Hron
BRATISLAVA
Danube (Dunaj)
Kolárovo
Little Alföld
Levice
Lučenec
Rimavská Sobota
Komárno

AUSTRIA

HUNGARY

Gerlachovský štít
2,655 m (8,711 ft)

POLAND

Carpathian Mountains
Tatra Mountains
Bardejov
Poprad
Brezno
Hornád
Prešov
Slovenské rudohorie
Košice
Michalovce
Poloniny

UKRAINE

N

Mountain bears

A growing population of more than a thousand brown bears roams the Tatra Mountains. They break up rocky ground with strong claws to find food.

Playing the *fujara*

Originally played by Slovakian shepherds, the fujara flute can now be heard at local festivals.

The open flower petals curve backward.

Wild blooms

The Turk's cap lily can grow to a height of 6 ft (1.8 m), with each stem holding up to 50 bowl-shaped flowers. These flowers grow wild on the slopes of the Carpathian Mountains.

⤢ 18,933 sq miles (49,035 sq km)

👥 5.4 million

★ Bratislava

🗨 Slovak, Hungarian (Magyar), Czech

Slovakia became an **independent nation** in **1993**. Its **mountainous landscape** is dotted with **historic castles**. The **capital** city of **Bratislava** has a well-preserved **Old Town**.

Hungary

Hungarian flavor
The national spice is paprika, which is made from ground hot, sweet red peppers. It is featured in traditional dishes such as goulash, a beef soup.

*With an area of 231 sq miles (598 sq km), **Lake Balaton** is the largest lake in Central Europe.*

Nagy Magyar Alföld is the name given by Hungarians to the Great Hungarian Plain.

Kékes
1,014 m
(3,326 ft)

AUSTRIA

Danube (Duna)

SLOVAKIA

UKRAINE

Sopron

Little Alföld

Győr

Tatabánya

Vác

Mátra

Bükk

Miskolc

Salgótarján

Eger

Nyíregyháza

Szombathely

Pilis

BUDAPEST

Székesfehérvár

Debrecen

SLOVENIA

Zalaegerszeg

Veszprém

Bakony

Lake Balaton

Tisza

Great Alföld

Keszthely

Szolnok

Kecskemét

Berettyo

ROMANIA

Great Hungarian Plain

Danube (Duna)

Drava

Kaposvár

Mecsek

Szekszárd

Békéscsaba

N

Barcs

Pécs

Baja

Szeged

Makó

0   50 km
0   50 miles
(approximate scale)

CROATIA

SERBIA

Striking floral designs are the most common pattern.

Hungarian embroidery
Folk art enjoyed a revival in 19th-century Hungary as the nation found its identity. Embroidered costumes are worn for celebrations.

⊘ 35,918 sq miles
(93,028 sq km)

👥 9.8 million

★ Budapest

⬤ Hungarian (Magyar)

Rubik's Cube
In 1974, the Hungarian inventor Ernő Rubik created the Rubik's Cube—a color-coded 3-D puzzle toy. More than 400 million Rubik's Cubes have been sold worldwide.

Water polo
Both the Hungarian men's and women's national teams excel at the sport of water polo. The men's team has won 15 Olympic medals and 11 World Championships.

Known by its people as the "**Land of Magyars**," this country lost two-thirds of its land after World War I. Today, it is known for **folk art**, **music**, and **thermal baths** as well as **Lake Balaton**.

The Széchenyi Chain Bridge is one of eight bridges linking Buda (on the left) with Pest (on the right).

Budapest
The Danube River divides the city in two. On the west bank lies quiet Buda, home to Buda Castle and the Old Town. Across the river is lively Pest, where the Parliament and shopping district lie.

Serbia

The coat of arms has a two-headed eagle on a red shield.

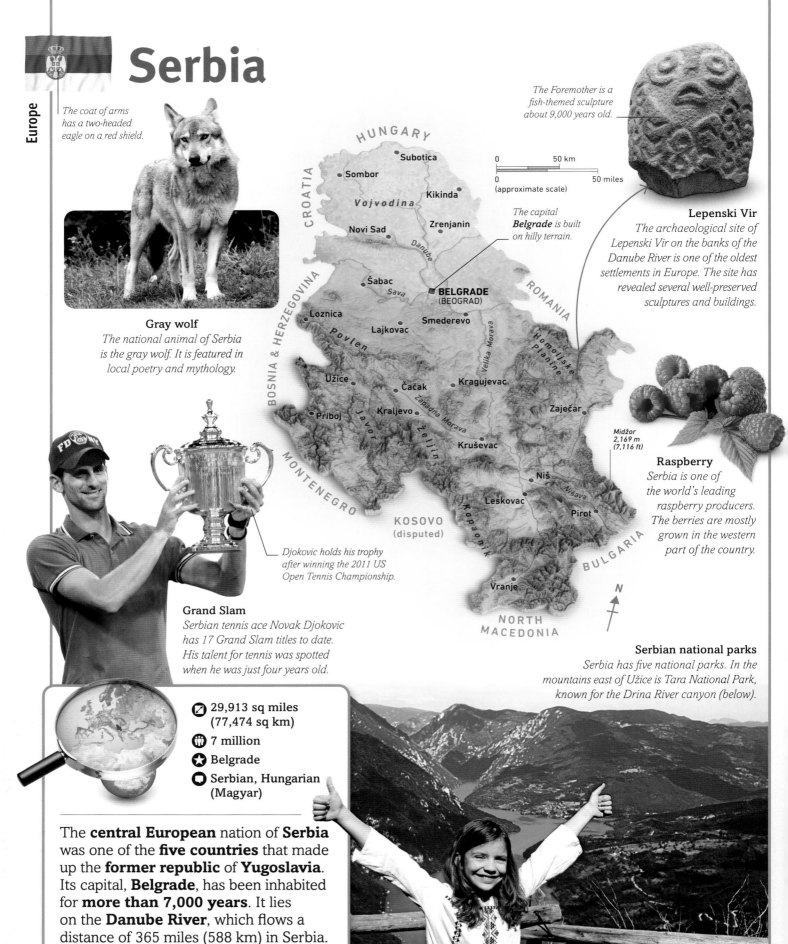

Gray wolf
The national animal of Serbia is the gray wolf. It is featured in local poetry and mythology.

The Foremother is a fish-themed sculpture about 9,000 years old.

Lepenski Vir
The archaeological site of Lepenski Vir on the banks of the Danube River is one of the oldest settlements in Europe. The site has revealed several well-preserved sculptures and buildings.

HUNGARY

Subotica

Sombor

Kikinda

Vojvodina

CROATIA

Novi Sad

Zrenjanin

Danube

The capital **Belgrade** is built on hilly terrain.

Šabac

Sava

BELGRADE
(BEOGRAD)

ROMANIA

Loznica

Smederevo

Lajkovac

Povlen

BOSNIA & HERZEGOVINA

Velika Morava

Homoljske Planine

Užice

Čačak

Kragujevac

Zapadna Morava

Javor

Priboj

Kraljevo

Zaječar

Željin

Kruševac

Midžor
2,169 m
(7,116 ft)

MONTENEGRO

Niš

Nišava

Leskovac

Pirot

Kopaonik

KOSOVO
(disputed)

BULGARIA

Vranje

N

NORTH
MACEDONIA

0   50 km

0   50 miles
(approximate scale)

Raspberry
Serbia is one of the world's leading raspberry producers. The berries are mostly grown in the western part of the country.

Djokovic holds his trophy after winning the 2011 US Open Tennis Championship.

Grand Slam
Serbian tennis ace Novak Djokovic has 17 Grand Slam titles to date. His talent for tennis was spotted when he was just four years old.

Serbian national parks
Serbia has five national parks. In the mountains east of Užice is Tara National Park, known for the Drina River canyon (below).

⊘ 29,913 sq miles
(77,474 sq km)

👥 7 million

★ Belgrade

◯ Serbian, Hungarian
(Magyar)

The **central European** nation of **Serbia** was one of the **five countries** that made up the **former republic** of **Yugoslavia**. Its capital, **Belgrade**, has been inhabited for **more than 7,000 years**. It lies on the **Danube River**, which flows a distance of 365 miles (588 km) in Serbia.

Pula Arena
Built in the 1st century BCE in Pula, this Roman amphitheater was used as a battleground for gladiators. It could hold up to 23,000 spectators.

Croatia

Windsurfing
The strong winds along the Croatian coastline make perfect conditions for windsurfers. Many international windsurfing competitions are held here.

*The capital **Zagreb** lies on the Sava River.*

SLOVENIA

Krapina
Čakovec
Varaždin
Koprivnica
Samobor
Bjelovar
Bilo Gora
ZAGREB
Rijeka
Karlovac
Sisak
Virovitica
Drava
HUNGARY
SERBIA
Rovinj   Istria
Crikvenica
Krk
Slavonia
Osijek
Danube
Pula
Cres
Sava
Požega
Vukovar
Slavonski
Brod

Plitvice Lakes National Park
This vast nature reserve has many waterfalls, including the 52 ft (16 m) tall Galovački Buk waterfall.

Pag
Velebit
Dinaric Alps
BOSNIA
&
HERZEGOVINA

Dugi Otok
Zadar

Dinara
1,831m
(6,007 ft)

Šibenik

N

0   50 km
0   50 miles
(approximate scale)

Griffon vulture
With a wingspan of up to 8.7 ft (2.65 m), the griffon vulture is among the world's largest birds. It nests on the northern islands, including Cres and Krk.

⤢ 21,851 sq miles
(56,594 sq km)

👥 4.2 million

★ Zagreb

⬭ Croatian

Split
Brac
Vis
Hvar
Korčula
Dalmatia
Mljet
Dubrovnik

Adriatic Sea

Croatia has 3,700 miles (6,000 km) of **Adriatic coastline**, as well as **idyllic islands** and **national parks**, making it popular with tourists. The country was a part of **Yugoslavia** until **1991**.

Walled city
Overlooking the Adriatic Sea in southern Croatia is Dubrovnik, known for the stone walls, red-roofed buildings, and historic forts of the Old Town as well as its popular beaches.

Bosnia and Herzegovina

Outdoor chess
Giant chess boards are scattered around the streets and parks of Sarajevo so locals can challenge each other to a game.

Natural spring
The Vrelo Bune spring feeds from a cliff cave into the Buna River at Blagaj, a scenic spot with a monastery.

- ⤢ 19,767 sq miles (51,197 sq km)
- 👥 3.8 million
- ⭐ Sarajevo
- ⬭ Bosnian, Serbian, Croatian

This country is made up of the **two regions** of **Bosnia** and **Herzegovina**. It has popular **ski slopes**, **striking waterfalls**, and the **historic city** of **Mostar**, a mix of Ottoman architecture and modern street art.

Map labels:
CROATIA · Sava · Bosanski Novi · Bihać · Vrbas · Banja Luka · Bosna · Doboj · Brčko · Gradačac · Bijeljina · Ključ · Jajce · Vlašić Mountains · Tuzla · Zvornik · Drina · SERBIA · Zenica · Livno · Dinaric Alps · Lake Buško · Srebrenica · **SARAJEVO** · Goražde · Mostar · Foča · Capljina · Buna · Maglić 2,386 m (7,828 ft) · MONTENEGRO · Trebinje · Adriatic Sea · N

0 — 40 km
0 — 40 miles
(approximate scale)

Standing 574 ft (175 m) tall, the Avaz Twist Tower is the tallest building in Sarajevo.

Connected capital
Dating back to 1885, Sarajevo's tram network is thought to be one of the oldest in Europe. A total of 95 trams connect different parts of the city.

Spectacular bridge
Meaning "Old Bridge," Stari Most links the two halves of the city of Mostar. Fearless divers jump off the bridge into the Neretva River, 75 ft (23 m) below.

Montenegro

River rafting
With more than 11 miles (18 km) of fast-flowing rapids, the Tara River is a popular spot for white-water rafting.

A two-headed eagle on the flag of Montenegro represents unity between church and state.

⬚ 5,333 sq miles (13,812 sq km)

👥 609,900

⭐ Podgorica

🗣 Montenegrin, Serbian, other languages (+3)

*The capital **Podgorica** sits at the meeting point of the Morača and Ribnica rivers.*

Bay of Kotor
This picturesque bay on the Adriatic coast has limestone cliffs and is home to several medieval towns.

In the **tiny nation** of Montenegro, **medieval towns** nestle in the rugged **Dinaric Alps**, while **rivers** cut through dramatic **limestone canyons**. With a depth of 4,265 ft (1,300 m), the **Tara River canyon** is **Europe's deepest**.

Map labels: BOSNIA AND HERZEGOVINA, SERBIA, Pljevlja, Plužine, Bobotov Kuk 2,523 m (8,278 ft), Tara, Bijelo Polje, Nikšić, Kolašin, Rožaje, CROATIA, Vilusi, Zeta, Plav, KOSOVO, Dinaric Alps, Crkvice, Adriatic Sea, Kotor, PODGORICA, ALBANIA, Bay of Kotor, Lake Scutari, Petrovac na Moru, Ulcinj

0 20 km / 0 20 miles (approximate scale)

N

Kosovo

National Library of Kosovo
Designed by the Croatian architect Andrija Mutnjaković, this domed building in Pristina holds more than 2 million items, including books, manuscripts, and maps.

Tasty treat
A popular dish in Kosovo is burek, *a baked pastry with fillings such as cheese, spinach, or meat.*

Champion judoka
Sporting star Majlinda Kelmendi (in white) is a two-time judo world champion and the first Kosovar to win Olympic gold.

Kosovo was a part of Serbia before it declared itself **independent** in **2008**. It is bordered by steep mountains, and **Mount Gjeravica** is its highest point. **Most people live** in the fertile **central plains**.

⬚ 4,203 sq miles (10,887 sq km)

👥 1.9 million

⭐ Pristina

🗣 Albanian, Serbian, other languages (+4)

Map labels: SERBIA, Kopaonik, Mitrovica/Mitrovica, Podujevë/Podujevo, Sitnicë/Sitnica, Pejë/Peć, PRISTINA (PRISHTINË/PRIŠTINA), MONTENEGRO, Gjeravica/Đeravica 2,656 m (8,714 ft), Gjakovë/Đakovica, Gjilan/Gnjilane, ALBANIA, Prizren, Ferizaj/Uroševac, Šar Mountains, Kaçanik/Kačanik, NORTH MACEDONIA

0 20 km / 0 20 miles (approximate scale)

N

Cyrus

Kyrenia Castle
There has been a castle overlooking the harbor of Kyrenia for hundreds of years. Its present structure dates from the 16th century.

This intricately decorated copper pot is used for serving coffee.

Copper pot
Copper has been mined in Cyprus for 6,000 years. People have traditionally used it to make copperware, such as cooking utensils and this pot.

Grape candy
Made with grapes and nuts, shoushouko is a traditional Cypriot dessert. The grape juice gives it a chewy texture.

Cat island
Since ancient times, Cyprus has been full of cats. There are almost 300,000 more cats than people on the island.

Mediterranean Sea

Northern Cyprus has been occupied by Turkey since 1974

Cape Kormakitis
Cape Arnaouti
Erenköy (Kokkina)
Güzelyurt (Morphou)
Girne (Kyrenia)
Kyrenia Mountains
Dipkarpaz (Rizokarpaso)
Cape Apostolos Andreas
Yeni Erenköy (Yialousa)
Tatlısu (Akanthoú)
Karpasia
Polis
Mount Olympus 1,952 m (6,404 ft)
Troodos
NICOSIA
Mesaoria
Famagusta Bay
Paphos (Páfos)
Palaichóri
Dhali
Famagusta (Gazimağusa, Ammochostos)
Ársos
Mountains
Larnaca (Lárnaka)
Ayia Napa (Agia Napa)
Pachna (Pakhna)
Limassol (Lemesós)
Larnaca Bay
Dhekelia Sovereign Base Area (UK)
Akrotiri Sovereign Base Area (UK)
Cape Gata
Akrotiri
Mediterranean Sea

N

0   20 km
0   20 miles
(approximate scale)

Apollo, Greek god of the sun, is shown with his instrument, the lyre.

Mosaics of Paphos
Ancient floor mosaics depicting scenes from Greek mythology were discovered in Paphos in 1962 and are now on display at the city's Archaeological Park.

Divided city
The capital city of Nicosia is split into a Greek part and a Turkish part. The minarets of the historic Selimiye Mosque tower over the Turkish district.

- ⊘ 3,572 sq miles (9,251 sq km)
- 👥 1.3 million
- ★ Nicosia
- ⬭ Greek, Turkish

Traces of this **Mediterranean island's rich past** can be seen in its **Stone-Age settlements**, **Roman ruins**, and **Byzantine churches**. Since 1974, **Cyprus** has been **divided**, with **Turkey** running the **north**, and **Greek Cypriots** the **south**.

North Macedonia

Matka Canyon
Located to the west of Skopje, this canyon is known for its many caves and medieval monasteries and the artificial Matka Lake.

- ⬀ 9,928 sq miles (25,713 sq km)
- 👥 2.1 million
- ★ Skopje
- 💬 Macedonian, other languages (+4)

North Macedonia became **independent** in **1991** when the former state of **Yugoslavia split** into new nations. The country's **mountainous walking trails** are as popular as its **unspoiled lakes**, such as **Lake Ohrid**.

Map labels: KOSOVO, SERBIA, BULGARIA, ALBANIA, GREECE, Mount Korab 2,764 m (9,068 ft), Tetovo, Kumanovo, Osogovski Planini, SKOPJE, Gostivar, Delčevo, Veles, Vardar, Radoviš, Debrešte, Prilep, Negotino, Plakenska Planina, Struga, Ohrid, Crna Reka, Gevgelija, Lake Ohrid, Lake Prespa, Bitola

0 — 25 km / 0 — 25 miles (approximate scale)

Lakeside theater
A legacy of the area's Roman past, this amphitheater on the shore of Lake Ohrid was built in about 200 BCE but only rediscovered in the 1980s. It is now a venue for shows and concerts.

Albania

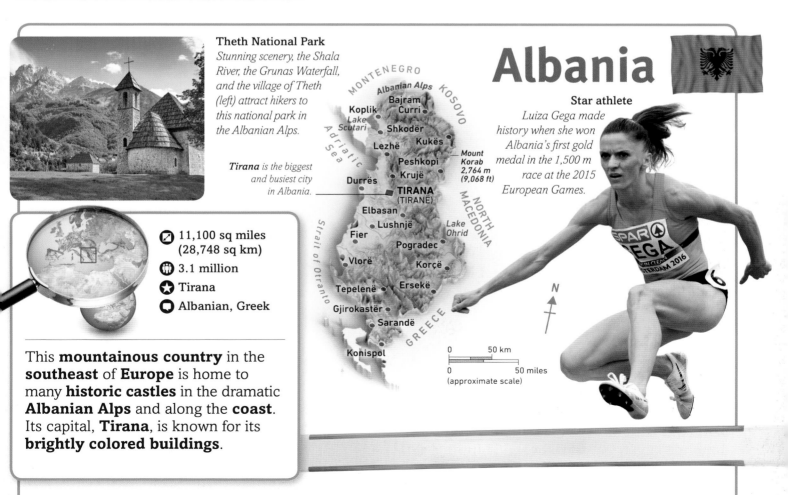

Theth National Park
Stunning scenery, the Shala River, the Grunas Waterfall, and the village of Theth (left) attract hikers to this national park in the Albanian Alps.

Tirana is the biggest and busiest city in Albania.

- ⬀ 11,100 sq miles (28,748 sq km)
- 👥 3.1 million
- ★ Tirana
- 💬 Albanian, Greek

This **mountainous country** in the **southeast** of **Europe** is home to many **historic castles** in the dramatic **Albanian Alps** and along the **coast**. Its capital, **Tirana**, is known for its **brightly colored buildings**.

Map labels: MONTENEGRO, KOSOVO, Albanian Alps, Koplik, Bajram Curri, Lake Scutari, Shkodër, Adriatic Sea, Lezhë, Kukës, Peshkopi, Mount Korab 2,764 m (9,068 ft), Krujë, Durrës, TIRANA (TIRANË), NORTH MACEDONIA, Elbasan, Lushnjë, Lake Ohrid, Fier, Pogradec, Vlorë, Korçë, Strait of Otranto, Tepelenë, Ersekë, Gjirokastër, GREECE, Sarandë, Konispol

0 — 50 km / 0 — 50 miles (approximate scale)

Star athlete
Luiza Gega made history when she won Albania's first gold medal in the 1,500 m race at the 2015 European Games.

Greece

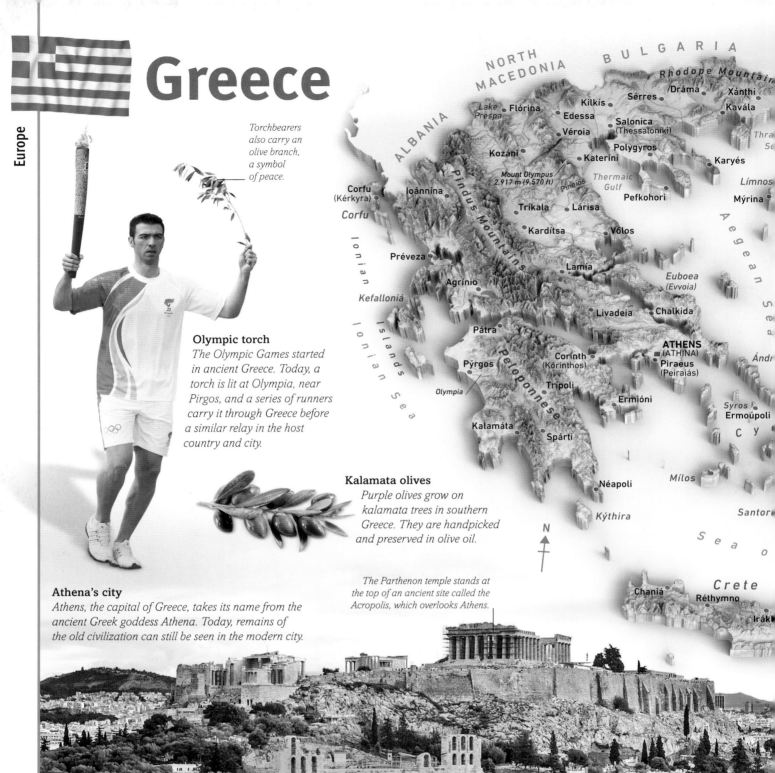

Torchbearers also carry an olive branch, a symbol of peace.

Olympic torch
The Olympic Games started in ancient Greece. Today, a torch is lit at Olympia, near Pirgos, and a series of runners carry it through Greece before a similar relay in the host country and city.

Kalamata olives
Purple olives grow on kalamata trees in southern Greece. They are handpicked and preserved in olive oil.

Athena's city
Athens, the capital of Greece, takes its name from the ancient Greek goddess Athena. Today, remains of the old civilization can still be seen in the modern city.

The Parthenon temple stands at the top of an ancient site called the Acropolis, which overlooks Athens.

Map labels:

NORTH MACEDONIA
BULGARIA
ALBANIA
Rhodope Mountains
Lake Prespa
Flórina
Kilkís
Sérres
Dráma
Xánthi
Kavála
Edessa
Salonica (Thessaloníki)
Véroia
Kozáni
Polygyros
Karyés
Kateríni
Mount Olympus 2,917 m (9,570 ft)
Thermaic Gulf
Pineiós
Límnos
Mýrina
Corfu (Kérkyra)
Ioánnina
Tríkala
Lárisa
Pefkohori
Corfu
Karditsa
Vólos
Aegean Sea
Préveza
Lamía
Euboea (Evvoia)
Agrinio
Kefalloniá
Chalkida
Livadeia
Pátra
Ermióni
Pýrgos
Corinth (Kórinthos)
ATHENS (ATHINA)
Ándr
Piraeus (Peiraiás)
Olympia
Tripoli
Peloponnese
Syros
Ermoúpoli
Kalamáta
Spárti
Cy
Néapoli
Mílos
Ionian Islands
Ionian Sea
Kýthira
Santor
N
Crete
Chaniá
Réthymno
Irák

Ancient Greece was one of the **first great civilizations** of **Europe**, where people prayed to the **gods** of **Mount Olympus**. Today, **tourists** flock to this **Mediterranean country** to see its **ancient ruins** and explore its **thousands** of **beautiful islands**. The country's **economy depends** largely on **tourism** and **shipping**.

- 50,948 sq miles (131,957 sq km)
- 10.6 million
- Athens
- Greek, other languages (+2)

Shipping industry
Together with tourism, shipping is one of Greece's biggest industries. This maritime nation has many busy ports, including Piraeus (above).

Jersey tiger moth
Known as the "Valley of the Butterflies," the Petaloúdes Valley on the Greek island of Rhodes is a sanctuary for thousands of migrating Jersey tiger moths.

The colorful moths have striped forewings and spotted underwings.

Greek pottery
For thousands of years, skilled Greek artisans have handcrafted pots. Many are decorated with scenes from Greek myths. This jar shows the Greek hero Theseus slaying the Minotaur.

Greek salad
A simple salad of tomatoes, cucumbers, onion, olives, feta cheese, and olive oil is eaten throughout the country.

Santorini island
Many island groups dot the seas around Greece. The volcanic island of Santorini, in the Aegean Sea, is famous for its whitewashed buildings.

Folk festivals
Greece has a busy calendar of national celebrations and local village festivals, such as this annual folk festival in the village of Pefkohori. Traditional music and dance, as well as outdoor feasts, accompany these special occasions.

Geography: Greece has a **rugged landscape**. Of its **6,000 islands**, only around **227** are **inhabited**.

History: More than **2,500 years ago**, the ancient Greeks led the way in **politics**, **philosophy**, and **science**.

Culture: Ancient Greek-inspired architecture can be seen worldwide. An example is the use of **Greek columns** on buildings.

Natural wonders: Greece's amazing **landscape** includes **Meteora's rock formations** and the **Samaria Gorge** on **Crete**.

Wildlife: The country's **terrain** is home to **bears**, **goats**, **lynx**, **wolves**, and **deer**.

Food and drink: Greeks enjoy a healthy Mediterranean diet of **grilled meat** and **fish**, **fresh fruit** and **vegetables**, **cheese**, and **olive oil**.

Map labels:
Orestiáda
omotiní
Alexandroúpoli
T U R K E Y
Mytilíni
Lesbos
Chíos
Chíos
Sámos
nos
Pátmos
des
Kos
kos
Amorgós
Kos
Rhodes (Ródos)
Lindos
Rhodes
rete
Kárpathos
Dodecanese
Sitía
Mediterranean Sea

0   50 km
0   50 miles
(approximate scale)

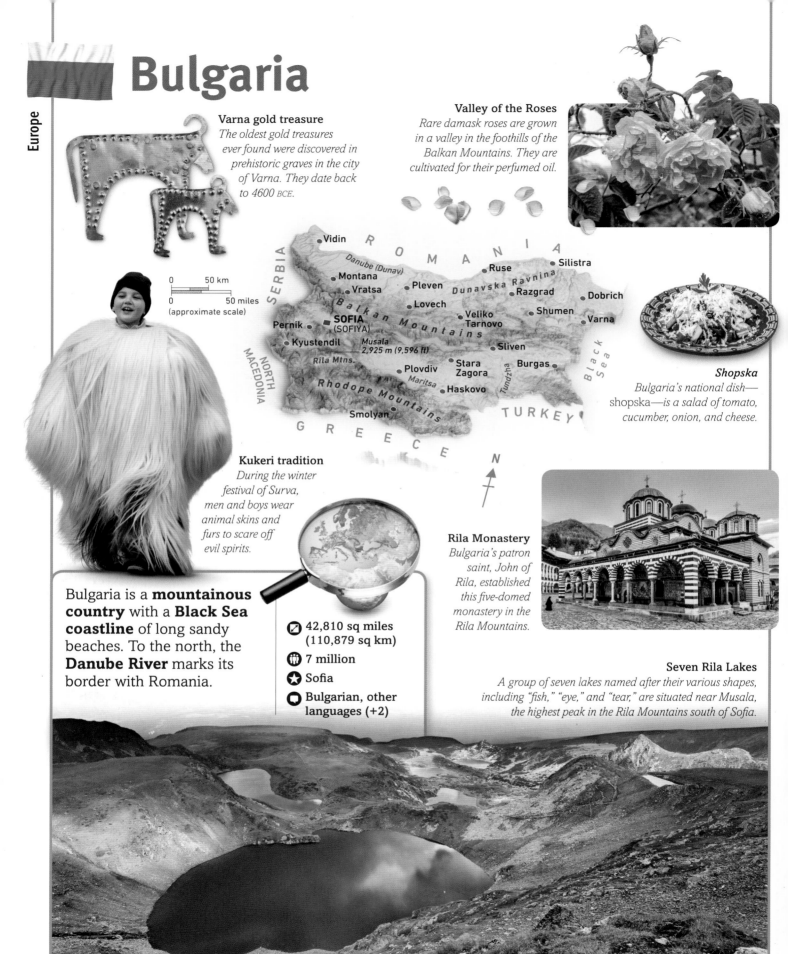

Bulgaria

Varna gold treasure
The oldest gold treasures ever found were discovered in prehistoric graves in the city of Varna. They date back to 4600 BCE.

Valley of the Roses
Rare damask roses are grown in a valley in the foothills of the Balkan Mountains. They are cultivated for their perfumed oil.

Kukeri tradition
During the winter festival of Surva, men and boys wear animal skins and furs to scare off evil spirits.

Shopska
Bulgaria's national dish—shopska—is a salad of tomato, cucumber, onion, and cheese.

Rila Monastery
Bulgaria's patron saint, John of Rila, established this five-domed monastery in the Rila Mountains.

Bulgaria is a **mountainous country** with a **Black Sea coastline** of long sandy beaches. To the north, the **Danube River** marks its border with Romania.

- 42,810 sq miles (110,879 sq km)
- 7 million
- Sofia
- Bulgarian, other languages (+2)

Seven Rila Lakes
A group of seven lakes named after their various shapes, including "fish," "eye," and "tear," are situated near Musala, the highest peak in the Rila Mountains south of Sofia.

Romania

Wall paintings
Monasteries in the Bucovina region, near Suceava, are painted with colorful 15th-century frescoes that depict Biblical stories.

Bran Castle
Some say this 14th-century castle in the Carpathian Mountains was Bram Stoker's inspiration for the setting of his fictional story of Dracula.

***Mărțișor* amulets**
Every Mărțișor (meaning "March 1"), at the start of spring, Romanians give their loved ones lucky amulets.

Red and white trinkets are worn around the neck or wrist in March.

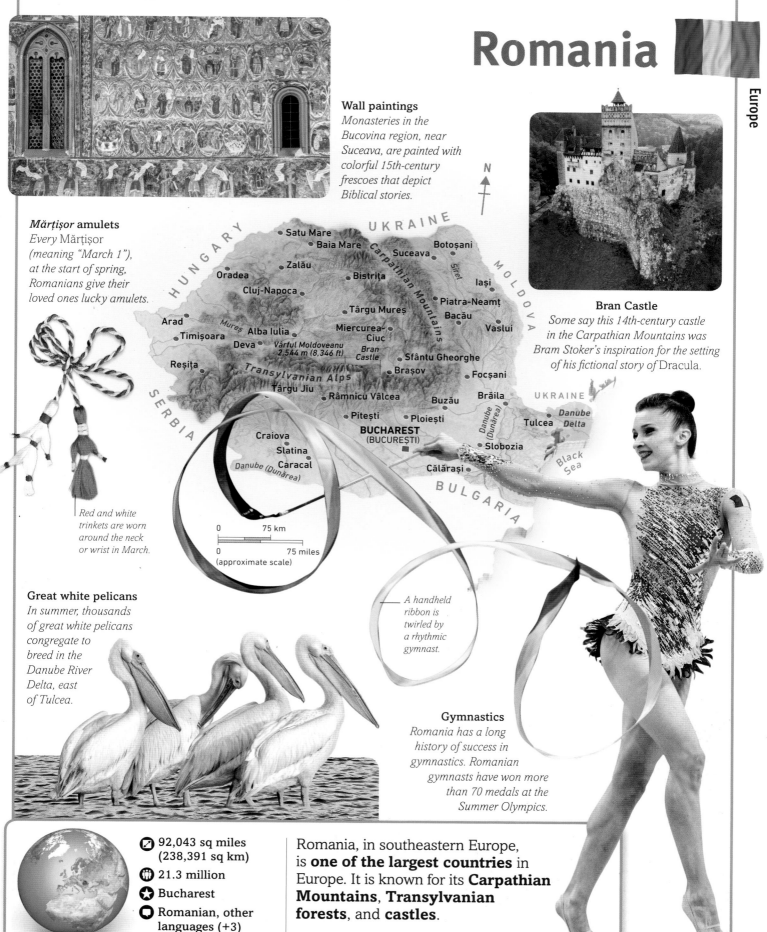

HUNGARY
UKRAINE
MOLDOVA
SERBIA
UKRAINE
BULGARIA

N

Satu Mare
Baia Mare
Suceava
Botoșani
Zalău
Bistrița
Iași
Oradea
Cluj-Napoca
Piatra-Neamț
Târgu Mureș
Bacău
Arad
Miercurea-Ciuc
Vaslui
Timișoara
Deva
Alba Iulia
Mureș
Vârful Moldoveanu 2,544 m (8,346 ft)
Bran Castle
Sfântu Gheorghe
Reșița
Brașov
Focșani
Transylvanian Alps
Târgu Jiu
Râmnicu Vâlcea
Buzău
Brăila
Danube (Dunărea)
Tulcea
Danube Delta
Pitești
Ploiești
Craiova
BUCHAREST (BUCUREȘTI)
Slatina
Slobozia
Black Sea
Caracal
Danube (Dunărea)
Călărași

Siret
Carpathian Mountains

0   75 km
0   75 miles
(approximate scale)

A handheld ribbon is twirled by a rhythmic gymnast.

Great white pelicans
In summer, thousands of great white pelicans congregate to breed in the Danube River Delta, east of Tulcea.

Gymnastics
Romania has a long history of success in gymnastics. Romanian gymnasts have won more than 70 medals at the Summer Olympics.

⬙ 92,043 sq miles (238,391 sq km)

👥 21.3 million

★ Bucharest

⬭ Romanian, other languages (+3)

Romania, in southeastern Europe, is **one of the largest countries** in Europe. It is known for its **Carpathian Mountains**, **Transylvanian forests**, and **castles**.

Ukraine

Domes of gold
St. Michael's Golden-Domed Cathedral in Kyiv is a working monastery as well as a cathedral of the Orthodox Church of Ukraine.

The Antonov Serial Production Plant in Kyiv has been manufacturing planes since 1920.

Aircraft industry
For decades, Ukraine has been an industrial powerhouse producing many types of aircrafts, including large cargo planes, such as this An-225 Mriya.

BELARUS

Pripet Marshes

POLAND

Chernobyl (Chornobyl')
Chernihiv
Luts'k
Korosten
Kyiv Reservoir
Rivne
L'viv
Pryluky
Sumy
Ternopil'
Zhytomyr
KYIV
Dnieper Lowland
Dnieper

SLOVAKIA
Carpathian Mountains
Ivano-Frankivs'k
Khmel'nyts'kyy
Kharkiv
Vinnytsya
Cherkasy
Poltava
Donets'
Uzhhorod
Hoverla 2,061m (6,762 ft)
Uman'
HUNGARY
Podil's'ka Vysochyna
Kremenchuk Reservoir
Kremenchuk
Khust
Chernivtsi
Kropyvnyts'kyy (Kirovohrad)
Dnipro (Dnipropetrovs'k)
Luhans'k

ROMANIA
MOLDOVA
Dniester
Kryvyi Rih
Zaporizhzhya
Donets'k
Black Sea Lowland
Kakhovka Reservoir
Nikopol'

The male roe deer grows a new pair of antlers every year.

Mykolayiv
Mariupol'
Odessa (Odesa)
Berdyans'k
Kherson
Gulf of Taganrog
Artsyz
Black Sea
Sea of Azov
RUSSIA

RUSSIA

N

0 — 100 km
0 — 100 miles
(approximate scale)

Yevpatoriya
Crimea
Kerch
Simferopol'
(annexed by Russia since 2014)
Sevastopol'
Yalta

Roe deer
This solitary mammal with a distinctive white rump and short tail thrives in Ukraine's forests.

Farming crops
Ukraine's vast fertile plains and mild climate make it one of the top producers of wheat, corn, barley, and soy beans. In 2019, nearly 82.7 millions tons (75 million metric tons) of grain were harvested.

- ⬈ 233,032 sq miles (603,550 sq km)
- 👥 43.9 million
- ★ Kyiv
- ⬡ Ukrainian, Russian, Tatar

Formerly part of the **Soviet Union**, Ukraine became an **independent republic** in **1991**. The nation is sometimes known as the "**Breadbasket of Europe**" for its **fertile fields**.

The bandura is a stringed instrument that resembles a lute.

Young musicians
Traditional folk music is popular throughout Ukraine. Their tunes range from love melodies to political songs.

Belarus

Belovezhskaya Pushcha National Park
This ancient forest protects nearly 579 sq miles (1,500 sq km) of old oak, pine, and fir trees. Half of the park lies in the neighboring country of Poland, where it is called Białowieża National Park.

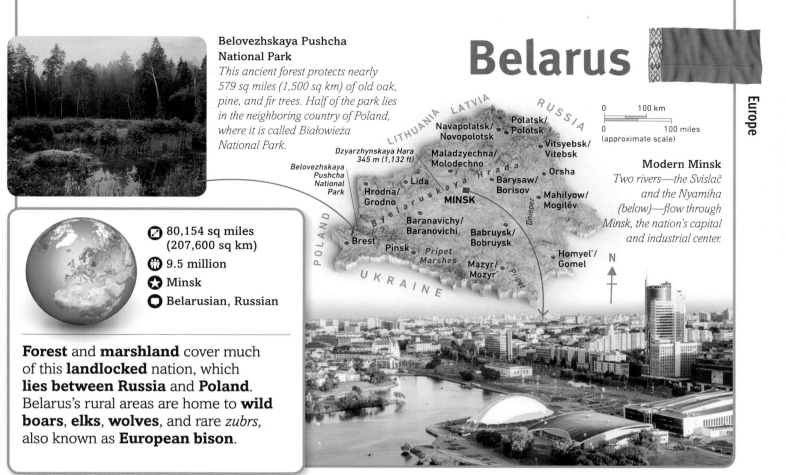

LITHUANIA LATVIA RUSSIA

Navapolatsk/ Novopolatsk
Polatsk/ Polotsk
Vitsyebsk/ Vitebsk

Dzyarzhynskaya Hara 345 m (1,132 ft)
Maladzyechna/ Molodechno
Orsha

Belovezhskaya Pushcha National Park
Lida
Barysaw/ Borisov
Byelaruskaya Hrada
Mahilyow/ Mogilëv

Hrodna/ Grodno
MINSK

POLAND
Baranavichy/ Baranovichi
Babruysk/ Bobruysk

Brest
Pinsk
Pripet Marshes
Mazyr/ Mozyr'
Homyel'/ Gomel

Dnieper

UKRAINE
Pripet

N

0 100 km
0 100 miles
(approximate scale)

Modern Minsk
Two rivers—the Svislač and the Nyamiha (below)—flow through Minsk, the nation's capital and industrial center.

- ⊘ 80,154 sq miles (207,600 sq km)
- 👥 9.5 million
- ★ Minsk
- ⬭ Belarusian, Russian

Forest and **marshland** cover much of this **landlocked** nation, which **lies between Russia** and **Poland**. Belarus's rural areas are home to **wild boars**, **elks**, **wolves**, and rare *zubrs*, also known as **European bison**.

Moldova

Soroca fortress
This 15th-century fortress was built to protect Moldova from invaders. The round towers helped it resist cannon fire.

Edineţ
Soroca
Bălţi
Ribniţa
UKRAINE

Falesti
Bălăneşti Hill 430 m (1,411 ft)
Dubăsari
Dniester

ROMANIA
CHIŞINĂU
Bender (Tighina)
Tiraspol

Leova
Basarabeasca

Cahul
N

0 60 km
0 60 miles
(approximate scale)

Lavender harvest
Lavender thrives in Moldova's dry, warm climate and rich soil. The flowers are distilled to produce a fragrant essential oil.

- ⊘ 13,070 sq miles (33,851 sq km)
- 👥 3.4 million
- ★ Chişinău
- ⬭ Moldovan, Ukrainian, Russian

This landlocked nation, lying on a hilly plateau, declared its **independence** from the **Soviet Union** in **1991**. **Orchards** and **vineyards** dot the country's rolling hills and produce an abundance of **fruit** and **wine**.

Russia

Russia became the first country to send a person into space when Soviet cosmonaut Yuri Gagarin circled Earth for 108 minutes aboard the Vostok 1 spacecraft in 1961.

Moscow skyscrapers

The biggest city in Russia is the capital, Moscow, situated on the Moskva River. Modern skyscrapers in the business district contrast with the historic architecture of Red Square.

Matryoshka dolls

Wooden stacking dolls called matryoshkas, *meaning "little matrons," have been handmade in Russia since the 1890s. They fit inside one another and form part of a set.*

St. Petersburg

The golden dome of St. Isaac's Cathedral dominates the skyline of Russia's former imperial capital. The historic port city and its palaces are home to world-class museums.

Map labels:

Franz Josef Land · Baltic Sea · FINLAND · Murmansk · Kaliningrad · Kola Peninsula · Barents Sea · Nova Zemlya · POLAND · LITHUANIA · LATVIA · ESTONIA · St Petersburg (Sankt-Peterburg) · Neva · Lake Ladoga · Petrozavodsk · Lake Onega · Archangel (Arkhangel'sk) · Kara Sea · Diks · Pskov · BELARUS · Smolensk · Tver · Vologda · Yamal Peninsula · Nor · MOSCOW (MOSKVA) · Syktyvkar · Vorkuta · Bryansk · UKRAINE · Ryazan' · Nizhny Novgorod · Kirov · Ob · Taz · Voronezh · Penza · Kazan' · Perm' · Ural Mountains · Ob · West Siberian Plain · Rostov-na-Donu · Saratov · Ul'yanorsk · Samara · Ufa · Yekaterinburg · Surgut · Krasnodar · Volgograd · Sochi · Stavropol' · Volga · Chelyabinsk · Irtysh · Nal'chik · Orenburg · Ural · Omsk · Tomsk · Kemerovo · Mt. Elbrus 5,642 m (18,510 ft) · Grozny · Astrakhan' · Caspian Sea · KAZAKHSTAN · Novosibirsk · Krasnoya · AZERBAIJAN · Barnaul · Abakan · Kyzyl

0 — 500 km
0 — 500 miles
(approximate scale)

Russia is the **largest country** in the world. Spanning **11 time zones**, it is spread over two continents, from **eastern Europe** to the **Pacific coast** of **Asia**. The **Ural Mountains** divide Russia in **two**. The **Siberian wilderness** in the east has the **coldest inhabited place** on Earth: **Oymyakon**, east of Yakutsk. Here, the **temperature** falls below **−58°F** (−50°C) in the **winter**.

- 6,601,668 sq miles (17,098,242 sq km)
- 141.7 million
- Moscow
- Russian, Tatar, Ukrainian, Chavash, other languages

Nenet people
Deep in the Siberian Arctic, on the Yamal Peninsula, live the Nenets. These nomadic reindeer herders wear thick furs to survive the subzero temperatures.

Lake Baikal
The world's largest freshwater lake is Lake Baikal in southern Siberia. This 25-million-year-old lake holds about 20 percent of the planet's fresh surface water.

Dancers from Moscow's famous Bolshoi Ballet perform Don Quixote.

N

A R C T I C   O C E A N

Severmaya Zemlya

New Siberian Islands

East Siberian Sea

Bering Strait

Chukot Range

Poluostrov Taymyr

Laptev Sea

Ambarchik

Anadyr'

Khatanga

Tiksi

Chokurdakh

Nizhneyansk

Batagay

Khrebet Cherskogo

Koryak Range

Central Siberian Plateau

Verkhoyanskiy Khrebet

Ust-Nera

Oymyakon

Palana

Zhigansk

Lena

Kamchatka

i b e r i a

Mirnyy

Yakutsk

Magadan

Lensk

Okhotsk

Sea of Okhotsk

Petropavlovsk-Kamchatsky

Ust-Ilimsk

Aldan

Lena

Stanovoy Khrebet

atsk

Okha

Lake Baikal

Yablonovyy Khrebet

Sakhalin

Irkutsk

Bukachacha

Kuril Islands

Ulan-Ude

Chita

Blagoveshchensk

Yuzhno-Sakbalinsk

M O N G O L I A

C H I N A

Khabarovsk

Dal'negorsk

Vladivostok

Sea of Japan (East Sea)

J A P A N

Russian ballet
Russia is renowned for its classical ballet tradition and is where some of the most famous ballets, such as Swan Lake, *were created.*

Long journey
Trains running on the main line of the Trans-Siberian Railway network take eight days to complete the journey from Moscow in the west to Vladivostok in the east, a distance of 5,772 miles (9,289 km).

Siberian tiger
The Siberian, or Amur, tiger has thick fur for extra warmth in the icy forests of eastern Russia. Only about 500 of these big cats survive in the wild today.

Geography: The **vast terrain** covers **mountains**, **forests**, treeless **tundra**, grassy **steppes**, and **deserts**. Europe's longest river, the **Volga**, flows through central Russia.

History: Russia was **ruled by** monarchs called **czars** until the **1917 Revolution**, when **Communists** took control and created the **Soviet Union**. This fell in 1991.

Culture: Russia's **rich culture** includes the **literature of Tolstoy**, the **music of Tchaikovsky**, and athletes such as **tennis star Maria Sharapova**.

Wildlife: Russia's **diverse** habitats are home to the **Eurasian lynx**, **Amur leopards**, **red deer**, **brown bears**, **beluga whales**, and **Oriental storks**.

EUROPE

Ural Mountain

West
Sideri
Plain

AFRICA

CYPRUS
LEBANON
ISRAEL
JORDAN

TURKEY

Black Sea

GEORGIA
ARMENIA
AZERB.
AZERBAIJAN

SYRIA

Tigris

Euphrates

IRAQ

KUWAIT

Caspian Sea

Aral
Sea

KAZAKHSTAN

Lake
Balkhash

SAUDI
ARABIA

IRAN
Iranian
Plateau

TURKMENISTAN

UZBEKISTAN

KYRGYZSTAN

TAJIKISTAN

BAHRAIN
QATAR

Persian Gulf

AFGHANISTAN

Kunlun Mountains

Red Sea

Arabian
Peninsula

U.A.E.

PAKISTAN

Plateau
of Tibet

YEMEN

OMAN

Gulf of Oman

Indus

Thar Desert

H
I
M
A
L
A
Y
A
S

Mount Everest
8,848 m (29,029 ft)

Gulf of Aden

Socotra
(to Yemen)

Arabian
Sea

Ganges

NEPAL

BHUTAN

INDIA

BANGLADESH

Deccan

MYANMA
(BURM

Laccadive Islands
(to India)

MALDIVES

SRI
LANKA

Bay
of
Bengal

Andaman Islands
(to India)

Andaman
Sea

Nicobar Islands
(to India)

INDIAN
OCEAN

MALAYS

SINGAPOR

Sumatra

0   750 km
0   750 miles
(approximate scale)

N

ASIA

Kara
Sea

Laptev
Sea

East
Siberian
Sea

Wrangel
Island

NORTH
AMERICA

Bering
Sea

*Central
Siberian
Plateau*

Lena

Siberia

RUSSIA

Kamchatka

*Sea of
Okhotsk*

*Altai
Mountains*

MONGOLIA

Gobi

Inner Mongolia

Sakhalin

Kuril Islands

CHINA

Yellow River

NORTH
KOREA

SOUTH
KOREA

JAPAN

Honshu

Yangtze

*Yellow
Sea*

*East
China
Sea*

LAOS

HAILAND

TAIWAN

Hainan
Dao

Ryukyu Islands

PACIFIC
OCEAN

CAMBODIA

VIETNAM

*South
China
Sea*

Luzon

*Philippine
Sea*

PHILIPPINES

Mindanao

BRUNEI

*Sulu
Sea*

MALAYSIA

Borneo

*Celebes
Sea*

NDONESIA

Celebes

Moluccas

Java

Java Sea

Flores Sea

*Banda
Sea*

Flores

EAST
TIMOR

New Guinea

*Timor
Sea*

*Arafura
Sea*

Turkey

Patara beach
One of Turkey's beauty spots is the 11-mile (18 km) long Patara Beach, south of Mugla. It lies close to the ruins of an ancient city.

Tasty pastry
Among the sweetest treats in Central Asia is baklava, a popular honey and nut pastry dessert.

Suleiman the Magnificent
Turkey was the heartland of the Ottoman Empire. During the reign of sultan Suleiman I (1520–1566), the empire expanded all the way into Europe, northern Africa, and western Asia.

Majestic Mosque
The spectacular 17th-century Sultan Ahmed Mosque dominates the Istanbul skyline. Also known as the Blue Mosque, it has patterned blue tiles on its inside walls.

One of six towering minarets from which worshippers are called to prayer.

BULGARIA
GREECE
Edirne · Kırklareli
Tekirdağ · İstanbul · Bosporus · Zonguldak · Küre Dağları · Sinop
Sea of Marmara · İzmit · Adapazarı · Kastamonu · Bafr
Çanakkale · Bursa · Bolu · Çankırı · Sams
Aegean Sea · Balıkesir · Bilecik · Çorum · Ca
Manisa · Eskişehir · ANKARA · Amas
Kütahya · Kırıkkale
İzmir · Uşak · Afyon · Kırşehir
Selçuk · Lake Tuz (Tuz Gölü) · Kızıl
Söke · Aydın · Denizili · Eğirdir Gölü · Nevşehir · Kayser
Muğla · Burdur · İsparta · Beyşehir Gölü · Konya · Ana t
Antalya · Karaman · Nigde
Taurus Mountains (Toros Dağları) · Tarsus · Osmaniye
Mersin (İçel) · Adana
İskenderun
Antakya

Black Sea

Mediterranean Sea

CYPRUS

Turkey stretches from **eastern Europe** to **western Asia**. Straddling both continents, this country has a mix of **Islamic** and **Western traditions**. Turkey's largest city, **Istanbul**, was once the **center of the Byzantine Empire**, before the region was taken over by the **Ottomans**, who ruled Turkey for **more than 600 years**.

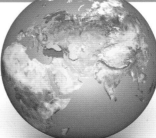

- 302,535 sq miles (783,562 sq km)
- 82 million
- Ankara
- Turkish, other languages (+7)

Hot-air balloons carry tourists over the Cappadocia rock formations so they can get a bird's-eye view.

N

0   125 km
0   125 miles
(approximate scale)

Fairy chimneys
Otherworldly rocky spires jut out from the arid landscape of Cappadocia. These boulders were formed over millions of years by volcanic eruptions.

Ordu   Trabzon
Doğu Karadeniz Dağları
Artvin
GEORGIA
Sivas
Kars
ARMENIA
Euphrates
Erzurum
Aras
Ağri
Mount Ararat
5,137 m (16,854 ft)
Elazig   Bingöl
Lake Van
(Van Gölü)
Malatya
Güney Dağları
Van
Adıyaman   Diyarbakır
Tigris   Batman
amanmaraş   Atatürk Baraji
Kurdistan
Gaziantep   Şanlıurfa
Mardin
Hakkâri
SYRIA
IRAQ
IRAN

The patterns, colors, and symbols of the rugs reflect local traditions and cultures.

Hand-woven carpets
Beautiful rugs and carpets called kilims *have been made in Turkey for centuries.*

Library of Celsus
The ancient site of Ephesus is located near Selçuk. Once a prosperous Roman city, its well-preserved ruins include this impressive 2nd-century library.

Grand Bazaar
Istanbul's famous bazaar is among the world's oldest covered markets. Its stalls sell everything from spices to jewelry.

Whirling dervishes
In Turkey, there are Muslim worshippers called dervishes *who perform whirling dances, songs, and prayers to express their faith.*

History: After the **defeat of the Ottoman Empire** in World War I, the **Republic of Turkey** formed in 1923.

Culture: The country's **art and architecture** reflect a unique mix of **Eastern and Western influences**.

Natural wonders: Grand sites include the clear green waters of the **Turquoise Coast** around Mugla and Antalya and the rare spires of **Cappadocia**.

Food and drink: From **kebabs** and **kofte** to **meze mixes**, Turkish dishes use ingredients from **Arab**, **Greek**, and **Western cuisine**.

Azerbaijan

Mud volcanoes
In Gobustan National Park, southwest of Baku, there are almost 300 mud volcanoes. These are not true volcanoes (made of lava) but formed by eruptions of mud and gas.

Mugham **music**
These musicians and poets have gathered together to make improvised traditional Azerbaijani folk music called mugham.

City landmark
The Heydar Aliyev Center in Baku is a hub for Azerbaijani culture. It is famous for its wavelike design.

- 🧭 33,436 sq miles (86,600 sq km)
- 👥 10.2 million
- ⭐ Baku
- 🔴 Azeri, Russian

Azerbaijan is **rich** in **petroleum** and **natural gas reserves**. In some places, **burning gas** seeps out of the ground and **stays ablaze** for years on end. For this reason, **Azerbaijan** has been called "the **land of fire**."

Syria

Raising water
Giant waterwheels called norias *were once used to raise water in irrigation systems around the city of Hama. The wheels (below) date from the 14th century.*

The waterwheels are turned by the flow of the Orontes River.

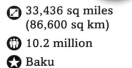

Bustling bazaar
The Al-Hamidiyah souk in Damascus is Syria's biggest market. It sells handicrafts, clothes, and groceries.

- 🧭 72,370 sq miles (187,437 sq km)
- 👥 19.4 million
- ⭐ Damascus
- 🔴 Arabic, other languages (7+)

Syria has a **rich history**—its capital, Damascus, has been **inhabited since 8000 BCE**. The country has experienced **turbulence** in recent years due to **a civil war** that began in **2011**, which has forced millions of people to flee their homeland.

Georgia

Chidaoba wrestling
These boys are taking part in chidaoba, an ancient form of one-on-one martial arts. Each five-minute match is accompanied by folk music and dance.

RUSSIA
Gagra
Sokhumi
Abkhazia
Caucasus
Shkhara
5,193 m (17,037 ft)
Ochamchire
Black Sea
Poti
Kutaisi
Batumi
Tskhinvali
Akhaltsikhe
Lesser Caucasus
TBILISI
Rustavi
TURKEY
ARMENIA
AZERBAIJAN

0   75 km
0   75 miles
(approximate scale)

Land of mountains
The spectacular Caucasus Mountains sweep through Georgia. The remote village of Ushguli (pictured below) sits at the foot of Mount Shkhara, the country's highest peak.

Sitting at the **crossroads** of **Asia** and **Europe**, Georgia is a small nation on the **eastern shore** of the **Black Sea**. Its colorful capital, **Tbilisi**, has many **historic sites** as well as **modern architecture**.

- 26,911 sq miles (69,700 sq km)
- 4 million
- Tbilisi
- Georgian, other languages (+6)

Armenia

Etchmiadzin Cathedral
Located west of Yerevan, this cathedral is the heart of the Armenian Christian Church. Floral and geometric patterns decorate its interiors.

GEORGIA
Lesser Caucasus
AZERBAIJAN
Gyumri
Mount Aragats
4,090 m
(13,420 ft)
Vanadzor
Ashtarak
Sevan
Lake Sevan
YEREVAN
Artashat
TURKEY
Jermuk
AZERBAIJAN
Goris
Yerevan is located in the Armenian highlands.
Meghri
IRAN

0   50 km
0   50 miles
(approximate scale)

N

Golden fruit
The national fruit of Armenia is the apricot, which has grown in this country for at least 3,000 years.

Armenia's **mountainous terrain** has many fast-flowing **rivers, canyons**, and **extinct volcanoes**. **Many people** in this landlocked country are **farmers**, but **mining** and **tourism** are growing industries in Armenia.

- 11,484 sq miles (29,743 sq km)
- 3 million
- Yerevan
- Armenian, Azeri, Russian

Symphony of stones
A rock formation in Garni Canyon, southeast of Yerevan, is called the Symphony of Stones. Its tall basalt columns resemble the pipes of an organ.

Lebanon

The cedar tree is the national symbol of Lebanon.

Beirut is one of the busiest ports on the Mediterranean coastline.

Pigeon Rocks
This pair of giant limestone rocks stands in the sea off the coast of Beirut, where they are a popular landmark for locals and visitors.

Ancient wine
Lebanon's Bekaa Valley is one of the world's oldest wine-making regions. Its wine has been famous since biblical times, almost 3,000 years ago, and has enjoyed a revival in recent years.

SYRIA
Qurnat al-Sawda 3,087 m (10,128 ft)
Tripoli
Bsharri (Bcharre)
Hermel
Lebanon Mountains
Beqaa Valley
Baalbek
Mediterranean Sea
BEIRUT (BEYROUTH)
Sidon
Nabatieh (Nabatîye)
Tyre
ISRAEL
S Y R I A
N

0   40 km
0   40 miles
(approximate scale)

A farmer holds a freshly harvested basket of grapes.

Meaty treat
The national dish is kibbeh— a mix of meat, onions, spices, herbs, and bulgur wheat that is fried until crispy.

- 4,015 sq miles (10,400 sq km)
- 5.5 million
- Beirut
- Arabic, French, Armenian, Assyrian

This **Mediterranean** country has been a **trading center** for thousands of years. Lebanon's population is unique in the Middle East for its almost even mix of **Muslim** and **non-Muslim faith groups**, including **Maronite Christians**, and **Druze**.

Israel

More than 5 million Palestinians live in the West Bank and Gaza.

Tree-planting festival
The Jewish "New Year for Trees" is when fruit trees are planted and Jews eat the fruit of Israel, such as grapes, figs, dates, and pomegranates.

LEBANON
Mount Hermon 2,814 m (9,232 ft)
Haifa (Hefa)
Tiberias
Golan Heights
Lake Tiberias
SYRIA
Nazareth
Mediterranean Sea
Tel Aviv-Yafo
Jordan
Holon
WEST BANK
GAZA
JERUSALEM *(not internationally recognized)*
Be'er Sheva
'Arad
Dead Sea
Currently, the United Nations does not recognize Jerusalem as the capital of Israel.
N e g e v
E G Y P T
J O R D A N
Mitspe Ramon
Elat
N

0   40 km
0   40 miles
(approximate scale)

Ancient Jerusalem
Dating back to 2000 BCE, the Old City is considered holy in Judaism, Christianity, and Islam. Its sacred sites include the Jewish Western Wall and the Islamic Dome of the Rock shrine.

Vibrant Tel Aviv
A lively city on the Mediterranean Sea, Tel Aviv has engulfed the old port of Yafo. It is known for its modern buildings and popular beaches.

- 8,470 sq miles (21,937 sq km)
- 8.7 million
- Jerusalem
- Hebrew, Arabic, other languages (+6)

Israel was **created** in 1948 as a homeland for the **Jewish people**. The state has been in conflict with the **displaced Palestinians**, now living in the **West Bank** and **Gaza**, ever since.

More than 20 muscles move each ear, helping the caracal hear the quietest of sounds.

Wild hunter
A wildcat found in the semideserts of Jordan, the caracal is an agile predator that uses its powerful hind legs and keen sense of hearing to catch prey such as birds and rodents.

Jordan

Red and white are two of the national colors of Jordan.

Traditional headdress
The kaffiyeh *is a patterned Arab headdress, often worn by men in the Middle East.*

Bedouin feast
Derived from Bedouin cuisine and popular in Jordan, mansaf is a dish of lamb cooked with yogurt and accompanied by rice.

Map labels:
SYRIA
IRAQ
Irbid
Jarash
Al Mafraq
Az Zarqa'
AMMAN
Madaba
Al 'Umarí
Syrian Desert
Dead Sea
Jordan
ISRAEL
Al Karak
At-Tafilah
Ard as Sawwan
Wadi Musa' (Petra)
Bayir
Ma'an
Jabal al Adhriyat
Al 'Aqabah
Jebel Umm El Dami 1,854 m (6,083 ft)
Al Mudawwarah
SAUDI ARABIA
N

0   50 km
0   50 miles
(approximate scale)

Lost city
The ancient city of Petra was at its peak 2,000 years ago. Among its buildings were temples and tombs carved into sandstone cliffs. Ruins at the site include the Ad Deir Monastery, which has huge chambers cut out of the rock.

- 34,495 sq miles (89,342 sq km)
- 10.8 million
- Amman
- Arabic

The modern-day **nation** of **Jordan** was **founded** in **1921**. Vast areas of the country are **desert land**, where **Bedouin people** follow a **nomadic lifestyle**. Millions of Jordanians also live in **modern cities** such as **Amman**.

Historic Amman
Originally built on seven hills, Amman is one of the Arab world's largest cities. At its heart, the ruins of the ancient Amman Citadel (fort), including a Roman temple, sit on a hill overlooking the Old City.

Dead Sea
This famous lake is one of the saltiest bodies of water in the world, almost 10 times saltier than the oceans. This makes the water so dense that people can float without swimming.

Iraq

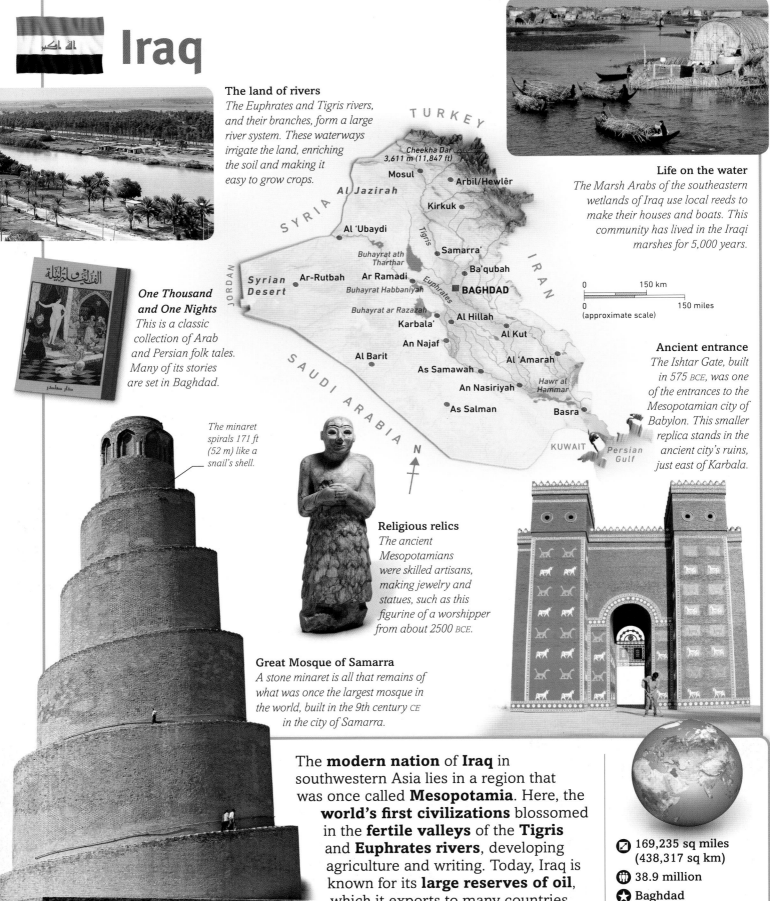

The land of rivers
The Euphrates and Tigris rivers, and their branches, form a large river system. These waterways irrigate the land, enriching the soil and making it easy to grow crops.

Life on the water
The Marsh Arabs of the southeastern wetlands of Iraq use local reeds to make their houses and boats. This community has lived in the Iraqi marshes for 5,000 years.

One Thousand and One Nights
This is a classic collection of Arab and Persian folk tales. Many of its stories are set in Baghdad.

Ancient entrance
The Ishtar Gate, built in 575 BCE, was one of the entrances to the Mesopotamian city of Babylon. This smaller replica stands in the ancient city's ruins, just east of Karbala.

Map labels:
TURKEY
Cheekha Dar 3,611 m (11,847 ft)
Mosul
Arbil/Hewlêr
Al Jazirah
Kirkuk
SYRIA
Al 'Ubaydi
Tigris
Samarra'
Buhayrat ath Tharthar
Ba'qubah
JORDAN
Syrian Desert
Ar-Rutbah
Ar Ramadi
BAGHDAD
Buhayrat Habbaniyah
Euphrates
IRAN
Buhayrat ar Razazah
Karbala'
Al Hillah
An Najaf
Al Kut
Al Barit
Al 'Amarah
SAUDI ARABIA
As Samawah
An Nasiriyah
Hawr al Hammar
As Salman
Basra
KUWAIT
Persian Gulf
N

0 — 150 km
0 — 150 miles
(approximate scale)

The minaret spirals 171 ft (52 m) like a snail's shell.

Religious relics
The ancient Mesopotamians were skilled artisans, making jewelry and statues, such as this figurine of a worshipper from about 2500 BCE.

Great Mosque of Samarra
A stone minaret is all that remains of what was once the largest mosque in the world, built in the 9th century CE in the city of Samarra.

The **modern nation** of **Iraq** in southwestern Asia lies in a region that was once called **Mesopotamia**. Here, the **world's first civilizations** blossomed in the **fertile valleys** of the **Tigris** and **Euphrates rivers**, developing agriculture and writing. Today, Iraq is known for its **large reserves of oil**, which it exports to many countries.

- 169,235 sq miles (438,317 sq km)
- 38.9 million
- Baghdad
- Arabic, other languages (4+)

Iran

Grand Bazaar of Tehran
Ornate arches top the busy walkways in this historic market in Tehran where people have come to shop for goods for centuries.

Gardens of paradise
The ancient Persians were the first to design landscaped gardens, which became common in Islamic architecture. Eram Garden, in the city of Shiraz, ranks among the finest in Iran.

Guided by the stars
Brass astrolabes helped the ancient Persians measure the positions of the sun and stars and find the direction of the holy city of Mecca.

Tehran is sheltered by the snowcapped Elburz Mountains in the north.

Khvoy
Lake Urmia
Tabriz
Ardabil
Maragheh
Zanjan
Qazvin
Sanandaj
Kermanshah (Bakhtaran)
Arak
Qom
TEHRAN
Semnan
Kashan
Isfahan
Dezful
Ahvaz
Yazd
Yasuj
Shiraz
Bushire
Fasa
Kerman
Sirjan
Gavbandi
Bandar-e 'Abbas
Bampur
Chabahar

Gorgan
Bojnurd
Sabzevar
Mashhad
Kashmar
Birjand
Bam
Zabol
Zahedan

Mount Damavand 5,671 m (18,606 ft)

Caspian Sea
TURKMENISTAN
Elburz Mountains
Dasht-e Kavir
Iranian Plateau
Dasht-e Lut
Zagros Mountains
Karkheh
Persian Gulf
Strait of Hormuz
Gulf of Oman

TURKEY
ARMENIA
AZERBAIJAN
IRAQ
AFGHANISTAN
PAKISTAN
U.A.E.

N

0   200 km
0   200 miles
(approximate scale)

The ancient city of Susa is located at the foot of the Zagros Mountains.

Zereshk polo
This Iranian steamed rice dish is flavored with aromatic saffron and zesty barberries and is usually served with chicken.

Elite fighters
This mosaic from the ancient city of Susa depicts the first Persian Empire's most elite warriors. This force was called the "Immortals" because whenever a soldier died, they were replaced by another so the unit always had 10,000 members.

Harvesting by hand
Most of the world's saffron spice comes from Iran. It is obtained from the delicate purple flowers of the saffron crocus, which are picked by hand.

- 🧭 636,372 sq miles (1,648,195 sq km)
- 👥 84.9 million
- ⭐ Tehran
- ⬡ Farsi, Azeri, other languages (+7)

Iran, formerly called **Persia**, is home to a civilization dating back to the 6th century BCE, known for **poetry**, **rug weaving**, and **metalwork**. Iran's rich cultural heritage is seen in its mix of **ethnic groups**, **architectural styles**, and **local customs**.

Saudi Arabia

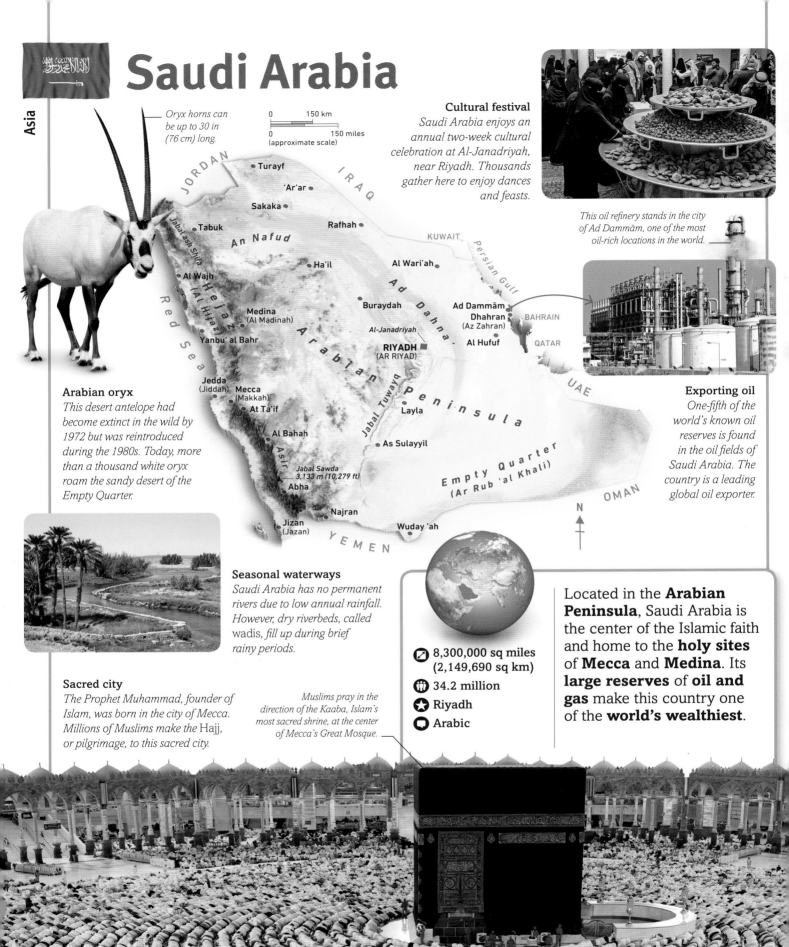

Oryx horns can be up to 30 in (76 cm) long.

0   150 km
0   150 miles
(approximate scale)

JORDAN

Turayf

'Ar'ar

Sakaka

Tabuk

Rafhah

IRAQ

KUWAIT

An Nafud

Ha'il

Al Wari'ah

Persian Gulf

Jabal ash Shifa

Hejaz (Al Hijaz)

Red Sea

Al Wajh

Medina (Al Madinah)

Buraydah

Ad Dahna

Ad Dammām
Dhahran
(Az Zahran)

BAHRAIN

QATAR

Yanbu' al Bahr

Al-Janadriyah

Arabian

RIYADH
(AR RIYAD)

Al Hufuf

UAE

Jedda (Jiddah)

Mecca (Makkah)

At Ta'if

Peninsula

Layla

Jabal Tuwayq

Al Bahah

Asir

Jabal Sawda
3,133 m (10,279 ft)

Abha

As Sulayyil

Empty Quarter
(Ar Rub 'al Khali)

OMAN

Najran

Jizan (Jazan)

Wuday 'ah

YEMEN

N

Cultural festival
Saudi Arabia enjoys an annual two-week cultural celebration at Al-Janadriyah, near Riyadh. Thousands gather here to enjoy dances and feasts.

This oil refinery stands in the city of Ad Dammām, one of the most oil-rich locations in the world.

Exporting oil
One-fifth of the world's known oil reserves is found in the oil fields of Saudi Arabia. The country is a leading global oil exporter.

Arabian oryx
This desert antelope had become extinct in the wild by 1972 but was reintroduced during the 1980s. Today, more than a thousand white oryx roam the sandy desert of the Empty Quarter.

Seasonal waterways
Saudi Arabia has no permanent rivers due to low annual rainfall. However, dry riverbeds, called wadis, fill up during brief rainy periods.

Sacred city
The Prophet Muhammad, founder of Islam, was born in the city of Mecca. Millions of Muslims make the Hajj, or pilgrimage, to this sacred city.

Muslims pray in the direction of the Kaaba, Islam's most sacred shrine, at the center of Mecca's Great Mosque.

⊘ 8,300,000 sq miles (2,149,690 sq km)

👥 34.2 million

★ Riyadh

◯ Arabic

Located in the **Arabian Peninsula**, Saudi Arabia is the center of the Islamic faith and home to the **holy sites** of **Mecca** and **Medina**. Its **large reserves** of **oil and gas** make this country one of the **world's wealthiest**.

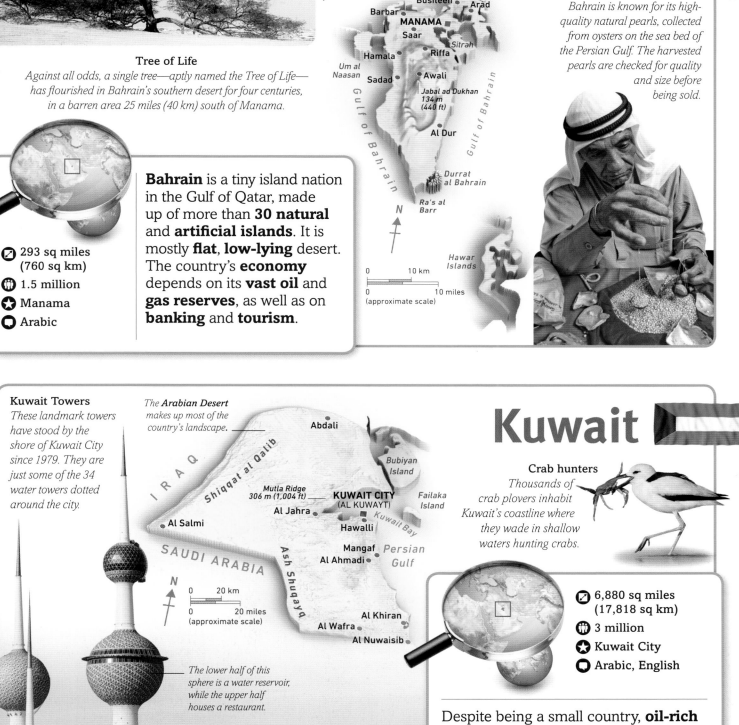

Bahrain

Tree of Life
Against all odds, a single tree—aptly named the Tree of Life—has flourished in Bahrain's southern desert for four centuries, in a barren area 25 miles (40 km) south of Manama.

Persian Gulf

Busiteen
Arad
Barbar
MANAMA
Saar
Sitrah
Hamala
Riffa
Um al
Naasan
Sadad
Awali
Jabal ad Dukhan
134 m
(440 ft)

Gulf of Bahrain

Al Dur

Durrat
al Bahrain

N

Ra's al
Barr

Hawar
Islands

0   10 km
0   10 miles
(approximate scale)

Bahraini pearls
Bahrain is known for its high-quality natural pearls, collected from oysters on the sea bed of the Persian Gulf. The harvested pearls are checked for quality and size before being sold.

- 📐 293 sq miles (760 sq km)
- 👥 1.5 million
- ⭐ Manama
- ⬤ Arabic

Bahrain is a tiny island nation in the Gulf of Qatar, made up of more than **30 natural** and **artificial islands**. It is mostly **flat**, **low-lying** desert. The country's **economy** depends on its **vast oil** and **gas reserves**, as well as on **banking** and **tourism**.

Kuwait Towers
These landmark towers have stood by the shore of Kuwait City since 1979. They are just some of the 34 water towers dotted around the city.

Kuwait

*The **Arabian Desert** makes up most of the country's landscape.*

Abdali

IRAQ

Shiqqat al Qalib

Bubiyan
Island

Mutla Ridge
306 m (1,004 ft)
KUWAIT CITY
(AL KUWAYT)
Failaka
Island
Al Jahra
Kuwait Bay

Al Salmi

Hawalli

SAUDI ARABIA
Mangaf
Al Ahmadi
Persian
Gulf

Ash Shuqayq

N

0   20 km
0   20 miles
(approximate scale)

Al Khiran
Al Wafra

Al Nuwaisib

The lower half of this sphere is a water reservoir, while the upper half houses a restaurant.

Crab hunters
Thousands of crab plovers inhabit Kuwait's coastline where they wade in shallow waters hunting crabs.

- 📐 6,880 sq miles (17,818 sq km)
- 👥 3 million
- ⭐ Kuwait City
- ⬤ Arabic, English

Despite being a small country, **oil-rich** Kuwait is one of the **richest** in the world. Most of its population lives in **Kuwait City**, a **sprawling capital** of **modern skyscrapers**. **Camel racing** is a **popular pastime**.

The United Arab Emirates

The four colors of the UAE flag represent different Arab dynasties.

Vertical city
At 2,716.5 ft (828 m), the Burj Khalifa in Dubai is the tallest building in the world, with the tallest service elevator.

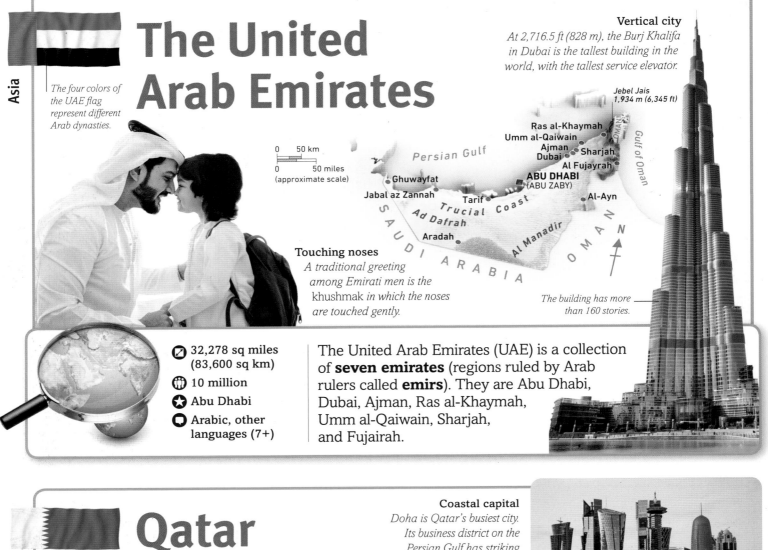

Jebel Jais
1,934 m (6,345 ft)

Ras al-Khaymah
Umm al-Qaiwain
Ajman
Dubai — Sharjah
Al Fujayrah
ABU DHABI
(ABU ZABY)
Al-Ayn

Ghuwayfat
Jabal az Zannah
Tarif
Trucial Coast
Ad Dafrah
Aradah
Al Manadir

Persian Gulf

0   50 km
0   50 miles
(approximate scale)

SAUDI ARABIA

OMAN

Gulf of Oman

The building has more than 160 stories.

Touching noses
A traditional greeting among Emirati men is the khushmak *in which the noses are touched gently.*

- ⬚ 32,278 sq miles (83,600 sq km)
- 🌐 10 million
- ★ Abu Dhabi
- ⬡ Arabic, other languages (7+)

The United Arab Emirates (UAE) is a collection of **seven emirates** (regions ruled by Arab rulers called **emirs**). They are Abu Dhabi, Dubai, Ajman, Ras al-Khaymah, Umm al-Qaiwain, Sharjah, and Fujairah.

Qatar

Coastal capital
Doha is Qatar's busiest city. Its business district on the Persian Gulf has striking waterfront skyscrapers.

0   40 km
0   40 miles
(approximate scale)

BAHRAIN

Ar-Ruwais
Ad-Dahirah
Al Ghuwayriyah
Al-Jumayliyah
Al-Khawr
Dukhan
Ash-Shahaniyah
Umm Bab
Ar Rayyan   **DOHA**
(AD DAWHAH)
Qurayn Abu al-Bawl
103 m (338 ft)
Al-Wakrah
Abu Samra

SAUDI ARABIA

Persian Gulf

N

Bedouin people
Many Qatari traditions, such as playing music and singing songs in a camplike environment, come from the Bedouin people, who are nomadic desert herders.

The rababa is a traditional one-stringed fiddle.

- ⬚ 4,473 sq miles (11,586 sq km)
- 🌐 2.4 million
- ★ Doha
- ⬡ Arabic

The country of Qatar occupies a **small peninsula** in the **Persian Gulf**. It has **large reserves** of **natural gas** and **oil**, which have helped it become a **wealthy nation**. Most of its landscape is **sandy desert** and **dunes**.

Oman

Mountain village
The village of Balad Sayat on the slopes of the Al-Hajar Mountains is known for its fertile agricultural terraces. Many people live on Oman's mountains, where the climate is cooler.

Irrigation system
The aflaj are ancient Omani irrigation channels that carry water from wells on high ground down to farms and villages below.

Omani tunic
The dishdasha is a long-sleeved, ankle-length tunic. For ceremonial occasions, it is worn with a dagger called a khanjar.

Map labels: IRAN, Gulf of Oman, UNITED ARAB EMIRATES, SAUDI ARABIA, YEMEN, Al-Hajar, al-Gharbi, Suhar, Rustaq, Ibri, MUSCAT (MASQAT), Nizwa, Sur, Jabal ash Sham 3,009 m (9,872 ft), Wahibah Sands, Al-Ghabah, Dawwah, Hayma, Zufar, Duqm, Thamarit, Sawqirah, Jabal al Qamar, ARABIAN SEA, Salalah

0 — 100 km
0 — 100 miles
(approximate scale)

- 119,499 sq miles (309,500 sq km)
- 4.7 million
- Muscat
- Arabic, other languages (+4)

Oman has one of the most **diverse landscapes** on the Arabian Peninsula, with rolling sand dunes, soaring mountains, lush oases, and a rugged coastline. Its capital, **Muscat**, is nestled in a **fertile zone** between the **Al-Hajar Mountains** and the **Gulf of Oman**.

Yemen

Desert defenses
Al-Hajjarah is a 12th-century village. Built on a steep cliff face, its towering, fortified houses helped ward off invaders in the past.

Map labels: Jabal An-Nabi Shu'ayb 3,666 m (12,028 ft), SAUDI ARABIA, OMAN, Red Sea, Sa'dah, Minwakh, Sanaw, SANAA (ṢAN'A'), Al Mahrah, Al-Hajjarah, Marib, Say'un, Hodeida, Dhamar, Hadhramaut, Al-Ghaydah, Taizz, Shuqrah, Al-Mukalla, Sayhut, Aden (Adan), Gulf of Aden, Socotra, Hadiboh

0 — 100 km
0 — 100 miles
(approximate scale)

Dragon's blood tree
Growing only on the islands of the Socotra archipelago, this unusual tree gets its name from the red resin that oozes from its bark.

- 203,850 sq miles (527,968 sq km)
- 29.9 million
- Sanaa
- Arabic

Yemen is a mostly mountainous country. In **ancient times**, its **position** on the **Red Sea** made it an important **trading nation**, especially for **coffee**, **frankincense**, and **myrrh**. Since 2015, Yemen has been devastated by **civil war**.

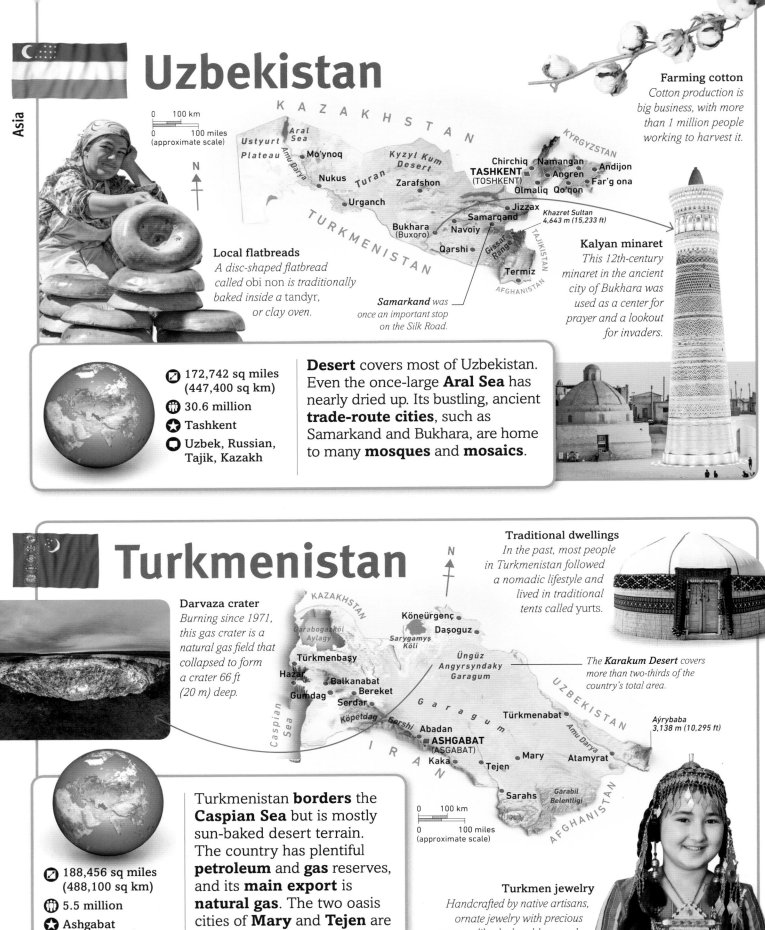

Uzbekistan

Farming cotton
Cotton production is big business, with more than 1 million people working to harvest it.

Local flatbreads
A disc-shaped flatbread called obi non *is traditionally baked inside a tandyr, or clay oven.*

Samarkand was once an important stop on the Silk Road.

Kalyan minaret
This 12th-century minaret in the ancient city of Bukhara was used as a center for prayer and a lookout for invaders.

- 172,742 sq miles (447,400 sq km)
- 30.6 million
- Tashkent
- Uzbek, Russian, Tajik, Kazakh

Desert covers most of Uzbekistan. Even the once-large **Aral Sea** has nearly dried up. Its bustling, ancient **trade-route cities**, such as Samarkand and Bukhara, are home to many **mosques** and **mosaics**.

Turkmenistan

Darvaza crater
Burning since 1971, this gas crater is a natural gas field that collapsed to form a crater 66 ft (20 m) deep.

Traditional dwellings
In the past, most people in Turkmenistan followed a nomadic lifestyle and lived in traditional tents called yurts.

*The **Karakum Desert** covers more than two-thirds of the country's total area.*

Turkmenistan **borders** the **Caspian Sea** but is mostly sun-baked desert terrain. The country has plentiful **petroleum** and **gas** reserves, and its **main export** is **natural gas**. The two oasis cities of **Mary** and **Tejen** are big **cotton-growing centers**.

- 188,456 sq miles (488,100 sq km)
- 5.5 million
- Ashgabat
- Turkmen, other languages (+4)

Turkmen jewelry
Handcrafted by native artisans, ornate jewelry with precious stones—like the headdress and necklace shown here—was a traditional symbol of wealth.

Kazakhstan

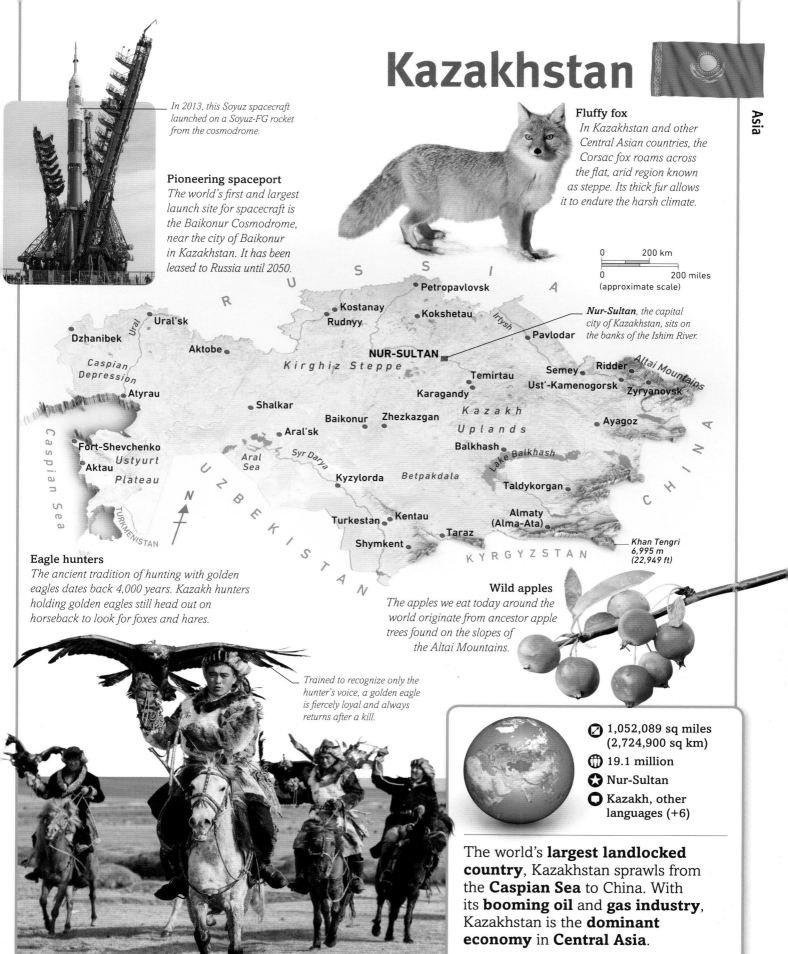

Pioneering spaceport
The world's first and largest launch site for spacecraft is the Baikonur Cosmodrome, near the city of Baikonur in Kazakhstan. It has been leased to Russia until 2050.

In 2013, this Soyuz spacecraft launched on a Soyuz-FG rocket from the cosmodrome.

Fluffy fox
In Kazakhstan and other Central Asian countries, the Corsac fox roams across the flat, arid region known as steppe. Its thick fur allows it to endure the harsh climate.

0   200 km
0   200 miles
(approximate scale)

Nur-Sultan, the capital city of Kazakhstan, sits on the banks of the Ishim River.

Petropavlovsk
Kostanay
Kokshetau
Rudnyy
Pavlodar
Ural'sk
Irtysh
Dzhanibek
Aktobe
NUR-SULTAN
Semey   Ridder
Altai Mountains
Caspian Depression
Kirghiz Steppe
Temirtau
Ust'-Kamenogorsk   Zyryanovsk
Atyrau
Karagandy
Kazakh Uplands
Shalkar
Zhezkazgan
Ayagoz
Baikonur
Fort-Shevchenko
Ustyurt Plateau
Aral'sk
Aral Sea
Syr Darya
Balkhash   Lake Balkhash
Aktau
N
Kyzylorda
Betpakdala
Taldykorgan
Caspian Sea
UZBEKISTAN
TURKMENISTAN
Turkestan   Kentau
Almaty (Alma-Ata)
CHINA
Taraz
Shymkent
KYRGYZSTAN
Khan Tengri 6,995 m (22,949 ft)

Eagle hunters
The ancient tradition of hunting with golden eagles dates back 4,000 years. Kazakh hunters holding golden eagles still head out on horseback to look for foxes and hares.

Trained to recognize only the hunter's voice, a golden eagle is fiercely loyal and always returns after a kill.

Wild apples
The apples we eat today around the world originate from ancestor apple trees found on the slopes of the Altai Mountains.

- 1,052,089 sq miles (2,724,900 sq km)
- 19.1 million
- Nur-Sultan
- Kazakh, other languages (+6)

The world's **largest landlocked country**, Kazakhstan sprawls from the **Caspian Sea** to China. With its **booming oil** and **gas industry**, Kazakhstan is the **dominant economy** in **Central Asia**.

Afghanistan

Great Mosque of Herat
Decorated with ornate patterned tiles, the Great Mosque has stood in the city of Herat for 800 years.

This goblet-shaped drum is made of bone, leather, metal, and wood.

Kabul is a city of palaces, parks, and markets, located in a valley of the Hindu Kush Mountains.

Traditional drum
The beat of this zerbaghali drum is still heard in folk music played by Afghan musicians.

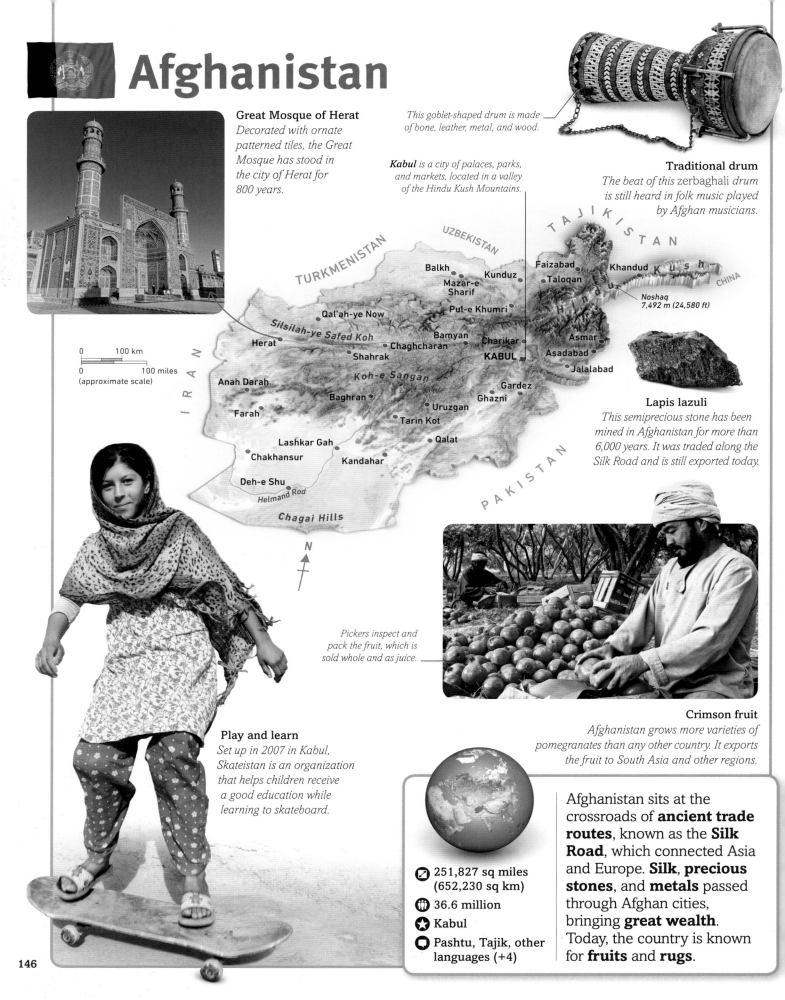

TURKMENISTAN

UZBEKISTAN

TAJIKISTAN

Balkh
Kunduz
Mazar-e Sharif
Faizabad
Taloqan
Khandud **Kush**
CHINA

Hindu
Noshaq 7,492 m (24,580 ft)

0 100 km
0 100 miles
(approximate scale)

Qal'ah-ye Now
Pul-e Khumri

Silsilah-ye Safed Koh
Bamyan
Charikar
KABUL
Asmar
Asadabad

IRAN
Herat
Chaghcharan
Shahrak
Koh-e Sangan
Jalalabad

Lapis lazuli
This semiprecious stone has been mined in Afghanistan for more than 6,000 years. It was traded along the Silk Road and is still exported today.

Anah Darah
Baghran
Gardez
Ghazni

Farah
Uruzgan
Tarin Kot

Lashkar Gah
Qalat

Chakhansur
Kandahar

Deh-e Shu
Helmand Rod

PAKISTAN

Chagai Hills

N

Pickers inspect and pack the fruit, which is sold whole and as juice.

Crimson fruit
Afghanistan grows more varieties of pomegranates than any other country. It exports the fruit to South Asia and other regions.

Play and learn
Set up in 2007 in Kabul, Skateistan is an organization that helps children receive a good education while learning to skateboard.

⤢ 251,827 sq miles (652,230 sq km)

👥 36.6 million

★ Kabul

◯ Pashtu, Tajik, other languages (+4)

Afghanistan sits at the crossroads of **ancient trade routes**, known as the **Silk Road**, which connected Asia and Europe. **Silk, precious stones,** and **metals** passed through Afghan cities, bringing **great wealth.** Today, the country is known for **fruits** and **rugs.**

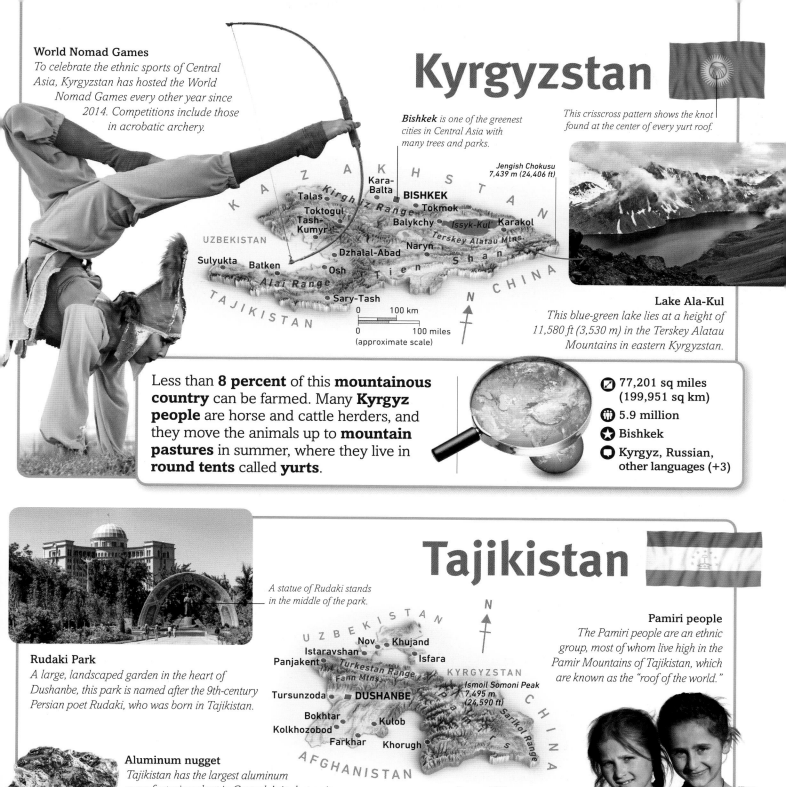

Kyrgyzstan

World Nomad Games
To celebrate the ethnic sports of Central Asia, Kyrgyzstan has hosted the World Nomad Games every other year since 2014. Competitions include those in acrobatic archery.

Bishkek is one of the greenest cities in Central Asia with many trees and parks.

This crisscross pattern shows the knot found at the center of every yurt roof.

Jengish Chokusu 7,439 m (24,406 ft)

KAZAKHSTAN

Kara-Balta
Talas
Kirghiz Range
BISHKEK
Toktogul
Tokmok
Tash-Kumyr
Balykchy
Issyk-Kul
Karakol
UZBEKISTAN
Terskey Alatau Mtns.
Naryn
Sulyukta
Batken
Dzhalal-Abad
Osh
Tien Shan
Alai Range
CHINA
TAJIKISTAN
Sary-Tash

0 — 100 km
0 — 100 miles
(approximate scale)
N

Lake Ala-Kul
This blue-green lake lies at a height of 11,580 ft (3,530 m) in the Terskey Alatau Mountains in eastern Kyrgyzstan.

Less than **8 percent** of this **mountainous country** can be farmed. Many **Kyrgyz people** are horse and cattle herders, and they move the animals up to **mountain pastures** in summer, where they live in **round tents** called **yurts**.

- ⬡ 77,201 sq miles (199,951 sq km)
- 👥 5.9 million
- ★ Bishkek
- ⬭ Kyrgyz, Russian, other languages (+3)

Tajikistan

Rudaki Park
A large, landscaped garden in the heart of Dushanbe, this park is named after the 9th-century Persian poet Rudaki, who was born in Tajikistan.

A statue of Rudaki stands in the middle of the park.

Pamiri people
The Pamiri people are an ethnic group, most of whom live high in the Pamir Mountains of Tajikistan, which are known as the "roof of the world."

UZBEKISTAN
Nov
Khujand
Istaravshan
Isfara
Panjakent
Turkestan Range
KYRGYZSTAN
Fann Mtns.
Ismoil Somoni Peak 7,495 m (24,590 ft)
Tursunzoda
DUSHANBE
Sarikol Range
Bokhtar
Kulob
CHINA
Kolkhozobod
Farkhar
Khorugh
AFGHANISTAN
N

0 — 100 km
0 — 100 miles
(approximate scale)

Aluminum nugget
Tajikistan has the largest aluminum manufacturing plant in Central Asia, but as it has no natural aluminum, it imports the raw ore. This metal is used in cans, foils, and utensils.

- ⬡ 55,637 sq miles (144,100 sq km)
- 👥 8.9 million
- ★ Dushanbe
- ⬭ Tajik, Uzbek, Russian

Many **customs** have been preserved in this mountainous country, such as **festivals** to celebrate the **first flowers of spring**. Tajikistan's **Ismoil Somoni Peak** is one of the **highest peaks** in **Central Asia**.

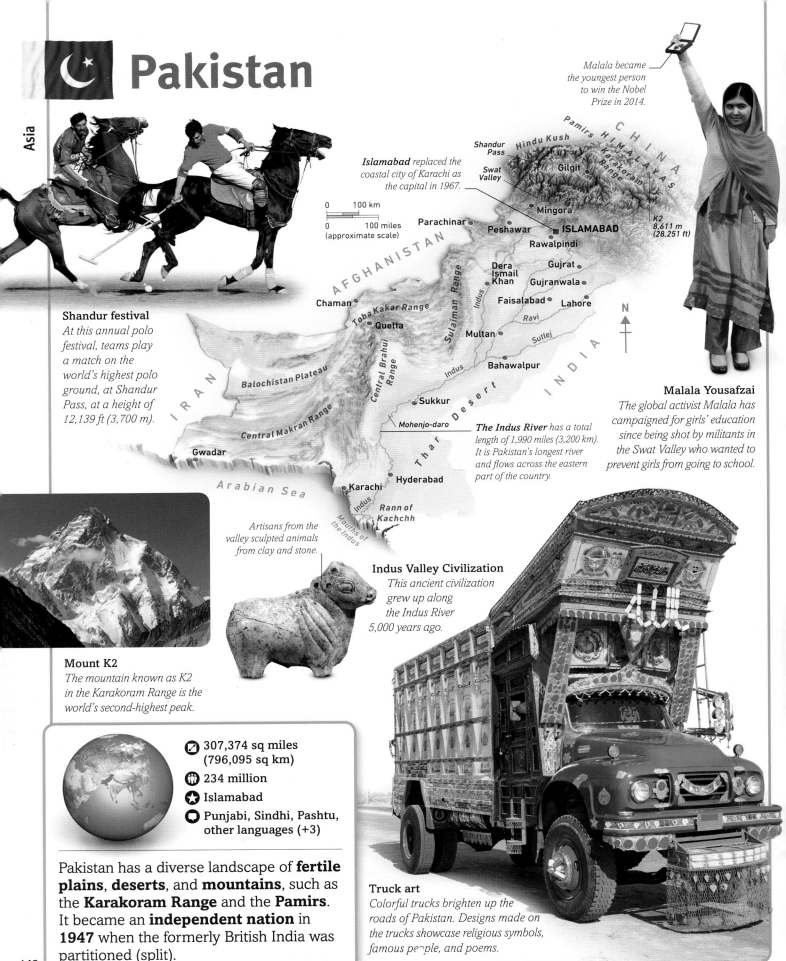

Pakistan

Asia

Malala became the youngest person to win the Nobel Prize in 2014.

Shandur festival
At this annual polo festival, teams play a match on the world's highest polo ground, at Shandur Pass, at a height of 12,139 ft (3,700 m).

Islamabad replaced the coastal city of Karachi as the capital in 1967.

0   100 km
0   100 miles
(approximate scale)

CHINA

Shandur Pass
Hindu Kush
Pamirs
HIMALAYAS
Karakoram Range

Gilgit
Swat Valley
Mingora
Parachinar
Peshawar **ISLAMABAD**
Rawalpindi
K2 8,611 m (28,251 ft)

AFGHANISTAN

Chaman
Toba Kakar Range
Quetta

Dera Ismail Khan
Gujrat
Gujranwala
Faisalabad
Lahore

Sulaiman Range

Indus
Ravi

Multan
Sutlej

IRAN

Balochistan Plateau

Central Brahui Range

Bahawalpur

INDIA

N

Central Makran Range

Indus

Thar Desert

Sukkur

Mohenjo-daro

The Indus River *has a total length of 1,990 miles (3,200 km). It is Pakistan's longest river and flows across the eastern part of the country.*

Gwadar

Arabian Sea

Karachi
Hyderabad

Indus
Mouths of the Indus
Rann of Kachchh

Malala Yousafzai
The global activist Malala has campaigned for girls' education since being shot by militants in the Swat Valley who wanted to prevent girls from going to school.

Artisans from the valley sculpted animals from clay and stone.

Indus Valley Civilization
This ancient civilization grew up along the Indus River 5,000 years ago.

Mount K2
The mountain known as K2 in the Karakoram Range is the world's second-highest peak.

⤢ 307,374 sq miles (796,095 sq km)

👥 234 million

⭐ Islamabad

🗨 Punjabi, Sindhi, Pashtu, other languages (+3)

Pakistan has a diverse landscape of **fertile plains**, **deserts**, and **mountains**, such as the **Karakoram Range** and the **Pamirs**. It became an **independent nation** in **1947** when the formerly British India was partitioned (split).

Truck art
Colorful trucks brighten up the roads of Pakistan. Designs made on the trucks showcase religious symbols, famous people, and poems.

Sri Lanka

INDIA

Palk Strait

Bay of Bengal

Jaffna
Kilinochchi
Delft
Vavuniya
Gulf of Mannar
Anuradhapura
Trincomalee
Puttalam
Mahaweli Ganga
Batticaloa
Kurunegala
Pidurutalagala 2,524 m (8,281 ft)
Negombo
COLOMBO
Kandy
Moratuwa
SRI JAYEWARDENEPURA KOTTE
Ratnapura
Hambantota
Galle
Matara

INDIAN OCEAN

0 50 km
0 50 miles
(approximate scale)

The lion represents the strength of the nation.

Stilt fishing
These Sri Lankan fishermen perch on wooden stilts high over shallow waters to catch fish. Generations of families have used this technique.

Kandy Esala Perahera
Also known as the "Festival of the Tooth," this annual event in the city of Kandy pays tribute to a relic said to be the Buddha's tooth. Decorated elephants join dancers and acrobats in processions.

- ◪ 25,332 sq miles (65,610 sq km)
- ⦿ 22.9 million
- ★ Sri Jayewardenepura Kotte, Colombo
- ◗ Sinhala, Tamil, Sinhala-Tamil, English

The **island country** of Sri Lanka lies off the **southern tip** of **India**. Its location in the **Indian Ocean** has attracted **traders** since ancient times. Today, the country is known for its **tea plantations** and **wildlife**.

Maldives

0 100 km
0 100 miles
(approximate scale)

INDIAN OCEAN

Eight Degree Channel

Ihavandippolhu Atoll
Thiladhunmathi Atoll
Makunudhoo Atoll
North Miladummadulu Atoll
North Maalhosmadulu Atoll
South Miladummadulu Atoll
South Maalhosmadulu Atoll
Faadhippolhu Atoll
Rasdu Atoll
Male' Atoll
Ari Atoll
MALE (MAALE)
North Nilandhe Atoll
Felidhu Atoll
South Nilandhe Atoll
Mulaku Atoll
Kolhumadulu Atoll
Hadhdhunmathi Atoll

One and Half Degree Channel

North Huvadhu Atoll
South Huvadhu Atoll
Equatorial Channel
Villingili Island 2 m (7 ft)
Fuammulah
Gan
Addu Atoll

Malé
One-third of the population inhabits the capital city of Malé, taking up a whole island in the Malé atoll.

Underwater cabinet meeting
In 2009, the Maldives government made history by holding the world's first underwater cabinet meeting to promote action against rising water levels and climate change.

Dr. Ibrahim Didi
Minister of Fisheries and Agriculture

- ◪ 115 sq miles (298 sq km)
- ⦿ 392,000
- ★ Malé
- ◗ Dhivehi, other languages (+3)

Famous for their picture-perfect **tropical beaches** and **clear waters**, the **flat, low-lying Maldives** risk being submerged by **rising sea levels**. This archipelago consists of **more than 1,000 coral islands**, grouped into **26 atolls**.

India

The *Chakra (wheel)* is a symbol of the Buddhist faith.

Indian movies
India produces more than 1,500 movies a year, in nearly 25 languages. Hindi movies are made in Bollywood and range from comedies (such as 3 Idiots) to musicals and dramas.

Symbolic hand movements, known as mudras, *help tell the story of the dance.*

Classical dance
There are many traditional Indian dance forms, each with their own unique costumes, music, and style. This dancer is performing Odissi—an ancient dance from eastern India.

The *Ganges River (Ganga) flows over a length of 1,616 miles (2,601 km).*

0   150 km
0   150 miles
(approximate scale)

Map labels:
CHINA, HIMALAYAS, Indus, Srinagar, Amritsar, Sutlej, Shimla, Chandigarh, PAKISTAN, Rohtak, **NEW DELHI**, Bareilly, NEPAL, Bikaner, Agra, Ganges, Lucknow, Ajmer, Jaipur, Chambal, Yamuna, Jodhpur, Gwalior, Varanasi, Patna, Udaipur, Kota, Allahabad, Thar Desert, Sagar, Chota Nagpur, Rar, Rann of Kachchh, Ahmadabad, Vindhya Range, Bhopal, Narmada, Jabalpur, Gandhidham, Bilaspur, Raurkela, Porbandar, Rajkot, Vadodara, Indore, Satpura Range, Bhavnagar, Surat, Nagpur, Raipur, Gulf of Khambhat, Nashik, Tapti, Aurangabad, Chandrapur, Brahmap, Mumbai (Bombay), Ahmadnagar, Godavari, Visakhapatnam, Pune, Nizamabad, Warangal, Solapur, Deccan, Hyderabad, Krishna, Rajahmundry, Kolhapur, Sangli, Machilipatnam, Raichur, Nandyal, Eastern Ghats, Panaji, Hubballi, Proddatur, Nellore, Arabian Sea, Shivamogga, Chennai (Madras), Mangaluru (Mangalore), Bengaluru (Bangalore), Vellore, Mysuru (Mysore), Puducherry (Pondicherry), Kozhikode (Calicut), Salem, Kaveri, Coimbatore, Tiruchchirappalli, Kochi (Cochin), Madurai, Palk Strait, Western Ghats, Cardamom Hills, Kollam (Quilon), Tuticorin, SRI LANKA, Thiruvananthapuram (Trivandrum), Nagercoil, Gulf of Mannar, INDIAN OCEAN

Lakshadweep Islands
Located off India's southwestern coast is this group of 36 coral islands, of which only 10 are inhabited.

Arabian Sea, Agatti Island, Kadamatt Island, **Kavaratti**, Lakshadweep (Laccadive Islands), Minicoy Island

0   100 km
0   100 miles
(approximate scale)

Bengal tiger
India's national animal is the endangered Bengal tiger, now protected in nature reserves.

Home to more than **1 billion people**, India is the world's **seventh-largest country** by area. India ranges from the **Himalayas** in the north, to **fertile river** and **coastal plains**, where most people live. A rich variety of **cultures**, **faiths**, and **languages** makes India one of the **most diverse nations** on Earth.

- 1,269,219 sq miles (3,287,263 sq km)
- 1.3 billion
- New Delhi
- Hindi, English, other languages (12+)

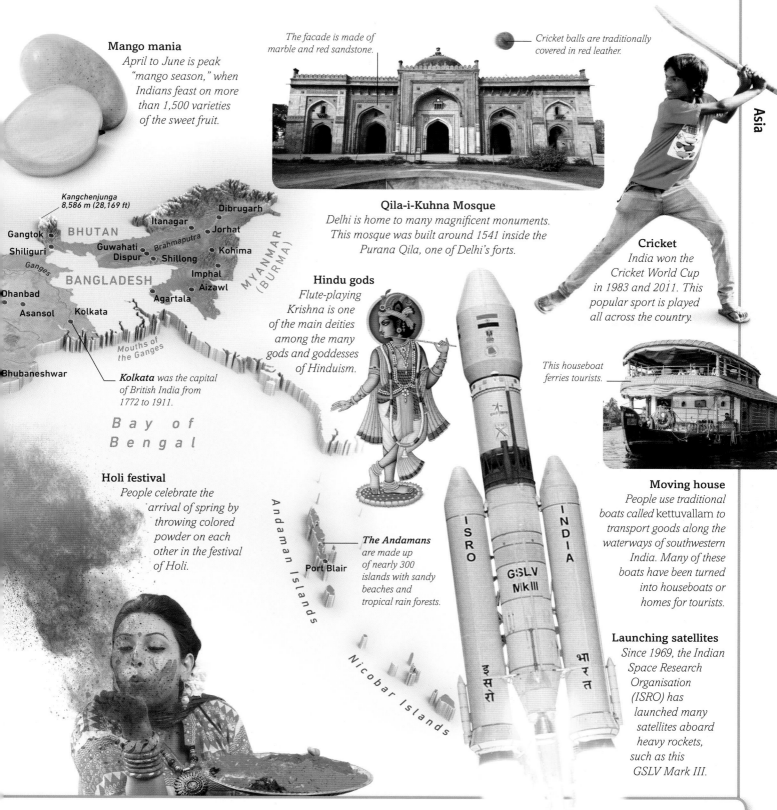

Mango mania
April to June is peak "mango season," when Indians feast on more than 1,500 varieties of the sweet fruit.

The facade is made of marble and red sandstone.

Cricket balls are traditionally covered in red leather.

Qila-i-Kuhna Mosque
Delhi is home to many magnificent monuments. This mosque was built around 1541 inside the Purana Qila, one of Delhi's forts.

Kangchenjunga
8,586 m (28,169 ft)

Dibrugarh

BHUTAN
Itanagar
Gangtok
Jorhat
Shiliguri
Guwahati
Kohima
Dispur
Shillong
Brahmaputra

Ganges
Imphal
BANGLADESH
Aizawl

Ohanbad
Agartala

Asansol
Kolkata

MYANMAR (BURMA)

Mouths of the Ganges

Bhubaneshwar

Kolkata was the capital of British India from 1772 to 1911.

Cricket
India won the Cricket World Cup in 1983 and 2011. This popular sport is played all across the country.

Hindu gods
Flute-playing Krishna is one of the main deities among the many gods and goddesses of Hinduism.

This houseboat ferries tourists.

B a y   o f   B e n g a l

Holi festival
People celebrate the arrival of spring by throwing colored powder on each other in the festival of Holi.

Andaman Islands

Port Blair

The Andamans are made up of nearly 300 islands with sandy beaches and tropical rain forests.

Nicobar Islands

ISRO
INDIA
GSLV Mk III
इसरो
भारत

Moving house
People use traditional boats called kettuvallam *to transport goods along the waterways of southwestern India. Many of these boats have been turned into houseboats or homes for tourists.*

Launching satellites
Since 1969, the Indian Space Research Organisation (ISRO) has launched many satellites aboard heavy rockets, such as this GSLV Mark III.

Geography: Forests, deserts, mountains, and **plains** make up India. Its climate is mostly **hot** and **tropical.**

History: Many kingdoms in the region were **under the British Empire,** until the **independent** country of **India** formed in **1947.**

Culture: The wide variety in **music, dance, festivals,** and **art** from all across the country reflects the **cultural diversity** of the nation.

Natural wonders: The **Himalayas** are the world's **highest mountain range.** They cross 10 Indian states.

Wildlife: Many of the planet's **most loved,** and **feared, creatures** are found in India—**tigers, elephants, crocodiles,** and **cobras.**

Food and drink: Rice, flour, and **lentils** are staple foods, typically flavored with a range of **spices.**

Bangladesh

The Sundarbans
Mangrove forests grow in the delta of the Ganges River. Called the Sundarbans, these are home to animals, including the rare Bengal tiger and chital deer (left).

Tea picking
This worker picks tea leaves by hand on a tea plantation in Sylhet. Bangladesh ranks among the world's top 10 tea producers.

- ⤢ 57,320 sq miles (148,460 sq km)
- 👥 162.6 million
- ★ Dhaka
- 💬 Bengali, other languages (+8)

The **small**, **South Asian** country of Bangladesh is situated on the **Bay of Bengal**. It has a changing landscape of sweeping **hillsides**, **mangrove forests**, and **riverside communities**.

Driving rickshaws
Two-wheeled and three-wheeled vehicles called rickshaws *are a common mode of transportation in Bangladesh. About a million people earn a livelihood by driving a rickshaw.*

Sweet dumplings
Traditional rice cakes made of rice flour, milk, and coconut, called pitha, *are a special treat.*

0   50 km
0   50 miles
(approximate scale)

N

Map labels:
Saidpur
Dinajpur
Rangpur
INDIA
Jamuna Nadi
Nawabganj
Rajshahi
Jamalpur
Mymensingh
Sylhet
Sirajganj
Tangail
Habiganj
Pabna
DHAKA
Brahmanbaria
Chuadanga
Padma
Comilla
Jessore
Meghna Nadi
Khulna
Barisal
Satkhira
Chittagong Hills
Sundarbans
Karnaphuli Reservoir
Chittagong
Saka Haphong 1,052 m (3,451 ft)
Mouths of the Ganges
Bay of Bengal
MYANMAR
INDIA

New Year's mask
Pôhela Boishakh is an important festival that celebrates the Bengali New Year. People take part in processions and make decorative masks.

Festival masks feature colorful depictions of characters from Bengali folklore.

Flower harvest
The water lily grows wild in many of Bangladesh's lakes and rivers. It is harvested for its stalks—for eating—and the flowers.

Bhutan

Buddhist prayer flags
From monastery doorways to village entrances, prayer flags can be seen fluttering everywhere in Bhutan.

Thimphu lies high in the Himalayas.

CHINA

HIMALAYAS

Gangkhar Puensum
7,570 m (24,840 ft)

THIMPHU
Punakha
Paro
Tongsa
Wangdue Phodrang
Mongar
Phuntsholing
Samdrup Jongkhar

INDIA

Smiling nation
Bhutan favors policies that focus on the happiness and well-being of its people. This country is called the happiest country in Asia.

Tiger's Nest Monastery
High up in the Paro Valley sits this 17th-century Buddhist temple, which marks the spot where Buddhism was first practiced in Bhutan.

0   50 km
0   50 miles
(approximate scale)

- ⬭ 14,824 sq miles (38,394 sq km)
- 👥 782,000
- ⭐ Thimphu
- 🗨 Dzongkha, Nepali, Assamese

Bhutan is a small **Buddhist kingdom** in the eastern **Himalayas**. The country's **main export** is **hydropower**, generated by the **rivers** that flow down its **steep valleys**.

Nepal

N

CHINA

HIMALAYAS

INDIA

Dipayal
Birendranagar
Nepalganj
Salyan
Pokhara
Butwal
KATHMANDU
Bharatpur
Lalitpur
Bhaktapur
Birganj
Dhankuta
Janakpur
Dharan
Biratnagar

Kathmandu is Nepal's largest city.

Mount Everest
8,848 m (29,029 ft)

0   100 km
0   100 miles
(approximate scale)

The Bhairavnath Temple is dedicated to Bhairava, a form of the Hindu god Shiva.

Top of the world
Mount Everest is the world's highest peak, located in southeastern Nepal. Many mountaineers climb its steep slopes, but fewer than 10,000 people have reached its summit.

Temple town
Magnificent temples and a former royal palace line the wide squares in the ancient city of Bhaktapur.

- ⬭ 56,827 sq miles (147,181 sq km)
- 👥 30.3 million
- ⭐ Kathmandu
- 🗨 Nepali, Maithili, Bhojpuri

Three-quarters of Nepal is covered in **mountains**, including many of the world's most **majestic peaks**. Its wildlife includes the **Asiatic elephant**, the **one-horned rhinoceros**, and the very rare **snow leopard**.

Myanmar

Bagan is a popular destination for hot-air ballooning.

Bagan skyline
The beautiful city of Bagan features a stunning skyline of Buddhist temples built by its ancient rulers from the 11th century onward.

Traditional parasols are made of bamboo, waxed cotton, or silk.

Buddhists in Myanmar wear maroon robes.

Young monks
Most of the country's population is Buddhist, and there are about 500,000 Buddhist monks. Boys train to be monks from the age of seven.

Hkakabo Razi
5,885 m (19,308 ft)

INDIA

BANGLADESH

Rakhine Mountains

Kumon Range

CHINA

Myitkyina
Banmauk
Hakha
Monywa · Shwebo
Pakokku · Mandalay
Myingyan
Bagan · Taunggyi
Magway
NAY PYI TAW
Sittwe
Ramree Island
Munaung Island
Bay of Bengal
Pyay
Phyu
Hinthada
Pathein · Bago
Yangon (Rangoon) · Thaton
Mawlamyine
Ye
Dawei
Myeik

Kengtung
Shan Plateau

Thanlwin

LAOS

THAILAND

Ayeyarwady

Sittang

Gulf of Mottama

Mouths of the Ayeyarwady

Preparis

Great Coco Island

Andaman Sea

Letsok-aw Kyun
Lanbi Kyun
Zadetkyi Kyun

THAILAND

0 — 150 km
0 — 150 miles
(approximate scale)

Kyaukse festival
A giant bamboo elephant takes center stage at this annual festival where dancers dressed as elephants parade in the streets.

Eating tea
Although many nations drink tea, the people of Myanmar also eat it. Among the national favorites is laphet thoke, a pickled tea leaf salad.

Yangon city
Myanmar's largest and busiest city is Yangon (formerly Rangoon), which was the capital from 1948 to 2006.

- 261,228 sq miles (676,578 sq km)
- 56.6 million
- Nay Pyi Taw
- Burmese (Myanmar), other languages (+7)

Formerly called **Burma**, Myanmar is the **second-largest country** in **Southeast Asia**. It is known as **"the land of golden pagodas"** because of its **thousands of spectacular temples**.

Laos

Natural materials

Bamboo is a giant grass that thrives in Laos. The long stems make poles for building things, and the leaves can be woven into baskets.

Phongsali
Louangnamtha
Houayxay
Louangphabang
Phou Bia 2,819 m (9,249 ft)
Xam Nua
Xaignabouli
Plateau de Xiangkhoang
VIENTIANE (VIANGCHAN)
Pakxan
Thakhèk
Khanthabouli
Salavan
Pakxe
Champasak
Attapu

CHINA / MYANMAR / THAILAND / VIETNAM / CAMBODIA

Mekong

Vientiane sits on the banks of the Mekong River.

0   100 km
0   100 miles
(approximate scale)

Morning markets

Markets in Laos sell a variety of local produce, such as noodles made from rice. Textiles, handcrafted goods, and traditional cuisine are all traded at busy stalls.

Mekong River

The lifeline of the country is the Mekong River. It is used for transportation and watering crops.

- 91,428 sq miles (236,800 sq km)
- 7.4 million
- Vientiane
- Lao, other languages (+5)

Laos is a **landlocked country** in Southeast Asia with a **landscape** of mountains, forests, and waterfalls. The **Mekong River** runs the length of the country.

Cambodia

Apsara dance

Apsaras *are heaven's female dancers in Hindu mythology. This traditional style of Cambodian dance was named after them.*

Sisophon
Battambang
Siem Reap
Tonle Sap
Pursat
Virôchey
Stung Treng
Lumphat
Kampong Thum
Phnom Aural 1,813 m (5,948 ft)
Mekong
Kompong Cham
PHNOM PENH
Sihanoukville
Kampot
Gulf of Thailand
Cardamom Mountains

THAILAND / LAOS / VIETNAM

0   50 km
0   50 miles
(approximate scale)

Phnom Penh is known as "the Pearl of Asia."

Angkor Wat

The Buddhist temple of Angkor Wat is the largest religious monument in the world. It is featured on the Cambodian flag.

The **mountains** of Cambodia are covered in **dense tropical forests**. Most people live in **lowland areas** where **crops** such as **rice** can be **farmed** and **cattle graze.**

- 69,898 sq miles (181,035 sq km)
- 16.9 million
- Phnom Penh
- Khmer, other languages (+4)

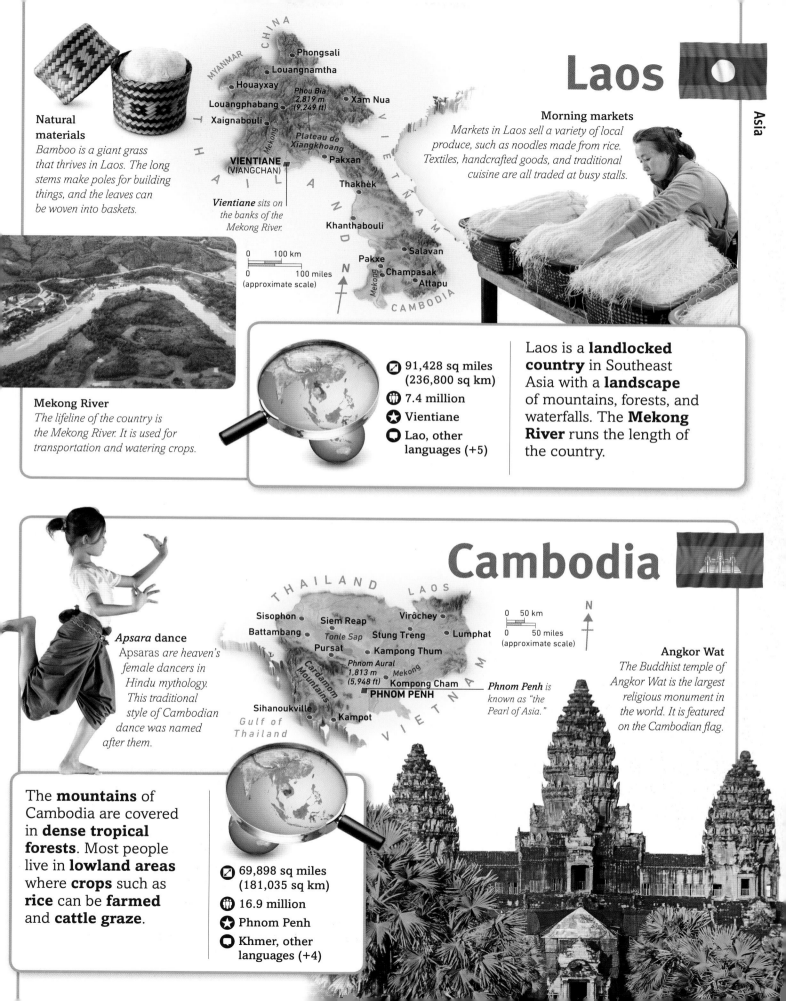

Thailand

Doi Inthanon
Waterfalls, forests, shrines, and the country's highest mountain can all be found in Doi Inthanon National Park.

Tropical beaches
To the south of Thailand are thousands of remote islands and unspoiled beaches that are accessible only by boat. Railay Beach, near Phuket, is a favorite with rock climbers and swimmers.

Khon dance
For centuries, masked Thai performers have taken part in khon, *a spectacular dance-drama.*

This character battles a demon in a scene from the epic poem Ramakien.

Queen of fruit
The mangosteen is a purple tropical fruit with a soft, juicy pulp that is grown in Thailand.

Muay Thai
The national sport of Thailand is a form of boxing called Muay Thai. *Fighters can use their fists, elbows, knees, and shins to combat their opponent.*

Floating markets
In Thailand, vendors fill boats called sampans *with fresh produce to sell to locals and tourists. Damnoen Saduak in Ratchaburi is one of Thailand's largest floating markets.*

MYANMAR

Doi Inthanon
2,565 m (8,415 ft)

0 — 100 km
0 — 100 miles
(approximate scale)

LAOS

Chiang Mai • Nan
Lampang • Phrae
Uttaradit
Tak
Phitsanulok
Loei • Udon Thani
Korat Plateau
Khon Kaen
Chaiyaphum
Nakhon Sawan
Lop Buri
Buriram • Surin
Ubon Ratchathani
Saraburi
Tane Range
Tha Chin
Mun
Chi

BANGKOK
(KRUNG THEP)
Ratchaburi
Phetchaburi
Chon Buri
Ao Krung Thep
Rayong
Hua Hin
Chanthaburi

CAMBODIA

Ko Chang

Gulf of Thailand

Chumphon

Ko Phangan
Ko Samui

Surat Thani

Nakhon Si Thammarat
Ko Phuket • Phuket
Ko Lanta
Trang
Hat Yai
Ko Tarutao
Narathiwat
Pattani

Andaman Sea

MALAYSIA

N

- 198,116 sq miles (513,120 sq km)
- 69 million
- Bangkok
- Thai, other languages (+6)

The **bustling capital** of Bangkok and **tropical southern islands** draw millions of visitors to Thailand every year. **Buddhism** is the **main religion** here, and thousands of **temples** and statues of **the Buddha** dot the country.

Vietnam

Fansipan
3,143 m (10,312 ft)

CHINA

Ha Giang
Lao Cai
Cao Bang
Lai Chau
Yen Bai
Lang Son
Son La
HANOI
Cam Pha
Hoa Binh
Hai Phong
Nam Dinh
Thanh Hoa

Hoang Lien Son
Red River

Gulf of Tonkin

0   100 km
0   100 miles
(approximate scale)

Vinh

LAOS

Dong Hoi

South China Sea

Hue
Da Nang

Quang Ngai

Kon Tum
Play Cu

Quy Nhon
Buon Ma Thuot
Tuy Hoa

Nha Trang
Da Lat
Cam Ranh

CAMBODIA

Tay Ninh

Chau Doc
Bien Hoa
Phan Thiet
Ho Chi Minh
Phu Quoc
Vinh Long
Vung Tau
Rach Gia
Tra Vinh
Gulf of Thailand
Soc Trang
Ca Mau
Bac Lieu
Mouths of the Mekong

Mekong

Annamite Mountains

Con Son Island

N

Red-shanked douc
Bright red legs give this eye-catching monkey its name. It lives high in the trees of Vietnamese rain forests.

Golden Bridge
Two big stone hands support this scenic walkway in the hills near Da Nang. People walk on the bridge at a height of 4,590 ft (1,400 m).

Hanoi Train Street
Twice a day, a train speeds through this narrow, residential street in Hanoi's Old Quarter. Locals stay clear of the tracks for their own safety.

Rice terraces
Rice is an important crop in Southeast Asia. It is grown in wet paddy fields or on steplike "terraced" fields in hilly areas. Vietnam ranks among the world's top five rice producers.

Noodle soup
Every region of Vietnam has a different recipe for making pho— a traditional noodle soup made with broth, meat, and herbs.

Ha Long Bay
Rocky limestone islands covered in rain forest dot the waters of this bay near Hai Phong in northeastern Vietnam. Tourists visit this popular spot on daily boat trips.

⊘ 127,880 sq miles (331,210 sq km)

⊕ 98.7 million

★ Hanoi

◯ Vietnamese, other languages (+8)

Vietnam lies on the **eastern edges** of the **Southeast Asian peninsula**. There are **mountains** to the north and **central highlands**. To the south of **Ho Chi Minh City**, the **Mekong River** ends its 2,800-mile (4,500 km) journey across Asia in a **vast, fertile delta**.

Philippines

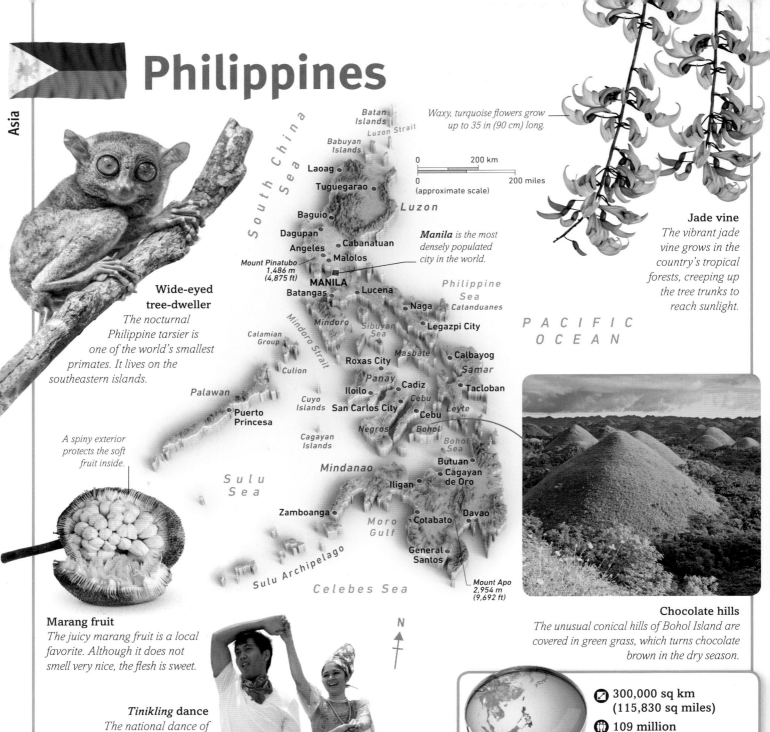

Batan Islands

Luzon Strait

Babuyan Islands

Laoag

Tuguegarao

Luzon

Baguio

Dagupan

Angeles · Cabanatuan

Mount Pinatubo 1,486 m (4,875 ft)

Malolos

MANILA

Manila is the most densely populated city in the world.

Batangas · Lucena

Mindoro

Naga

Philippine Sea

Catanduanes

Legazpi City

Calamian Group

Sibuyan Sea

Mindoro Strait

Culion

Masbate

Roxas City

Panay

Cadiz

Samar

Calbayog

Iloilo

Cuyo Islands

San Carlos City

Cebu

Cebu

Leyte

Tacloban

Palawan

Puerto Princesa

Cagayan Islands

Negros

Bohol

Bohol Sea

Sulu Sea

Mindanao

Butuan

Cagayan de Oro

Iligan

Zamboanga

Moro Gulf

Cotabato

Davao

General Santos

Sulu Archipelago

Celebes Sea

Mount Apo 2,954 m (9,692 ft)

N

0 — 200 km
0 — 200 miles
(approximate scale)

South China Sea

PACIFIC OCEAN

Wide-eyed tree-dweller
The nocturnal Philippine tarsier is one of the world's smallest primates. It lives on the southeastern islands.

Jade vine
Waxy, turquoise flowers grow up to 35 in (90 cm) long.

The vibrant jade vine grows in the country's tropical forests, creeping up the tree trunks to reach sunlight.

Marang fruit
A spiny exterior protects the soft fruit inside.

The juicy marang fruit is a local favorite. Although it does not smell very nice, the flesh is sweet.

Chocolate hills
The unusual conical hills of Bohol Island are covered in green grass, which turns chocolate brown in the dry season.

Tinikling dance
The national dance of tinikling *involves dancers moving in rhythm over a pair of bamboo poles that are slid around on the ground.*

- 300,000 sq km (115,830 sq miles)
- 109 million
- Manila
- Filipino, English, other languages (4+)

The **Philippines** is a collection of **more than 7,000 islands** in southeastern Asia. Dotted across the country are **more than 20 active volcanoes**. The **eruption of Mount Pinatubo**, on Luzon, in 1991, was **one of the most powerful** in the 20th century.

Mongolia

Asia

Sand and snow
The towering dunes of the Gobi Desert dwarf a herd of two-humped Bactrian camels, kept by nomadic Mongols for transportation, wool, milk, and meat.

Naadam festival
Every July, people all over Mongolia take part in the Naadam sporting festival. They compete in horse racing, wrestling, and archery.

In bkyukl bökh, a form of Mongolian wrestling, wrestlers win by forcing their opponent to the ground.

Bergenia flower
Despite its delicate appearance, this resilient flower thrives in Mongolia's low temperatures.

Nayramadlin Orgil
4,374 m (14,350 ft)

Horsehead fiddle
A carved horsehead tops the morin khuur—a traditional bowed instrument played for centuries.

Nomadic life
Around a million Mongolians live as traditional nomads. They set up temporary camps known as gers and travel on horseback to tend their herds.

- 603,908 sq miles (1,564,116 sq km)
- 3.2 million
- Ulaanbaatar
- Khalkha Mongolian, other languages (+3)

Mongolia is a vast country in **Central Asia** with landscapes ranging from the snowcapped **Altai Mountains** in the west to the vast, cold **Gobi Desert** in the south.

159

China

Mooncake
Often eaten during lunar celebrations in fall, this cake is a rich, sweet baked dessert.

Great Wall of China
A huge stone wall was built across China over many centuries to protect it from invaders. The Great Wall spans more than 13,000 miles (21,000 km).

Dragons—symbols of good luck—are made to dance through the streets.

Giant pandas
These endangered bears live in forested mountains in China, where they survive on a diet of bamboo plants. Fewer than a thousand adults exist in the wild.

Chinese New Year
China's most important festival marks the New Year and the coming of spring. This event is also celebrated in some other parts of Southeast Asia.

KAZAKHSTAN

N

Altay

KYRGYZSTAN
Yining
Ürümqi

TAJIKISTAN
Kashi
Shache
Hami

Tien Shan

Takla Makan Desert

PAKISTAN
Hotan
Dunhuang
Jiayugu

Kunlun Mountains
Altun Shan
Qaidam Pendi

Golmud

Plateau of Tibet

Mount Everest
8,848 m
(29,029 ft)

Xigaze
Lhasa

HIMALAYAS

BHUTAN

INDIA

MYANMAR

Industry and trade
China is one of the largest and fastest-growing economies in the world. It manufactures most goods for export but imports goods, too.

More than **one-fifth** of the people in the world live in China, making it the **most populated nation** on Earth. Officially known as the **People's Republic of China**, it is also the world's **third-largest country**. China has a **varied landscape** of desert, mountains, and plains, but the majority of its inhabitants live in **towns** and **big cities**.

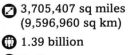

- 3,705,407 sq miles (9,596,960 sq km)
- 1.39 billion
- Beijing
- Mandarin, other languages (+6)

Chinese lanterns
Lanterns are featured in the decorations for Chinese New Year. The red stands for happiness and the gold signifies wealth.

0 250 km
0 250 miles
(approximate scale)

RUSSIA

MONGOLIA

Gobi

Hulun Buir (Hailar)
Qiqihar
Jiamusi
Ulanhot
Harbin
Jixi
Manchuria
Changchun
Tongliao
Jilin
Chifeng (Ulanhad)
Shenyeng
NORTH KOREA
Anshan
Jinzhou
Sea of Japan/ East Sea
Hohhot
gye
Baotou
BEIJING
Yinchuan
Yulin
Tianjin
Dalian
ei
Xining
Yellow River (Huang He)
Taiyuan
Shijiazhuang
Yantai
Lanzhou
Handan
Jinan
Qingdao
Zibo
Xi'an
Zhengzhou
Zaozhuang
Yellow Sea
Mianyang
Nanyang
Xuzhou
Nanchong
Huai'an
Sichuan Pendi
Three Gorges Dam
Huainan
Nanjing
Wuxi
gdu
Hefei
Yangtze (Chang Jiang)
Shanghai
Leshan
Wuhan
Suzhou
Ningbo
Yangtze
Guang'an
Hangzhou
Chongqing
Changsha
Nanchang
Wenzhou
Xuanwei
Pingxiang
Guiyang
Hengyang
East China Sea
Kunming
Fuzhou
Pearl River (Zhujiang)
Guilin
Gejiu
Shaoguan
Quanzhou
Laibin
Wuzhou
Xiamen
Nanning
Guangzhou
Dongguan
Shenzhen
TAIWAN
Zhanjiang
Hong Kong (S.A.R.)
VIETNAM
Hainan Dao
Haikou
South China Sea

Modern Shanghai
On the central coast of China lies Shanghai, a sprawling city known for industry and commerce. It is China's largest city.

Traditional opera
Since the 18th century, Chinese performers have used music, mime, and dance in their dramatic operatic plays.

The style of the headdress reveals information about the opera's characters—this is the crown of a noblewoman.

Fan Zhendong
Table tennis has been China's most popular sport since the 1950s, and Fan Zhendong is among its greatest players.

Geography: The **Yangtze** and the **Yellow Rivers** are the longest in China. To the north lies the **Gobi Desert**.

History: Until the Communist Revolution in 1949, China was **ruled by emperors** for **more than 4,000 years**.

Culture: The country is famous for **philosophy**, **architecture**, **martial arts**, and **visual arts**.

Food and drink: Rice, **noodles**, **meat**, **vegetables**, and **tea** are at the heart of Chinese cuisine.

Taiwan

Bubble tea
This popular drink was invented in Taiwan during the 1980s. It is a blend of milk, sugar, tea leaves, and tapioca balls, and it can come in many fruit flavors.

Rush-hour traffic
Motorbikes often outnumber cars in the storm of traffic that hits Taipei every morning and evening.

CHINA

Tanshui • Keelung
East China Sea
Chung-li • Keelung
Hsinchu •
Miaoli • **TAIPEI**
Kinmen Island
Taiwan Strait
T'aichung • Yilan
Changhua • Nantou
Hsueh Shan 3,884 m (12,743 ft)
Magong • Douliou • Hua-lien
P'enghu Islands
Chiaya •
T'ainan •
Kaohsiung • P'ingtung • T'ai-tung
Lü Tao
South China Sea
Lan Yü
Philippine Sea

0 — 30 km
0 — 30 miles
(approximate scale)
N

- 13,892 sq miles (35,980 sq km)
- 23.6 million
- Taipei
- Amoy Chinese, other languages (+2)

The **mountainous island** of Taiwan in the **Pacific Ocean** lies about 100 miles (160 km) off the southeastern coast of China. The country is famous for its **natural beauty** and the **fusion** of **different cultures**.

Ace students
Math and science are valued highly in Taiwan, and its students achieve some of the best scores in the world.

North Korea

No man's land
After a three-year war between North and South Korea, ending in 1953, a demilitarized zone was created between the two countries. Nature thrives in this 2.5-mile (4 km) strip of empty land.

Rhythmic gymnastics involves dance routines with balls.

0 — 50 km
0 — 50 miles
(approximate scale)

Paektu Mountain 2,744 m (9,002 ft)
Hoeryong • Rajin
Ch'ongjin •
CHINA
Manp'o • Hyesan
Kanggye • Kilchu
Ch'osan • Kimch'aek
Namsan-ni •
Sinuiju • Hamhung
Chongju • Hungnam
Anju • Yonghung
Sunch'on • Wonsan
P'YONGYANG
Yellow Sea
• Namp'o • Kosong
Sariwon •
Changyon • P'yongsan
Ongjin • Haeju • Kaesong
SOUTH KOREA
Sea of Japan / East Sea
N

Champion gymnasts
North Korea has won three Olympic gold medals for artistic gymnastics.

- 46,540 sq miles (120,538 sq km)
- 25.6 million
- Pyongyang
- Korean

North Korea separated from South Korea **after World War II.** The **border** between the countries was drawn across the middle of the **Korean peninsula** along **a line of latitude**.

South Korea

Sejong the Great
One of the most revered figures in Korean history, King Sejongdaewang was a brilliant scholar who ruled the nation in the 15th century.

The Hangul alphabet was introduced by King Sejongdaewang.

세 종 대 왕

Global pop
Korean pop (or K-pop) music has become hugely popular worldwide, with bands such as BTS (above) selling millions of singles and albums.

Delicious dish
The popular South Korean dish bibimbap is a mix of rice, vegetables, meat, and egg. It originated in the 15th century.

Lotus vase
Korea has a tradition of fine pottery and porcelain. Much was produced during the Goryeo Dynasty (918–1392 CE), including this ornate vase featuring a lotus flower.

Fighters must strike the colored areas of their opponent's body or head protector to score points.

Hats worn by military musicians are often decorated with bird feathers.

Map labels
NORTH KOREA
Sokcho
Chuncheon
Goyang
Bucheon
SEOUL
Gangneung
Incheon
Songnam
Ansan
Suwon
Wonju
Taebaek-sanmaek
Eumseong
Han
Cheongju
SEJONG CITY
Andong
Daejeon
Nakdong
Gunsan
Iksan
Pohang
Jeonju
Daegu
Gyeongju
Sobaek-sanmaek
Ulsan
Gwangju
Jinju
Changwon
Mokpo
Busan
Suncheon
Yeosu
Korea Strait
Yellow Sea
Sea of Japan / East Sea
Ulleung-do
Hallasan
1,947 m
(6,388 ft)
Jeju
Jeju Strait
Jeju-do
N

0   50 km
0   50 miles
(approximate scale)

Tae Kwon Do
The national sport of South Korea is Tae Kwon Do. Competitors are allowed to use both their hands and feet during matches. This ancient martial art was invented to help soldiers prepare for battle.

Marching music
Daechwita *is a traditional form of military marching music that uses instruments such as drums, brass horns, and gongs. It accompanies the ceremonial changing of the guards at the country's royal palaces.*

A yonggo is a barrel drum decorated with painted dragons.

- ⤢ 38,502 sq miles (99,720 sq km)
- 👥 51.8 million
- ★ Seoul
- ⬤ Korean

On the bottom half of a peninsula jutting out between the **Sea of Japan** and the **Yellow Sea**, South Korea is **one of Asia's biggest economies**, with booming businesses in **electronics** and **car manufacturing**.

Japan

The red disc stands for the sun and represents Japan as "the land of the rising sun."

Mount Fuji
At 12,390 ft (3,776 m) high, Mount Fuji is the country's tallest peak. This active volcano, which last erupted in 1707, is a sacred site.

Origami
The art of folding paper into imaginative shapes is called origami. Millions enjoy this artistic activity.

Earthquake drill
Japan has more than 75 active volcanoes, and one in five of all major earthquakes occurs here. Regular earthquake evacuation drills help school children learn what to do in the event of an emergency.

Traditional sweets
Japanese people enjoy eating handcrafted sweets called wagashi, *made from fruit, grains, and sugar.*

Torii gates are often painted bright red to ward off evil spirits.

Torii gate
This iconic gateway is seen all over Japan, marking the entrances to sacred shrines. Some shrines have more than one torii *gate.*

Pacific territories
Hundreds of inhabited and uninhabited islands belonging to Japan are scattered around a vast area of the Pacific Ocean and East China Sea.

Sea of Japan/ East Sea

Toyama
Kanazawa
Fukui
HONSHU
Gifu
Oki-shoto   Dogo
Dozen   Yonago   Tottori   Maizuru   Nagoya
Matsue   Kyoto   Otsu   Tsu
Chugoku-sanchi   Kobe   Osaka   Nara
Hamada   Okayama   Awajishima
Hiroshima   Takamatsu   Wakayama
Yamaguchi   Matsuyama   Tokushima
Shikoku-sanchi   Kochi
Kitakyushu   SHIKOKU
Fukuoka
Saga   Oita
Sasebo   KYUSHU
Nagasaki   Kumamoto
Kyushu-sanchi
Miyazaki
Kagoshima

SOUTH KOREA
Korea Strait
Tsushima
East China Sea
Goto-retto

Osumi-shoto

TOKYO
0   100 km
0   100 miles (approximate scale)
O-shima
Miyake-jima
Hachijo-jima
Aoga-shima
Izu-shoto
Tori-shima
N
PACIFIC OCEAN
Philippine Sea
Mukojima-retto
Chichijima-retto
Hahajima-retto
Kita-Io-jima
Io-jima
Minami-Io-jima
Ogasawara-shoto
Kazan-retto

0   100 km
0   100 miles (approximate scale)
East China Sea
Kagoshima
Osumi-shoto
Ryukyu Islands (Nansei-shoto)
Amami-O-shima
Naze
Tokuno-shima
Okinawa   Amami-gunto
Sakishima-shoto
Naha
Iriomote-jima   Okinawa-shoto
Ishigaki-jima   Miyako-jima   Philippine Sea   N

The **island country** of Japan celebrates the old and the new. **Ancient traditions** are honored as an important part of everyday life, while the nation still maintains its position as a **world leader** in **cutting-edge technology**. Japan is one of the world's **richest countries**, and its people enjoy a **high standard of living**.

- 145,913 sq miles (377,915 sq km)
- 125.5 million
- Tokyo
- Japanese

RUSSIA

Kuril
Islands

Sea of
Okhotsk

La Perouse Strait

Asahikawa
Kitami
Kushiro

HOKKAIDO

Sapporo
Obihiro

Hakodate

Hirosaki
Aomori
Iwate

Akita
Morioka

Sakata

Yamagata
Sendai

Niigata
Fukushima

Iwaki

gaoka
Utsunomiya
Hitachi

Oyama
Mito

Maebashi
Saitama

atsumoto
Kawasaki
TOKYO

Kofu
Chiba

Yokohama

Fuji

zuoka

namatsu

Mount Fuji
3,776 m
(12,388 ft)

PACIFIC
OCEAN

Ou-sanmyaku

Mikuni-sanmyaku

Izu-shoto

0   75 km
0   75 miles
(approximate scale)

*Japanese robot
ASIMO can
open doors, lift
objects, and
play soccer.*

ASIMO

HONDA

Robotics
*Japanese scientists
have developed robots
capable of moving
like humans.*

Cherry blossom
*Nature is celebrated
in Japan, with crowds
of people flocking to local
parks to view the pretty
pink cherry blossoms in
bloom every spring.*

Kimono
*For special occasions,
such as weddings and
temple visits, the kimono
is worn. Both men and
women wear this
formal clothing.*

日本

Calligraphy
Shodo, *a form of
calligraphy, is the
creation of decorative
symbols and lettering
by brush or pen. This
Japanese art form
dates back centuries.*

Capital city
*Tokyo is the world's
largest urban area,
with more than
35 million people.*

Japanese macaques
Monkeys called macaques *grow thick
fur to keep warm in snowy northern
Japan and even bathe in hot springs
to escape the freezing temperatures.*

Geography: Japan consists
of many **islands** on the
Pacific Ocean. Three-quarters of
the landscape is **mountainous**.

History: The earliest settlers
arrived about **30,000 years ago**.
Over the centuries, Japan has seen
both **imperial** and **military** rule.

Culture: From **calligraphy**,
poetry, and **theater** to **bonsai**,
origami, and **martial arts**, a wide
variety of customs and traditions
is at the heart of Japanese culture.

Natural wonders: More than
100 volcanoes dot the country.
The most famous is **Mount Fuji**.

Wildlife: Much of Japan is
covered in **forests**—a haven
for wildlife such as **macaques**,
bears, **squirrels**, and **wild boar**.

Food and drink: People eat
a healthy **diet rich in fish**. Japan
is known for its **green tea**, consumed
without milk.

Malaysia

Taking flight
Kite flying is popular in Malaysia. The wau bulan, meaning "moon kite," is a large kite with a bamboo frame and floral decorations.

The art of defense
A traditional Malaysian martial art, called Silat Melayu, *helps develop self-defense techniques. Many children learn it at school.*

Bare hands or weapons can both be used for this martial art.

Giant bloom
The world's biggest flower belongs to a plant called rafflesia, *found in some parts of Malaysia. It can reach 3 ft (1 m) wide and produces a foul smell to attract insects.*

THAILAND

Kota Bharu
George Town
Taiping
Ipoh
Teluk Intan
Kuala Terengganu
Taman Negara
Kuantan
KUALA LUMPUR
PUTRAJAYA
Klang
Melaka
Johor Bahru
SINGAPORE
INDONESIA
Malay Peninsula
Strait of Malacca

Noisy caller
Malaysia's national bird, the rhinoceros hornbill is recognized by its bright beak and a hollow hornlike structure on its head that amplifies its song.

Indonesia

Marine life
The Raja Ampat coral reef north of Sorong in New Guinea is home to whales and dolphins, more than 500 species of coral, and thousands of different fish.

Medan
Pematangsiantar
SINGAPORE
Singkawang
Pegunu
Pekanbaru
Pontianak
Borne
Padang
Jambi
Banjarmasi
Palembang
Sumatra
Pegunungan Barisan
N
MALAYS
Java Se
Serang
JAKARTA
Bandung
Semarang
Bogor
Java
Surab
Yogyakarta
Malang
Denpas
INDIAN OCEAN

Shadow puppetry
Used in traditional Indonesian storytelling, these puppets cast dramatic shadows when held in front of a screen and lit from behind. Puppeteers use rods to animate the characters.

- 735,358 sq miles (1,904,569 sq km)
- 267 million
- Jakarta
- Javanese, Sundanese, other languages (+3)

The **largest country** in Southeast Asia, Indonesia consists of **13,466 islands** across 3,100 miles (5,000 km) of sea. Most people live on the **island of Java**.

Taman Negara Park
Visitors can climb a ropeway to explore the canopy of one of the world's oldest deciduous rain forests at this enormous national park on the Malay Peninsula.

Stinky fruit
The durian is an unusual fruit with a smell so bad that it is banned on public transportation in Malaysia.

A spiky outer shell protects the soft, yellowish flesh of the fruit.

Gunung Kinabalu
4,101 m
(13,454 ft)
Kota Kinabalu
Sandakan
Sulu Sea
BRUNEI
Miri
South China Sea
Bintulu
Baram
Banjaran Crocker
Sibu
Kuching
Rajang
Borneo
INDONESIA

0 100 km
0 100 miles
(approximate scale)

N

Petronas Towers
The world's tallest twin towers are the Petronas Towers in Kuala Lumpur. With a height of 1,483 ft (452 m), these skyscrapers both have 88 floors.

- 127,354 sq miles (329,847 sq km)
- 32.6 million
- Kuala Lumpur
- Bahasa Malaysia, Malay, other languages (+3)

This **tropical, Southeast Asian country** is made up of the **Malay Peninsula** and **part of the island of Borneo**. Malaysia is known for its popular **beaches**, lush **rain forests**, and large **multicultural cities**.

Sensational satay
Among Indonesia's favorite dishes is skewered and grilled meat called satay, *served with a delicious peanut sauce.*

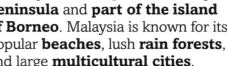

Rain forest rover
The island of Sumatra is home to the Sumatran Orangutan, a critically endangered primate. It spends most of its time in the trees and sleeps in a nest of branches.

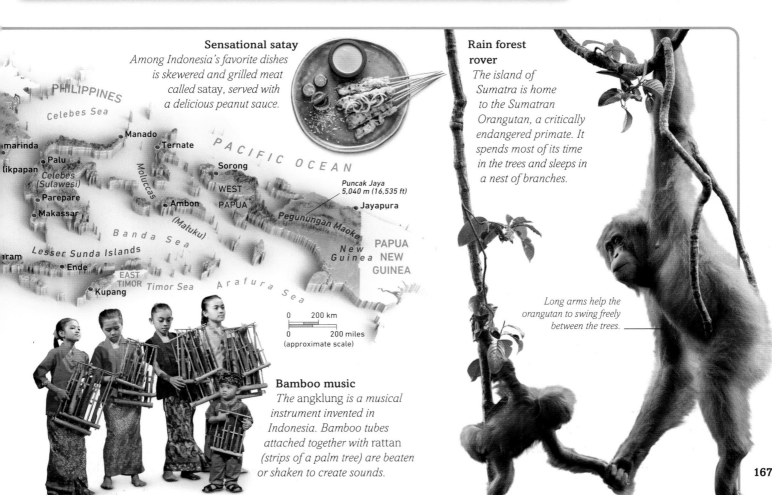

PHILIPPINES
Celebes Sea
Manado
marinda
Palu
Ternate
Sorong
PACIFIC OCEAN
likpapan
Celebes (Sulawesi)
Moluccas
WEST PAPUA
Puncak Jaya
5,040 m (16,535 ft)
Parepare
Ambon
PAPUA
Jayapura
Makassar
(Maluku)
Pegunungan Maoke
Banda Sea
aram
Lesser Sunda Islands
New Guinea
PAPUA NEW GUINEA
Ende
EAST TIMOR
Timor Sea
Arafura Sea
Kupang

0 200 km
0 200 miles
(approximate scale)

Long arms help the orangutan to swing freely between the trees.

Bamboo music
The angklung *is a musical instrument invented in Indonesia. Bamboo tubes attached together with* rattan *(strips of a palm tree) are beaten or shaken to create sounds.*

Singapore

Marina Bay Sands is a luxury hotel.

Bumboat travel
Brightly colored bumboats cruise the Singapore River, providing a water taxi service or taking tourists on trips.

Street food
The lively streets of Singapore are known for food stalls that serve a broad range of local dishes and international cuisine.

Mouse deer
At only 18 in (45 cm) tall, the mouse deer of Singapore is the world's smallest hoofed mammal.

N

MALAYSIA

Causeway

Sungai Buloh
Choa Chu Kang
Bukit Panjang
Jurong West
Jurong East
Tuas

Woodlands
Sembawang
Seletar Reservoir
Yishun
Bukit Timah Hill 182 m (597 ft)
Bukit Timah
SINGAPORE CITY
Queenstown
Telok Blangah

Punggol
Pulau Ubin
Serangoon
Bedok
Katong

Changi
Singapore Changi International Airport

Pulau Tekong

MALAYSIA

South China Sea

Pulau Jurong
Pandan Strait
Pulau Sudong
Pulau Pawai
Pulau Senang
Strait of Singapore

Pulau Bukum
Pulau Semakau
Sentosa
Pulau Sebarok

Strait of Singapore

Johore Strait

0   6 km
0   6 miles
(approximate scale)

⊘ **277 sq miles (719 sq km)**

👥 **6.2 million**

★ **Singapore**

◯ **Mandarin, Malay, Tamil, English**

A **bridge** connects this **tropical island country** in Southeast Asia to mainland Malaysia. Singapore is a **city-state** and a prosperous center of **finance** and **industry**.

Gardens by the Bay
Opened in 2012, this award-winning nature park of gardens and greenhouses is a star attraction in Singapore.

Buddha Tooth Relic Temple
This statue of the Buddha is displayed in a temple that also holds a tooth believed to be from the Buddha himself.

The Buddha is the founder of Buddhism.

The park features illuminated structures that reach up to 164 ft (50 m).

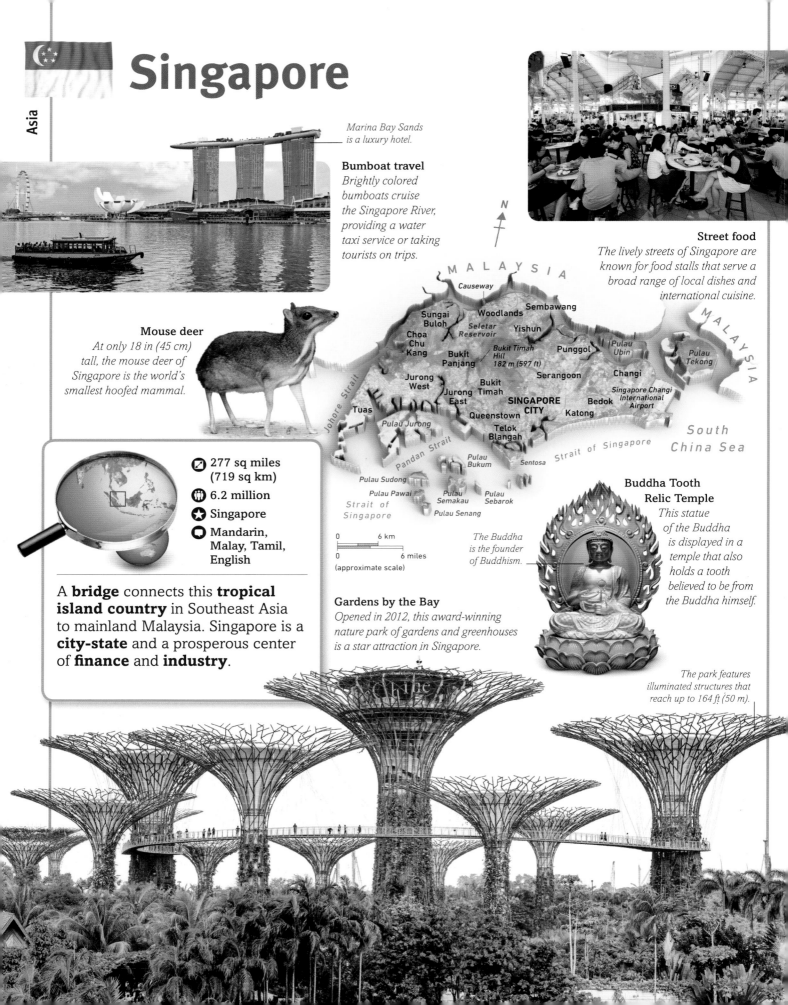

Brunei

- ⬈ 2,226 sq miles (5,765 sq km)
- 👥 464,480
- ★ Bandar Seri Begawan
- ⬭ Malay, English, Chinese

Despite being among the smallest, Brunei is **one of the richest nations** on Earth because of its plentiful **oil** and **gas** reserves. The **Sultan (ruler) of Brunei** is one of the world's **wealthiest** people.

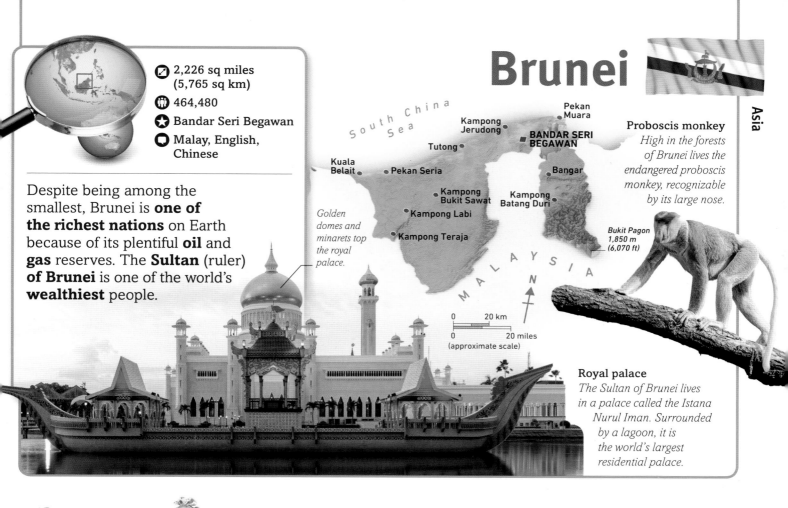

South China Sea

Kuala Belait
Pekan Seria
Tutong
Kampong Jerudong
BANDAR SERI BEGAWAN
Pekan Muara
Kampong Bukit Sawat
Kampong Labi
Kampong Teraja
Kampong Batang Duri
Bangar

Golden domes and minarets top the royal palace.

M A L A Y S I A

Bukit Pagon 1,850 m (6,070 ft)

0 20 km
0 20 miles
(approximate scale)

Proboscis monkey
High in the forests of Brunei lives the endangered proboscis monkey, recognizable by its large nose.

Royal palace
The Sultan of Brunei lives in a palace called the Istana Nurul Iman. Surrounded by a lagoon, it is the world's largest residential palace.

Timor-Leste

Traditional clothing
Tais *cloth is the traditional textile of Timor-Leste. These children are wearing golden headdresses and colorful sarongs called* tais mane.

Pulau Atauro
Ombai Strait
Wetar Strait
Liquica
DILI
Manatuto
Baucau
Tutuala
Laleia
Lospalos
Tatamailau 2,986 m (9,797 ft)
Maliana
Viqueque
I N D O N E S I A
Pante Makassar
Same
Suai
T i m o r   S e a

0 20 km
0 20 miles
(approximate scale)

Sacred huts
All over Timor-Leste, people visit sacred huts that stand as prayer houses and special places to remember their ancestors.

- ⬈ 5,743 sq miles (14,874 sq km)
- 👥 1.4 million
- ★ Dili
- ⬭ Tetum, Bahasa Indonesia, Portuguese

Timor-Leste sits on the eastern side of the **island of Timor**. **Dili** is the **capital** and **largest city**. The country has a tropical climate and a landscape of **mountains**, **grasslands**, and **coral reefs**.

MARSHALL ISLANDS

M i c r o n e s i a

K

Northern
Mariana
Islands
(to US)

Philippine Sea

Guam
(to US)

Caroline Islands

Pohnpei

Kosrae

Tungaru

MICRONESIA

M e l a n e s i a

NAURU

Bismarck Sea

New Ireland

Santa Cruz Islands

PALAU

New Britain

Solomon Sea

SOLOMON ISLANDS

VANUAT

ASIA

PAPUA NEW GUINEA

Coral Sea

New Caledonia (to France)

Gulf of Carpentaria

Great Barrier Reef

Joseph Bonaparte Gulf

Arnhem Land

QUEENSLAND

Timor Sea

Tanami Desert

AUSTRALIA

Darling

INDIAN OCEAN

Great Sandy Desert

NORTHERN
TERRITORY

Simpson Desert

Lake Eyre
North

NEW SOUTH WALES

AUSTRALIA
CAPITAL
TERRITORY

Gibson Desert

SOUTH
AUSTRALIA

Lake
Torrens

Great Dividing Range

Hamersley Range

WESTERN
AUSTRALIA

Great Victoria Desert

Nullarbor Plain

Murray

VICTORIA

Bass Strait

Tasman Sea

Tasmania

TASMANIA

Great Australian Bight

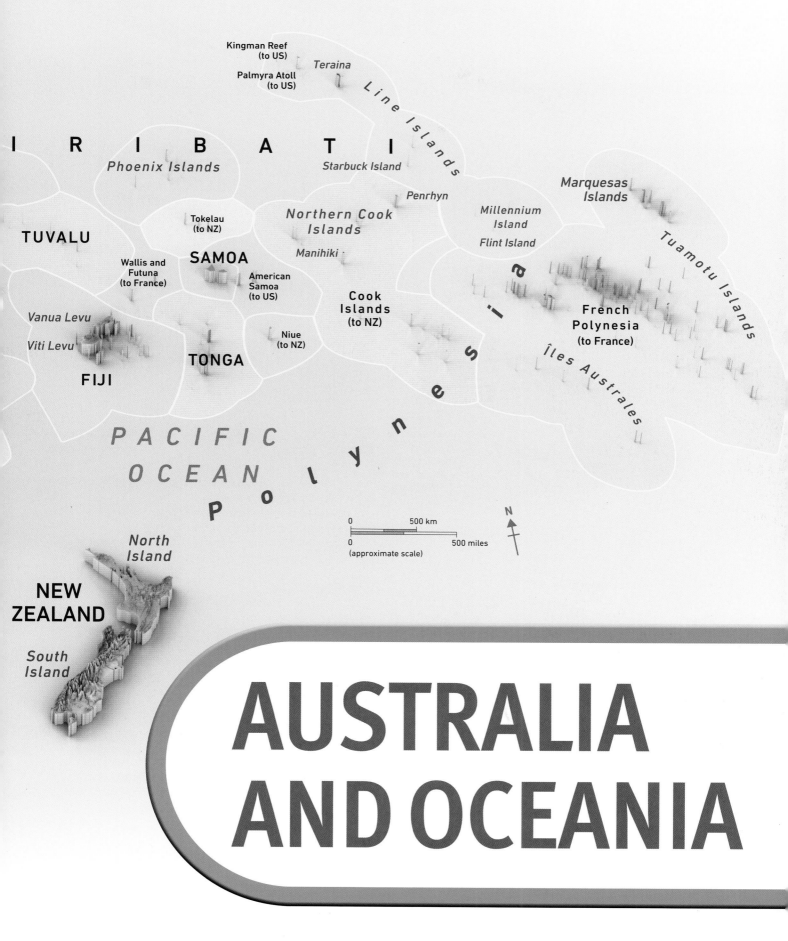

PACIFIC OCEAN

Kingman Reef
(to US)

Palmyra Atoll
(to US)

Teraina

Line Islands

KIRIBATI

Phoenix Islands

Starbuck Island

Marquesas
Islands

Penrhyn

Tuamotu Islands

TUVALU

Tokelau
(to NZ)

Northern Cook
Islands

Millennium
Island

Flint Island

Wallis and
Futuna
(to France)

SAMOA

American
Samoa
(to US)

Manihiki

Cook
Islands
(to NZ)

P o l y n e s i a

French
Polynesia
(to France)

Vanua Levu

Viti Levu

Niue
(to NZ)

FIJI

TONGA

Îles Australes

PACIFIC

OCEAN

P o l y n e s i a

0   500 km
0   500 miles
(approximate scale)

N

North
Island

NEW
ZEALAND

South
Island

AUSTRALIA AND OCEANIA

Australia

Flying doctors
Medics take to the skies in light aircraft to provide emergency care to people living in remote regions of the Outback.

Map labels: Timor Sea, Bathurst Island, Darw, Kimberley Plateau, Broome, Port Hedland, Karratha, Great Sandy Desert, Hamersley Range, Exmouth, Gibson Desert, Uluru (Ayers Rock) 863 m (2,831 ft), Barlee Range, WESTERN AUSTRALIA, Denham, Shark Bay, Musgrave Ranges, Kalbarri, Great Victoria Deser, Geraldton, INDIAN OCEAN, Kalgoorlie, Nullarbor Plain, Perth, Fremantle, Mandurah, Busselton, Great Australian Bight, Albany

Paradise for beachgoers
Millions of surfers flock to the Gold Coast and Sunshine Coast in the east to ride the waves.

Road train
Long trucks called "road trains" haul supplies vast distances across Australia. Some measure more than 164 ft (50 m) long.

Indigenous art
For centuries, Aboriginal artists have painted elements from their sacred tales called dreamtime stories. *The artist June Smith stands in front of her work* Flowers After the Rain.

Sacred rock
At the heart of Australia, near the remote town of Alice Springs, lies Uluru, an ancient sandstone rock sacred to the Aboriginal people. During sunrise and sunset, the sunlight gives it a reddish glow.

Australia is the **biggest island** on Earth. Situated in the southern hemisphere, it is the **largest nation** in Oceania and the **world's sixth-largest country**. Much of Australia is **desert**, so people live in coastal **towns** and **cities**. The **hot**, **dry areas** in the interior are known as the **Outback**.

- 2,988,901 sq miles (7,741,220 sq km)
- 25.5 million
- Canberra
- English, other languages (+6)

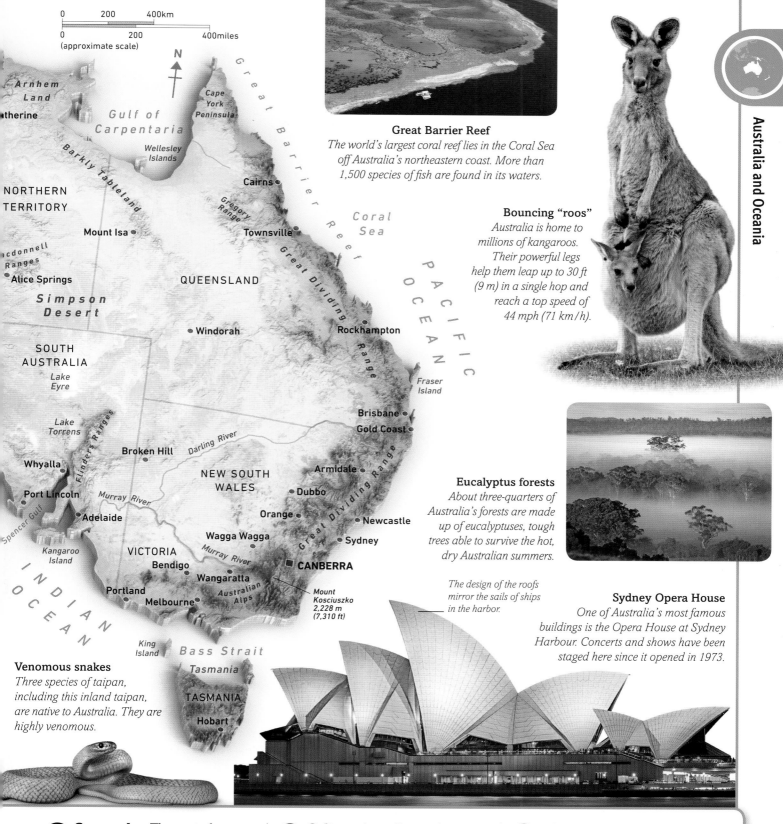

Great Barrier Reef

The world's largest coral reef lies in the Coral Sea off Australia's northeastern coast. More than 1,500 species of fish are found in its waters.

Bouncing "roos"

Australia is home to millions of kangaroos. Their powerful legs help them leap up to 30 ft (9 m) in a single hop and reach a top speed of 44 mph (71 km/h).

Eucalyptus forests

About three-quarters of Australia's forests are made up of eucalyptuses, tough trees able to survive the hot, dry Australian summers.

The design of the roofs mirror the sails of ships in the harbor.

Sydney Opera House

One of Australia's most famous buildings is the Opera House at Sydney Harbour. Concerts and shows have been staged here since it opened in 1973.

Venomous snakes

Three species of taipan, including this inland taipan, are native to Australia. They are highly venomous.

Map labels:

200 400km
(approximate scale)
200 400miles
N

Arnhem Land
Katherine
Gulf of Carpentaria
Cape York Peninsula
Wellesley Islands
Barkly Tableland
Great Barrier Reef
NORTHERN TERRITORY
Mount Isa
Macdonnell Ranges
Alice Springs
Simpson Desert
SOUTH AUSTRALIA
Lake Eyre
Lake Torrens
Flinders Ranges
Broken Hill
Whyalla
Port Lincoln
Spencer Gulf
Adelaide
Kangaroo Island
INDIAN OCEAN
Portland
Melbourne
VICTORIA
Bendigo
Wangaratta
Australian Alps
King Island
Bass Strait
Tasmania
TASMANIA
Hobart
Cairns
Gregory Range
Townsville
Coral Sea
QUEENSLAND
Great Dividing Range
Windorah
Rockhampton
PACIFIC OCEAN
Fraser Island
Brisbane
Gold Coast
Darling River
NEW SOUTH WALES
Armidale
Dubbo
Murray River
Orange
Newcastle
Wagga Wagga
Sydney
Murray River
CANBERRA
Mount Kosciuszko 2,228 m (7,310 ft)

Geography: The central **desert region** is edged by **grasslands**, **rain forests**, **mountains**, and **beaches**.

History: The **indigenous Australian Aboriginals** were the first people to arrive and settle in Australia more than 50,000 years ago.

Culture: Australians enjoy adventures in the **great outdoors** and the **water** and are a great **sporting nation**.

Natural wonders: The dramatic landscape ranges from the **Great Barrier Reef** to the **Great Dividing Range**.

Wildlife: Marsupials (animals that raise young in pouches), such as **kangaroos** and **koalas**, are **unique** to Australia.

Food and drink: Australian food is as **multicultural** as its people, with a **mix of local**, **Asian**, and **Mediterranean** dishes.

Papua New Guinea

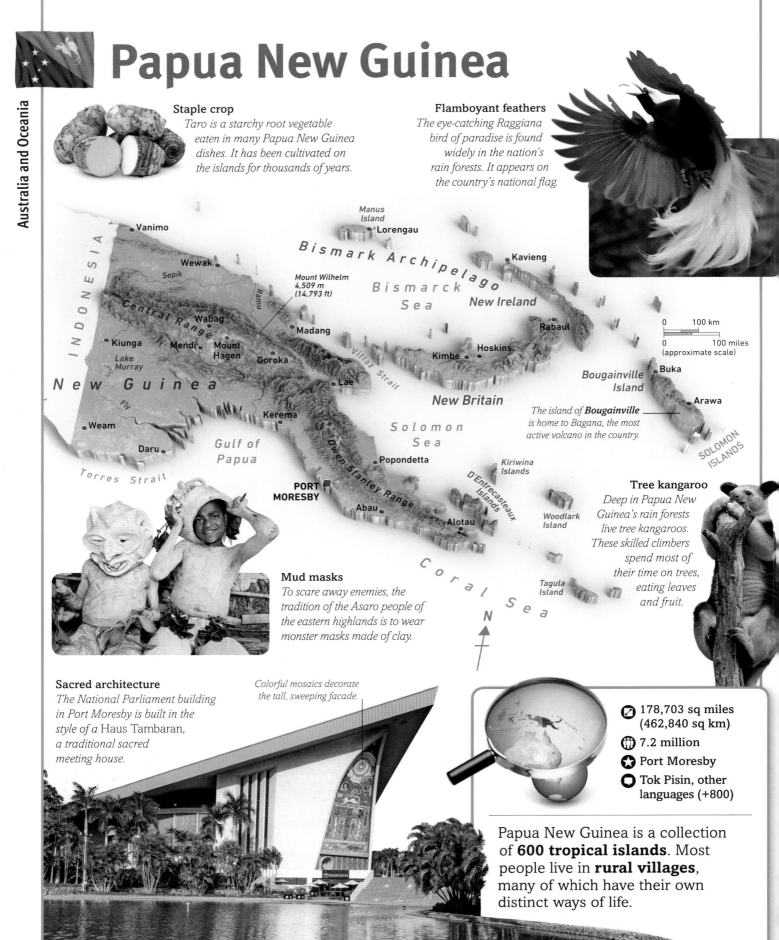

Staple crop
Taro is a starchy root vegetable eaten in many Papua New Guinea dishes. It has been cultivated on the islands for thousands of years.

Flamboyant feathers
The eye-catching Raggiana bird of paradise is found widely in the nation's rain forests. It appears on the country's national flag.

INDONESIA

Vanimo

Wewak

Sepik

Central Range

Ramu

Mount Wilhelm
4,509 m
(14,793 ft)

Wabag

Kiunga

Mendi

Mount Hagen

Lake Murray

Goroka

Madang

New Guinea

Fly

Weam

Daru

Kerema

Lae

Gulf of Papua

Torres Strait

PORT MORESBY

Abau

Owen Stanley Range

Popondetta

Manus Island

Lorengau

Bismark Archipelago

Kavieng

Bismarck Sea

New Ireland

Rabaul

Vittaz Strait

Kimbe

Hoskins

New Britain

Solomon Sea

Kiriwina Islands

D'Entrecasteaux Islands

Alotau

Woodlark Island

Tagula Island

Coral Sea

N

Buka

Bougainville Island

Arawa

SOLOMON ISLANDS

*The island of **Bougainville** is home to Bagana, the most active volcano in the country.*

0   100 km
0   100 miles
(approximate scale)

Tree kangaroo
Deep in Papua New Guinea's rain forests live tree kangaroos. These skilled climbers spend most of their time on trees, eating leaves and fruit.

Mud masks
To scare away enemies, the tradition of the Asaro people of the eastern highlands is to wear monster masks made of clay.

Sacred architecture
The National Parliament building in Port Moresby is built in the style of a Haus Tambaran, *a traditional sacred meeting house.*

Colorful mosaics decorate the tall, sweeping facade.

- 178,703 sq miles (462,840 sq km)
- 7.2 million
- Port Moresby
- Tok Pisin, other languages (+800)

Papua New Guinea is a collection of **600 tropical islands**. Most people live in **rural villages**, many of which have their own distinct ways of life.

New Zealand

This ornate, hand-painted wooden carving of Tangaroa, the Māori god of the sea, is on display in Auckland.

Dairy farming
New Zealand is one of the world's biggest dairy producers. Millions of cows graze in pastures across the country.

Beloved bird
Native to New Zealand, the flightless kiwi bird is the unofficial national symbol.

Extreme sports
Thrill seekers can enjoy a variety of extreme sports in the great outdoors. These include skydiving, white-water rafting, and bungee jumping.

0 | 100 km
0 | 100 miles
(approximate scale)

Māori carvings
The Māori are Polynesian settlers who first arrived in New Zealand in the 14th century. Their carvings are treasured artifacts.

The team performs the ceremonial Māori dance called the haka *before the start of every game.*

New Zealand All Blacks
The country's national sport is rugby. The national team, known as the All Blacks, has won the rugby union World Cup three times.

Milford Sound
Mountains and rain forest surround this fjord (deep sea inlet) in South Island. Dolphins and seals swim in its waters.

Map labels

Kaitaia
Whangarei
Great Barrier Island
Auckland
Hamilton
Tauranga
Bay of Plenty
Rotorua
Lake Taupo
Taupo
North Island
New Plymouth
Raukumara Range
Gisborne
Wanganui
Rangitikei
Napier
Hastings
Palmerston North
Lower Hutt
WELLINGTON
Nelson
Tasman Bay
Blenheim
Cook Strait
Tasman Sea
Aoraki (Mount Cook) 3,724 m (12,218 ft)
Greymouth
Hanmer Springs
Waipara
Southern Alps
Waitaki
Christchurch
Pegasus Bay
Milford Sound
Timaru
Fiordland
Queenstown
Oamaru
South Island
PACIFIC OCEAN
Gore
Dunedin
Invercargill
Stewart Island
N

- 103,798 sq miles (268,838 sq km)
- 4.9 million
- Wellington
- English, Māori

Two islands in the Pacific Ocean make up New Zealand. Its landscape is a mix of stunning **coastline**, active **volcanoes**, and fertile **farmland**. There are **30 million sheep** here—which far outnumber the people.

Palau

Palau is a nation of **more than 300 islands** in the western Pacific Ocean. Many Palauans make a living from **tourism**, **agriculture**, or **fishing**.

- ⬕ 177 sq miles (459 sq km)
- 👥 21,700
- ⭐ Ngerulmud
- ⬤ Palauan, English, other languages (+4)

Built in 1890, Airai Bai is a traditional Palauan men's meeting house.

Marshall Islands

Just **north** of the **equator** in the Pacific Ocean, this chain of **coral atolls** and more than 1,000 **islets** teems with **marine life**.

- ⬕ 70 sq miles (181 sq km)
- 👥 77,900
- ⭐ Majuro
- ⬤ Marshallese, English, other languages (+2)

Copra (dried coconut kernel) and coconut oil are exported by the islands.

Nauru

This **rocky island** nation has to import most of its **food**, **water**, and **other goods** from abroad.

- ⬕ 8 sq miles (21 sq km)
- 👥 11,000
- ⭐ Yaren
- ⬤ Nauruan, Kiribati, other languages (+3)

Nauruan Itte Detenamo is an international medal-winning weight lifter.

Federated States of Micronesia

The **600 islands** of this tropical country fall into two types: **forested volcanic islands** and **coral atolls**. Many Micronesians make a living from **fishing**.

- ⬕ 271 sq miles (702 sq km)
- 👥 102,450
- ⭐ Palikir
- ⬤ Trukese, other languages (+4)

Spicy peppercorns are grown on the island of Pohnpei.

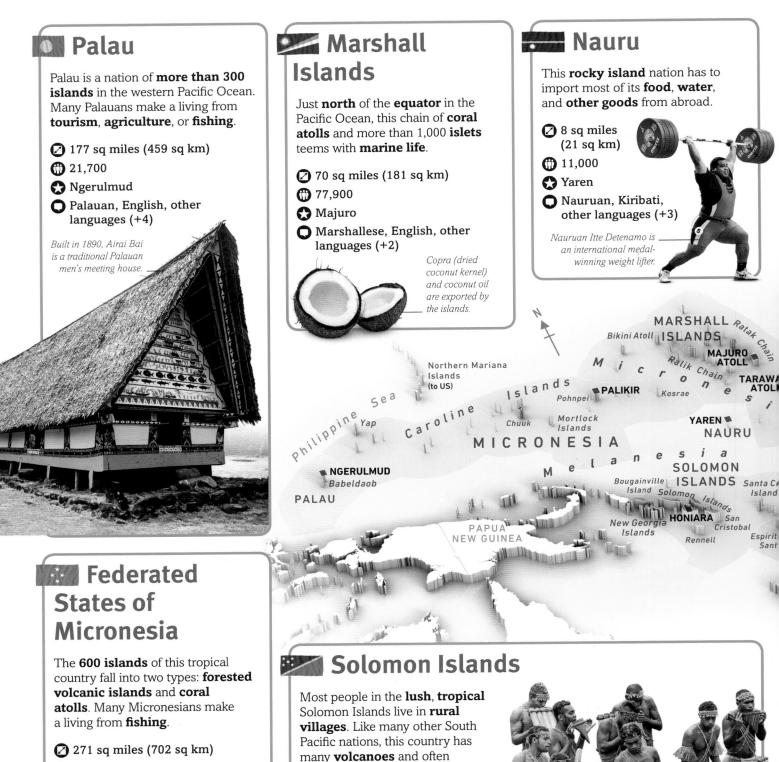

MARSHALL ISLANDS · Ratak Chain · Bikini Atoll · MAJURO ATOLL · Ralik Chain · TARAWA ATOLL

Northern Mariana Islands (to US) · PALIKIR · Pohnpei · Kosrae

Philippine Sea · Yap · Caroline Islands · Chuuk · Mortlock Islands · Micronesia · YAREN · NAURU

NGERULMUD · Babeldaob · PALAU · MICRONESIA · Melanesia · SOLOMON ISLANDS · Santa C... Island

PAPUA NEW GUINEA · Bougainville Island · Solomon Islands · New Georgia Islands · HONIARA · San Cristobal · Rennell · Espirit Sant... · New Georgia Islands

Solomon Islands

Most people in the **lush**, **tropical** Solomon Islands live in **rural villages**. Like many other South Pacific nations, this country has many **volcanoes** and often experiences **earthquakes** and **cyclones**.

Solomon Island bands play traditional music on bamboo instruments.

- ⬕ 11,157 sq miles (28,896 sq km)
- 👥 685,100
- ⭐ Honiara
- ⬤ English, Pidgin English, other languages (+121)

Tuvalu

White terns inhabit the Tuvalu islands.

Tuvalu is made up of **nine tiny Pacific Islands**. Around **half of the population** lives in **Funafuti**, where the government is based.

- ⤢ 10 sq miles (26 sq km)
- 👥 11,350
- ★ Funafuti
- ⬭ Tuvaluan, Kiribati, English

Kiribati

The **33 islands** of Kiribati are low-lying, making them at **risk of floods** due to **rising sea levels** caused by **climate change**.

- ⤢ 313 sq miles (811 sq km)
- 👥 111,800
- ★ Tarawa
- ⬭ English, Kiribati

Lava-lava—pieces of cloth wrapped around the waist like a sarong—are worn on Kiribati and other South Pacific islands.

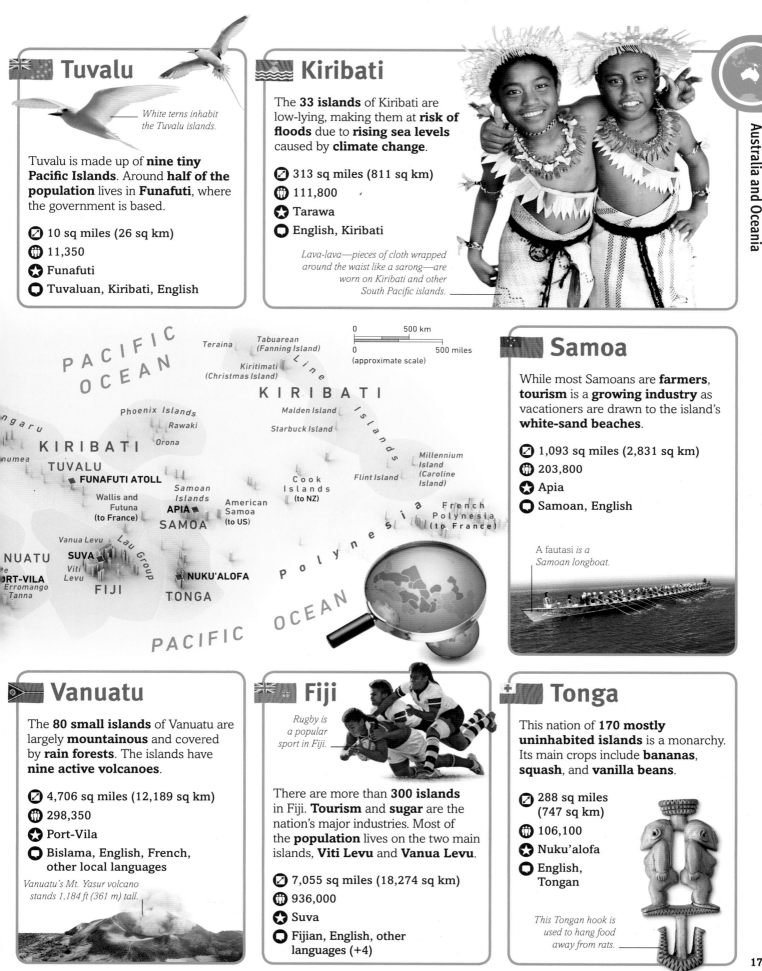

Samoa

While most Samoans are **farmers**, **tourism** is a **growing industry** as vacationers are drawn to the island's **white-sand beaches**.

- ⤢ 1,093 sq miles (2,831 sq km)
- 👥 203,800
- ★ Apia
- ⬭ Samoan, English

A fautasi is a Samoan longboat.

Vanuatu

The **80 small islands** of Vanuatu are largely **mountainous** and covered by **rain forests**. The islands have **nine active volcanoes**.

- ⤢ 4,706 sq miles (12,189 sq km)
- 👥 298,350
- ★ Port-Vila
- ⬭ Bislama, English, French, other local languages

Vanuatu's Mt. Yasur volcano stands 1,184 ft (361 m) tall.

Fiji

Rugby is a popular sport in Fiji.

There are more than **300 islands** in Fiji. **Tourism** and **sugar** are the nation's major industries. Most of the **population** lives on the two main islands, **Viti Levu** and **Vanua Levu**.

- ⤢ 7,055 sq miles (18,274 sq km)
- 👥 936,000
- ★ Suva
- ⬭ Fijian, English, other languages (+4)

Tonga

This nation of **170 mostly uninhabited islands** is a monarchy. Its main crops include **bananas**, **squash**, and **vanilla beans**.

- ⤢ 288 sq miles (747 sq km)
- 👥 106,100
- ★ Nuku'alofa
- ⬭ English, Tongan

This Tongan hook is used to hang food away from rats.

Map labels:
PACIFIC OCEAN
Teraina
Tabuarean (Fanning Island)
Kiritimati (Christmas Island)
Line Islands
KIRIBATI
Malden Island
Starbuck Island
Millennium Island (Caroline Island)
Flint Island
Phoenix Islands
Rawaki
Orona
ngaru
KIRIBATI
numea
TUVALU
FUNAFUTI ATOLL
Wallis and Futuna (to France)
Samoan Islands
APIA
SAMOA
American Samoa (to US)
Cook Islands (to NZ)
French Polynesia (to France)
Vanua Levu
Lau Group
NUATU
SUVA
Viti Levu
RT-VILA
Erromango
Tanna
FIJI
NUKU'ALOFA
TONGA
Polynesia
PACIFIC OCEAN

0   500 km
0   500 miles
(approximate scale)

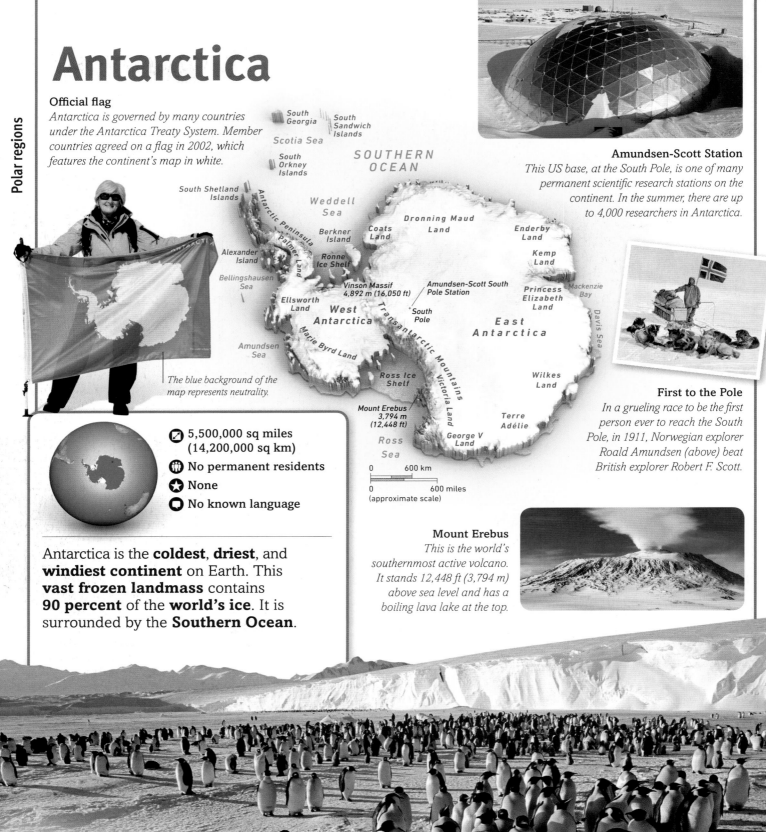

Antarctica

Official flag
Antarctica is governed by many countries under the Antarctica Treaty System. Member countries agreed on a flag in 2002, which features the continent's map in white.

The blue background of the map represents neutrality.

Amundsen-Scott Station
This US base, at the South Pole, is one of many permanent scientific research stations on the continent. In the summer, there are up to 4,000 researchers in Antarctica.

First to the Pole
In a grueling race to be the first person ever to reach the South Pole, in 1911, Norwegian explorer Roald Amundsen (above) beat British explorer Robert F. Scott.

Mount Erebus
This is the world's southernmost active volcano. It stands 12,448 ft (3,794 m) above sea level and has a boiling lava lake at the top.

- ⤢ 5,500,000 sq miles (14,200,000 sq km)
- 👥 No permanent residents
- ★ None
- ⬭ No known language

Antarctica is the **coldest**, **driest**, and **windiest continent** on Earth. This **vast frozen landmass** contains **90 percent** of the **world's ice**. It is surrounded by the **Southern Ocean**.

SOUTHERN OCEAN
South Georgia, South Sandwich Islands, Scotia Sea, South Orkney Islands, South Shetland Islands, Weddell Sea, Antarctic Peninsula, Palmer Land, Alexander Island, Bellingshausen Sea, Ellsworth Land, West Antarctica, Amundsen Sea, Marie Byrd Land, Berkner Island, Ronne Ice Shelf, Coats Land, Dronning Maud Land, Enderby Land, Kemp Land, Princess Elizabeth Land, Mackenzie Bay, Vinson Massif 4,892 m (16,050 ft), Amundsen-Scott South Pole Station, South Pole, East Antarctica, Davis Sea, Transantarctic Mountains, Victoria Land, Ross Ice Shelf, Wilkes Land, Mount Erebus 3,794 m (12,448 ft), Terre Adélie, Ross Sea, George V Land

0 600 km / 0 600 miles (approximate scale)

Penguin colony
About half a million emperor penguins—the biggest and tallest species of penguin—live in Antarctica. They gather in huge colonies to breed and raise chicks and walk long distances across the ice to feed from the sea.

The Arctic

Arctic tern
These birds have the longest migration of any animal in the world. Every year, they fly about 50,000 miles (80,000 km) from the Arctic to Antarctica and back.

Yu'pik people
The Arctic is home to many indigenous peoples, such as the Yu'pik of Siberia and Alaska, who travel on snowshoes and use animal furs for clothing.

Northern Lights Cathedral
This spiral-topped cathedral in the town of Alta, Norway, takes its name from the lights in the sky that can be seen in the far north.

Map labels
Bering Sea
Alaska (USA)
CANADA
Arctic Circle
Chukchi Sea
RUSSIA
Siberia
Hudson Bay
ARCTIC
North Pole
Laptev Sea
Severnaya Zemlya
OCEAN
Baffin Bay
Global Seed Vault
Kara Sea
Davis Strait
Greenland
Svalbard
Barents Sea
ATLANTIC OCEAN
Greenland Sea
Alta
ICELAND
NORWAY SWEDEN FINLAND
Norwegian Sea

*The **Arctic Ocean** is the world's smallest ocean, surrounded by snowy landmasses.*

0 — 800 km
0 — 800 miles
(approximate scale)

Water-resistant fur keeps the bear warm in the freezing Arctic.

Hardy plants
Lichen, moss, and other tough plants, such as these Arctic poppies, thrive in the light, short Arctic summer when the sun does not set.

Polar bears
Polar bears, the largest creatures in the Arctic, spend most of their lives on sea ice. Melting ice, due to a rise in global temperatures, is shrinking their habitat.

Arctic whales
A type of whale, narwhals are recognized by their up to 10 ft (3 m) long single tusks. They swim in Arctic waters all year round and can reach depths of 1 mile (1.5 km).

- ⬦ 5,600,000 sq miles (14,500,000 sq km)
- 👥 4 million
- ★ None
- ◯ Indigenous languages (+40), other languages (+7)

The **northernmost regions** of **North America**, **Russia**, and **Europe** lie within the **Arctic Circle**. Cold, treeless **tundra** cover the land, while the icy **Arctic Ocean** has the **North Pole** in its center.

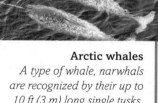

Global Seed Vault
To safeguard against any food crops becoming extinct, a vault inside a mountain in the Svalbard Islands of Norway contains millions of seeds from different crops. The Vault is preserved by permafrost and rock.

REFERENCE

Overseas Territories

Some territories around the world belong to countries that lie far away from them geographically. Many of these overseas lands were once part of past colonial empires. Some now have their own local governments, but many have decided against independence in order to keep strong trade connections, economic support, or military protection from the country they are linked to. A number of overseas territories are uninhabited islands. The UK administers the most overseas lands, followed by France, the US, and the Netherlands.

Australia

Ashmore and Cartier Islands

- Population: 0
- Area: 2 sq miles (5 sq km)

Lying about 199 miles (320 km) northwest of Australia, this territory consists of four uninhabited coral reef islets. The first Europeans to discover them were British Captain Nash, aboard his ship Cartier in 1800, and Captain Samuel Ashmore, in 1811.

Christmas Island

- Population: 2,200
- Area: 52 sq miles (135 sq km)

This island in the Indian Ocean was named, on Christmas Day, 1643, by a British sea captain. Flying Fish Cove is its main settlement and port, where most islanders live.

Thousands of red crabs migrate from Christmas Island to the ocean each year.

Cocos Islands

- Population: 600
- Area: 5.5 sq miles (14 sq km)

Two of the 27 tiny Cocos Islands in the Indian Ocean are inhabited. They are centers for fishing, snorkeling, and bird-watching.

Coral Sea Islands

- Population: 0
- Area: 1 sq mile (3 sq km)

On the edge of Australia's Great Barrier Reef, these tiny isles are visited by seabirds.

Heard and McDonald Islands

- Population: 0
- Area: 159 sq miles (412 sq km)

This territory in the southern Indian Ocean is about 1,050 miles (1,700 km) from Antarctica. The volcanic islands are a haven for wildlife.

Norfolk Island

- Population: 1,800
- Area: 14 sq miles (36 sq km)

Lying 994 miles (1,600 km) northeast of Sydney, Australia, Norfolk Island was formerly a prison colony for convicts exiled from the UK.

Denmark

Faroe Islands

- Population: 51,600
- Area: 538 sq miles (1,393 sq km)

The Faroe Islands are 18 rugged, volcanic isles in the North Atlantic Ocean. Viking warriors once lived on them, around 1,200 years ago.

Greenland

- Population: 57,600
- Area: 836,300 sq miles (2,166,000 sq km)

Greenland is the world's largest island that is not a country. Two-thirds of the territory lies in the Arctic Circle.

France

Clipperton Island

- Population: 0
- Area: 2.5 sq miles (6 sq km)

This remote island in the east Pacific Ocean takes its name from the 18th-century English pirate John Clipper, who is said to have hidden here. At its center is a large, nutrient-rich lagoon with an abundance of plant life.

French Guiana

- Population: 290,000
- Area: 35,135 sq miles (91,000 sq km)

On the northeast coast of South America is French Guiana, a region that is 90 percent dense jungle. Most people live in its largest city, Cayenne, or other towns on the coast.

French Polynesia

- Population: 295,100
- Area: 1,609 sq miles (4,167 sq km)

With 118 islands spanning the five archipelagos of Austral, Gambier, Marquesas, Society, and Tuamotu in the South Pacific, French Polynesia is rich in beaches, lagoons, and waterfalls. The largest island is mountainous Tahiti.

French Southern and Antarctic Lands

- Population: 0
- Area: 169,800 sq miles (439,781 sq km)

These remote, rugged islands lie in the southern Indian Ocean and off the Antarctic coast. Home to colonies of penguins and other seabirds, some of these isles are conservation areas with scientific research stations based on them.

Guadeloupe

- Population: 406,000
- Area: 629 sq miles (1,628 sq km)

This archipelago lies within the Lesser Antilles chain of islands in the Caribbean Sea. The two main islands of Basse-Terre and Grand-Terre are linked by a bridge over the Salée River.

La Soufrière volcano on Basse-Terre is the highest peak in the Lesser Antilles.

Martinique

- Population: 376,000
- Area: 436 sq miles (1,128 sq km)

This volcanic Caribbean island in the Lesser Antilles is some 4,400 miles (7,000 km) from France. Its French heritage is seen in the style of the buildings in its capital, Fort-de-France.

Mayotte

- Population: 270,300
- Area: 144 sq miles (374 sq km)

In the Indian Ocean, northwest of Madagascar, is the Mayotte archipelago. These picturesque islands have lush rain forest and mountains, and their coral reefs are popular with divers.

New Caledonia

- Population: 290,000
- Area: 7,172 sq miles (18,575 sq km)

About one-quarter of the world's reserves of the metal nickel are found in New Caledonia, a chain of islands in the South Pacific.

Réunion

- Population: 859,000
- Area: 970 sq miles (2,512 sq km)

One of the world's most active volcanoes, Piton de la Fournaise, meaning "Peak of the Furnace" in French, is situated on this island.

St. Barthélemy

- Population: 7,100
- Area: 9.5 sq miles (25 sq km)

Nicknamed St. Barts, this Caribbean island is a luxury holiday destination with white, sandy beaches and smart hotels.

St. Martin

- Population: 32,600
- Area: 21 sq miles (54 sq km)

This northeast Caribbean island is a French territory on the north side, while the south side (Sint-Maarten) is Dutch.

St. Pierre and Miquelon

- Population: 5,300
- Area: 93.5 sq miles (242 sq km)

Off the Canadian Atlantic Ocean lies an archipelago of eight French islands. Busy St. Pierre is home to most of the population, while Miquelon is a quiet haven for whales and seals.

Wallis and Futuna

- Population: 15,900
- Area: 55 sq miles (142 sq km)

These two small, remote volcanic islands lie in the South Pacific Ocean. Although they are governed by France, their Polynesian customs and communities are strong and diverse.

The Netherlands

Aruba

- Population: 119,400
- Area: 69 sq miles (180 sq km)

The picturesque island of Aruba lies off the Venezuelan coast in the Caribbean Sea.

Bonaire

- Population: 20,000
- Area: 113 sq miles (294 sq km)

With its coral reefs, diverse marine life, and sandy beaches, the Caribbean island of Bonaire is popular with divers and snorkelers.

Curaçao

- Population: 151,400
- Area: 171 sq miles (444 sq km)

This long, flat Caribbean island has a bustling coastal capital called Willemstad. The city's historic center boasts old Dutch-style buildings.

Willemstad—the colorful capital of Curaçao

Saba

- Population: 1,900
- Area: 5 sq miles (13 sq km)

The dormant volcano Mount Scenery lies at the heart of this tiny rain forest island in the Caribbean Sea. The Saba Marine Park protects the island's coral reefs and seagrass beds from damage by fishing, diving, and dumped waste.

Sint-Eustatius

- Population: 3,000
- Area: 8 sq miles (21 sq km)

Sint-Eustatius is a small island 16 miles (26 km) from Saba composed of two extinct volcanoes. Turtles nest on its beaches. This Caribbean island can be hit by tropical storms.

Sint-Maarten

- Population: 43,800
- Area: 13 sq miles (34 sq km)

Sint-Maarten is on the south side of the island that it shares with St. Martin (a French territory). Its bustling capital, Philipsburg, is popular with tourists on passing cruise ships.

New Zealand

Cook Islands

🏛 Population: 8,600

📐 Area: 91 sq miles (236 sq km)

The 15 Cook Islands are spread far and wide across 772,000 sq miles (2 million sq km) of South Pacific Ocean. The main exports of this self-governing territory are pearls and fish.

Niue

🏛 Population: 2,000

📐 Area: 100 sq miles (260 sq km)

Known as the "Rock of Polynesia," Niue is located 1,500 miles (2,400 km) off the coast of New Zealand. Its rugged interior is made up of cliffs, chasms, and forests.

Tokelau

🏛 Population: 1,600

📐 Area: 4.5 sq miles (12 sq km)

The three tiny coral atolls of Atafu, Fakaofo, and Nukunonu make up this territory in the South Pacific Ocean. Many of the population make their living by farming or fishing.

Red-footed boobies nest on Pacific islands.

Norway

Bouvet Island

🏛 Population: 0

📐 Area: 19 sq miles (49 sq km)

Situated in the south Atlantic Ocean, Bouvet Island is covered in ice. It is a nature reserve known for its penguin and seal populations.

Jan Mayen

🏛 Population: 0

📐 Area: 145 sq miles (377 sq km)

Between Greenland and Norway in the Atlantic Ocean is the small volcanic island of Jan Mayen. Scientists visit this uninhabited territory to study the glacial terrain and stormy weather.

Peter I Island

🏛 Population: 0

📐 Area: 69 sq miles (180 sq km)

A 19th-century Russian explorer named this volcanic island after Russian Tsar Peter I. This uninhabited territory in the Bellingshausen Sea is visited by petrels, terns, penguins, and seals.

Svalbard

🏛 Population: 2,900

📐 Area: 23,950 sq miles (62,045 sq km)

Nine islands form this archipelago in the Arctic Ocean north of Norway. Known for its snowy mountain peaks and glaciers, it is home to polar bears, reindeer, and Arctic foxes.

United Kingdom

Anguilla

🏛 Population: 18,100

📐 Area: 35 sq miles (91 sq km)

This beautiful island in the Caribbean Sea was named after the French word anguille *for "eel" because of its long, narrow shape. White-sand beaches and pretty islets attract many tourists.*

Sailboats race each other during the Anguilla Summer Festival.

Sailing is a national sport in Anguilla.

Ascension Island

🏛 Population: 800

📐 Area: 35 sq miles (91 sq km)

Roughly halfway between Brazil and Africa in the Atlantic Ocean is this small volcanic island once visited by celebrated British naturalist Charles Darwin. Green Mountain is the tallest peak on Ascension Island at 2,818 ft (859 m).

Bermuda

🏛 Population: 71,700

📐 Area: 21 sq miles (54 sq km)

Known for its pinkish-sand beaches, Bermuda is made up of seven Atlantic Ocean islands connected by bridges. It has a high number of wrecks in its waters, caused by ships hitting hidden coral reefs around its coastline.

Divers flock to the Bermuda coast to explore its shipwrecks.

British Indian Ocean Territory

🏛 Population: 0

📐 Area: 23 sq miles (60 sq km)

Lying in the middle of the Indian Ocean, this archipelago of 58 tropical islands serves as a military base. Its only visitors are military staff.

British Virgin Islands

🏛 Population: 37,400

📐 Area: 58 sq miles (151 sq km)

The clear, blue waters and warm, subtropical climate of these Caribbean islands make them very popular with tourists.

Cayman Islands

🌐 Population: 62,000

📐 Area: 102 sq miles (264 sq km)

The three islands of Grand Cayman, Cayman Brac, and Little Cayman make up this territory in the Caribbean Sea. It is famous for its financial services and for being a tax-free haven.

Falkland Islands

🌐 Population: 3,200

📐 Area: 4,700 sq miles (12,173 sq km)

Off the coast of Argentina in the Atlantic Ocean, this archipelago consists of two main islands and 776 smaller isles.

Gibraltar

🌐 Population: 30,000

📐 Area: 2.5 sq miles (6.5 sq km)

Gibraltar covers a tiny area on the south coast of Spain. This self-governing British territory is world famous for the mighty Rock of Gibraltar, a limestone rock 1,398 ft (426 m) tall.

Guernsey

🌐 Population: 67,000

📐 Area: 25 sq miles (65 sq km)

Guernsey is the second-largest of the Channel Islands in the English Channel. It has thousands of Guernsey cows known for their creamy milk.

Isle of Man

🌐 Population: 90,500

📐 Area: 221 sq miles (572 sq km)

In the Irish Sea off the northwest coast of England lies the rugged Isle of Man. This hilly island hosts the world-famous Tourist Trophy (TT) motorcycle races every year.

The TT courses are famous for being hazardous.

Jersey

🌐 Population: 101,000

📐 Area: 45 sq miles (116 sq km)

Lying close to the north coast of France, Jersey is the largest of the British Channel Islands. It is known for its historic castles, Jersey cows, and tunnels that date from World War II.

The 13th-century Mont Orgueil Castle in Jersey

Montserrat

🌐 Population: 5,400

📐 Area: 39 sq miles (102 sq km)

Named Montserrat by explorer Christopher Columbus in 1493, this Caribbean island has been an English territory since the 17th century. Since 1995, eruptions from the Soufrière Hills volcano have forced many islanders to leave.

Pitcairn Islands

🌐 Population: 50

📐 Area: 18 sq miles (47 sq km)

In 1789, British sailors on board the HMS Bounty staged a mutiny and settled on the remote, mid-Pacific Pitcairn Island. By 1838, Pitcairn and three surrounding islands had become a British territory.

St. Helena

🌐 Population: 6,000

📐 Area: 47 sq miles (122 sq km)

This volcanic island in the south Atlantic Ocean is rich in wildlife. French military commander Napoleon Bonaparte was in exile on St. Helena for six years until his death in 1821.

South Georgia and the South Sandwich Islands

🌐 Population: 0

📐 Area: 1,506 sq miles (3,903 sq km)

This group of southern Atlantic Ocean islands was claimed by British navigator James Cook in the 18th century. South Georgia is a haven for penguins, albatrosses, and elephant seals.

Tristan da Cunha

🌐 Population: 260

📐 Area: 38 sq miles (98 sq km)

The remote location of Tristan da Cunha in the Atlantic Ocean has attracted rare wildlife to these six tiny islands.

Turks and Caicos Islands

🌐 Population: 55,900

📐 Area: 366 sq miles (948 sq km)

Forty tropical islands form this archipelago in the Atlantic Ocean. Tourism, fishing, and financial services are important for its economy.

United States of America

American Samoa

🌐 Population: 49,400

📐 Area: 86 sq miles (224 sq km)

These islands were formed relatively recently—within the last seven million years—by volcanic activity.

Pink coral, American Samoa

Baker and Howland Islands

Population: 0

Area: 0.5 sq miles (1.4 sq km)

The two tiny Pacific islands of Baker and Howland are surrounded by coral reefs. Uninhabited, they are a refuge for marine life, including endangered sea turtles.

Guam

Population: 168,500

Area: 210 sq miles (544 sq km)

This tropical island in the western Pacific Ocean is the site of important US military bases. Its indigenous people are called the Chamorro.

Chamorro-style dancing

Jarvis Island

Population: 0

Area: 1.5 sq miles (4.5 sq km)

A tiny, flat island in the Pacific Ocean, Jarvis brought the US riches in the 19th century thanks to guano *(bird droppings), a valuable source of fertilizer. Today, Jarvis is a nature reserve.*

Johnston Atoll

Population: 0

Area: 1 sq mile (2.6 sq km)

Four islands form this atoll in the central Pacific Ocean. North and East islands were created artificially by dredging. An uninhabited nature refuge, this atoll is an oasis for reef and bird life.

Kingman Reef

Population: 0

Area: 0.4 sq miles (1 sq km)

This spectacular, submerged coral reef in the north Pacific Ocean is protected. More than 200 fish species thrive here, including eels, rays, and sharks. It is also home to giant clams.

Midway Islands

Population: 0

Area: 5.2 sq km (2 sq miles)

Named by the US Navy for its central location between California and Japan, Midway Islands form a small coral atoll in the Pacific Ocean. Its three islands support all sorts of nesting birds, including millions of albatrosses.

Navassa Island

Population: 0

Area: 2 sq miles (5.2 sq km)

Preserved as a wildlife sanctuary since 1999, Navassa is a tiny US territory in the Caribbean Sea. The landscape of limestone rock and craggy coastline provides an ideal habitat for native lizards and nesting sea birds.

Northern Mariana Islands

Population: 57,000

Area: 184 sq miles (477 sq km)

Totaling 22 islands in the Pacific Ocean, the self-governed Northern Mariana Islands have active volcanoes and fringing coral reefs.

Palmyra Atoll

Population: 0

Area: 5 sq miles (12 sq km)

The Palmyra Atoll in the Pacific Ocean is a protected area. Scientists visit it to study its landscape, wildlife, and climate.

Puerto Rico

Population: 3.2 million

Area: 3,515 sq miles (9,104 sq km)

This vibrant island in the Caribbean Sea has both mountains and tropical forests. With a diverse population, its culture includes a mix of Spanish, US, and Afro-Caribbean traditions.

Ponce Carnival is an annual celebration in Puerto Rico.

Virgin Islands

Population: 104,000

Area: 137 sq miles (355 sq km)

The Virgin Islands are part of a picturesque archipelago east of Puerto Rico. Their subtropical climate, white sands, and blue waters attract many visitors. These islands are sometimes hit by powerful hurricanes, including highly destructive Hurricane Irma in 2017.

Wake Island

Population: 0

Area: 2.5 sq miles (6.5 sq km)

This former World War II battleground is a tiny US territory in the Pacific Ocean made up of three coral islets over an underwater volcano. The public cannot visit them, but they have an emergency landing strip for military aircraft.

An aerial view of Palmyra Atoll

Glossary

alpine
Of or relating to high mountain areas.

amphitheater
An oval-shaped, open-air arena, usually where public events take place.

ancestor
An earlier person, animal, or object from the past of someone or something existing today.

annex
To take over territory that belongs to another country.

archipelago
A group of islands.

arid
Describes an area with little or no rainfall.

atoll
A ring-shaped coral reef that surrounds an area of shallow water, such as a lagoon.

bonsai
A Japanese art form of growing miniature trees and shrubs in pots using a special pruning technique.

calligraphy
The art of elegant or decorative handwriting.

casino
A space where gambling games are played.

cease-fire
An agreement to suspend fighting, usually to discuss terms of peace.

chateau
A large castle or stately home in France.

city-state
A city that is self-governing and does not belong to another country or state.

civilization
A group of people who share the same society, culture, and way of life.

climate
The average weather patterns of a particular area over a long period of time.

coastline
An area where land and ocean meet.

colonialism
A system by which one country takes political control of another country, and exploits its resources for financial or economic gain.

colony
An area that is ruled by another country.

communism
A system by which all property and industry is owned by the government. Wealth and resources are evenly distributed among the state's citizens.

constitution
A set of laws that describes the basic rights and duties of all citizens. A constitution also determines how a country should be governed.

currency
Anything that is widely accepted as money in a particular country.

delta
A flat area, sometimes triangular in shape, that forms from the settling of silt and sand at the mouth of a river.

democracy
A system of government in which people choose their leaders through elections.

diverse
Describes a population of people that includes many different races, cultures, societies, and religions.

dynasty
A ruling family whose power passes from one generation to the next.

empire
A group of countries or territories ruled by a single monarch or government.

endangered
A species with a low population that is at risk of becoming extinct.

endemic
A plant or animal species that is native to a particular area and found nowhere else.

ethnicity
The language, culture, and beliefs of a particular group of people.

exports
The sale of goods and services to other countries.

extinction
When all the members of a species die out.

fado music
A Portuguese style of singing in which the vocalist laments the hardships of daily life.

fjord
A long, thin body of water that extends inland from the sea, often between high cliffs.

folklore
The customs, traditions, and stories of a community passed down through generations, usually by word of mouth.

glacial lake
A lake formed when a glacier erodes the land and then melts, filling in the cavity left behind by the glacier.

Gothic
Describes a style of architecture used in western Europe between the 12th and 16th centuries.

Hangul
The Korean alphabet.

harbor
A place where ships may moor safely, usually due to the presence of piers, jetties, and other human-made structures.

imperial
Of or relating to an empire.

imports
Goods bought in from another country.

independence
The liberation of a country, state, or society, which then becomes self-governing.

indigenous
Native to a particular place.

irrigation
The method of supplying land with extra water by means of channels, pipes, or canals.

islet
A small island.

lagoon
An area of shallow water that has been cut off from the sea.

landlocked
An area of land (or water) that is completely surrounded by land.

marine
Of or relating to the sea.

marsupial
A type of mammal whose females carry their young in pouches.

medieval
From or relating to the Middle Ages, a time in history that lasted from 600 to 1500 CE.

minaret
A tall, thin tower that is part of a mosque.

monarchy
A form of government ruled by a king or queen.

oasis
A place in a dry area where there is water, and plants can grow.

Ottoman Empire
An empire that was founded in Anatolia (modern-day Turkey) in the 13th century. It controlled much of western Asia, southeastern Europe, and northern Africa from the 14th to 20th centuries.

peninsula
A piece of land that is connected to the mainland but that is almost entirely surrounded by water.

permafrost
Frozen ground found beneath the surface in polar regions.

Polynesia
An area in the central Pacific Ocean that includes many islands, such as Hawaii, Samoa, and New Zealand.

province
A large section of a country that may have its own administration or government.

regatta
A sporting event that involves boat and yacht races.

reggae
A style of music that originated in Jamaica in the 1960s.

relic
An ancient object.

Renaissance
A period of European history from the 14th to 16th centuries, during which an interest in the arts and learning was renewed.

republic
A form of government in which the supreme power lies with the people and their elected representatives.

rift (geology)
A widening crack caused by rocks pulling apart.

Sahel region
A semiarid region in northern Africa located directly south of the Sahara Desert and which stretches from the Atlantic Ocean to the Red Sea.

sarong
A long piece of cloth wrapped around the body and tucked in at the waist.

savanna
An area of grassland that has few trees.

sea level
The level of the sea's surface in relation to other geographical features such as hills.

souk
An Arab marketplace.

Soviet Union
Officially called the Union of Soviet Socialist Republics, or USSR. It was a collection of 15 federal socialist republics in what is now Russia and parts of eastern Europe and central Asia and which disbanded in 1991.

tapioca
A starch extracted from the cassava plant and which is used as a food thickening agent, especially for puddings.

terraces
A series of flat areas built into a slope-like steps, used for growing crops.

territory
An area of land that belongs to a ruler or state.

textile
A piece of cloth or woven fabric.

tropical
Of or in relation to the area near the Equator.

tundra
The cold, treeless areas around the North and South Pole, where the ground is frozen for most of the year.

volcanic beach
The beach on a volcanic island, where deposits of dark volcanic minerals and rocks are common.

Index

Acknowledgments

The publisher would like to thank the following people for their help with making the book: Kathakali Banerjee, Shatarupa Chaudhuri, Virien Chopra, Sukriti Kapoor, Sai Prasanna, Rupa Rao, Bipasha Roy, Neha Ruth Samuel, and Arani Sinha for editorial assistance; Rachel Lindfield and Pauline Ankunda for editorial assistance on the Africa chapter; Mansi Agrawal and Aparajita Sen for design assistance; Vagisha Pushp for picture research assistance; Nand Kishor Acharya, Dheeraj Singh, Vikram Singh, and Anita Yadav for DTP assistance; Rakesh Kumar, Priyanka Sharma, and Saloni Singh for the jacket; Hazel Beynon for proofreading; and Elizabeth Wise for indexing.

The publisher would like to thank the following for their kind permission to reproduce their photographs:

(Key: a-above; b-below/bottom; c-center; f-far; l-left; r-right; t-top)

123RF.com: 123mn 50ca, grigory_bruev 89cra, Olga Buiacova 144crb, Simon Dannhauer 17clb, Valery Egorov / valeryegorov 82cla, Ivan Fedorov 92clb (floor petals), Ramzi Hachicho 136ca, Eric Isselee / isselee 175cra (Kiwi), mehdi33300 15cra, 31tl, Margret Meyer 67b, mirco1 29tl, luca nichetti 92tr, photopips 42cla (Dates), possohh 18br, Korawee Ratchapakdee 173crb, RudyBalasko 94clb, server 99tr, Genadijs Stirans 45clb, Anek Suwannaphoom 72clb, Thawat Tanhai 15ca, Maria Tkach 15tc (frame), Allan Wallberg 88cla, Abi Warner 105cra, wklzzz 4bc, 76clb, Svetlana Yefimkina 11t, yelo34 19cr, 19clb, 19br; **4Corners:** Antonino Bartuccio 32cl, Paul Panayiotou 155clb, Aldo Pavan 31crb; **African Horseback Safari:** 72tr;

akg-images: Africa Media Online / ILAM Photographer 69clb; **Alamy Stock Photo:** AB Forces News Collection 185cl, Action Plus Sports Images 111tl, Aflo Co. Ltd. / Nippon News 102ca, Aflo Co. Ltd. / Nippon News / Naoki Morita 161cb, Africa Media Online 74ca, AGAMI Photo Agency / Daniele Occhiato 177tl, AGAMI Photo Agency / Dubi Shapiro 29clb, agefotostock / Gonzalo Azumendi 94cla, agefotostock / Jason Bazzano 17ca, agefotostock / Kevin O´Hara 46tr, Jerónimo Alba 15tc, Allstar Picture Library Ltd 73bl, Sally Anderson 179cla, arabianEye FZ LLC / Ali Al Mubarak 140clb, Arco Images GmbH / de Cuveland, J. 179tl, Arco Images GmbH / TUNS 173tr, Artokoloro 68cl, George Atsametakis 123tr, Backyard Productions 60tr, Javier Ballester 169br, Simon Balson 75br, John de la Bastide 25clb, Philip Berryman 172cla, Frank Bienewald 111cl, Biosphoto / Antoine Boureau 60crb, blickwinkel / AGAMI / A. Ouwerkerk 141crb, blickwinkel / artifant 64tr, blickwinkel / Hecker 179c, blickwinkel / Layer 157tl, Blue Jean Images 160clb, Blue Planet Archive MNO 34tc (butterfly), Joerg Boethling 37clb, 67cr, Julia Bogdanova 30tc, Ger Bosma 68cra, Myroslava Bozhko 78b, David Brennan 22cra, Thomas Brock 118cla, Michael Brooks 103tr, Roi Brooks 15br, Bob Burgess 51cl, Michele Burgess 57cra, Classic Image 178cra, Thornton Cohen 152ca, Dennis Cox 43cr, Zoltán Csipke 112tr, Cultura Creative (RF) / Alberto Bogo 106tc, Cultura RM / Tim E White 179b, Danita Delimont / Michele Westmorland 22cb, dbimages / Amanda Ahn 15tl, Viren Desai 74tl, Design Pics / Radius Images 10br, Design Pics Inc / Spencer Robertson / RM Level 2 52ca, Michael Diggin 84crb, Reinhard Dirscherl 43ca, V. Dorosz 116tr, dpa picture alliance 50clb, 149tl, dpa picture alliance / Daniel Bockwoldt 90cra, dpa picture alliance / Daniel Reinhardt 88crb, Mara Ducheti 154cla, Karin Duthie 72cr, Richard Ellis 19cla, Everett Collection Inc 116cl, Everett Collection Inc / © Netflix / Ron Harvey 58cb, Everett Collection, Inc. 150tc, eye35.pix 117b, Findlay 97cl, 157cl, S. Forster 154cra, FotoFlirt 151c, Nick Fraser 66cr, funkyfood London - Paul Williams 123c, Eric Gevaert 65ca, Vlad Ghiea 11cra, Granger Historical Picture Archive / NYC 99cr, Arthur Greenberg 155cra, Greenshoots Communications / GS International 61crb, Johnny Greig 58ca, 134bl, Natalia Harper 23tl, Helen Sessions 11tr, Gavin Hellier 83cra, Hemis.fr / Aurélien Brusini 22clb, 182cla, Hemis.fr / Bertrand Rieger 18tr, 61br, Hemis.fr / Bruno Morandi 44tr, Hemis.fr / Franck Charton 46cla, hemis.fr / Jean-Paul Azam 105cla, hemis.fr / Sylvain Cordier 28crb, Marc F. Henning 158bl, Heritage Image Partnership Ltd / © Fine Art Images 128tr, 132ca, Cindy Hopkins 178cla, Peter Horree 148cb, Jack Hoyle 151tr, Image Professionals GmbH / Don Fuchs 173cr, Image Professionals GmbH / Roetting / Pollex 93tr, imageBROKER / Günter Lenz 98-99b, imageBROKER / Juergen Hasenkopf 101tc, imageBROKER / Jürgen & Christine Sohns 169cra, 174crb, imageBROKER / Michael Peuckert 127b, imageBROKER / Michael Runkel 140tr, 144br, imageBROKER / Stephan Goerlich 95c, imageBROKER / Werner Lang 78cra, Images by Itani 136cla, Indiapicture / Hemant Mehta 151clb, Arif Iqball 153cra, Anton Ivanov 51tr, Ivoha 86cb, Jack Malipan Travel Photography 46br, jbdodane 61tl, David Jensen 19c, John Warburton-Lee Photography / Nigel Pavitt 49tl, Jon Arnold Images Ltd 79tr, Jon Arnold Images Ltd / Doug Pearson 21tc, Jon Arnold Images Ltd / John Coletti 16tr, Wolfgang Kaehler 86crb, katacarix 115crb, Keystone Press / Keystone Pictures USA 52tr, Micha Klootwijk 83cla, Ton Koene 33tl, Konstantin Kopachinskiy 167cb, Vladimir Kovalchuk 129tl, Petr Kovalenkov

Acknowledgments

98cla, LatitudeStock / David Forman 22cla, Dan Leeth 178crb, Lifestyle pictures 94tr, LightField Studios Inc. 132tr, Ronnachai Limpakdeesavasd 155cla, Alexander Ludwig 48cl, David Lyon 93cr, Johnny Madsen 79tl, Mandoga Media 105clb, Nino Marcutti 117cla, Borislav Marinic 89ca, MARKA / raffaele meucci 46cr, Stefano Politi Markovina 97bl, 111cra, Frederico Santa Martha 68tr, Iain Masterton 96b, Matthew Oldfield Editorial Photography 52cb, Jenny Matthews 146bl, mauritius images GmbH 70tr, mauritius images GmbH / Christopher Schmid 129clb, mauritius images GmbH / Dave Derbis 86cl, mauritius images GmbH / Hans Bleh 123cra, mauritius images GmbH / Jose Fuste Raga 164tr, mauritius images GmbH / Michael Obert 41crb, MB_Photo 173tc, Neil McAllister 78crb, mediacolor's 138bl, MehmetO 119cl, Michel & Gabrielle Therin-Weise 135br, Hercules Milas 103ca, Andrey Moisseyev 172tr, Jason Moore 136clb (Israeli family), Tuul and Bruno Morandi 143tl, 159clb, Marina Movschowitz 185cra, Guido Nardacci 116cla, Eric Nathan 126br, Nature Picture Library / Doug Perrine 16tl, Nature Picture Library / Eric Baccega 72br, Nature Picture Library / Jurgen Freund 181clb, Nature Picture Library / Wild Wonders of Europe / Giesbers 109crb, Nature Picture Library / Will Burrard-Lucas 69tl, Andrey Nekrasov 41cra, Alice Nerr 28tr, Quang Ngoc Nguyen 157c, Paul Mayall Birds 91tl, Sean Pavone 168b, Jeremy Pembrey 30cb, Wolfi Poelzer 24bl, Vova Pomortzeff 5cra, 19bc, Bart Pro 117cra, PvE 88fcla, Quagga Media 95cra, André Quillien 20clb, 62cra, 63tl, Niels Quist 87cra, Muhammad Mostafigur Rahman 152b, Hiren Ranpara 49crb, Janos Rautonen 79ca, Realy Easy Star / Giuseppe Masci 140cra, Mervyn Rees 13tr, Reimar 56cra, Edwin Remsberg 54cb, 54bl, 76tr, 76cra, robertharding / Christian Kober 163br, Robertharding / Michael DeFreitas 24cla, Robertharding / Michael Runkel 49clb, 60bl, 174b, 176cla, Erlantz Pérez Rodriguez 37crb, RZAF_Images 67cra, Octavio Campos Salles 33tc, Borges Samuel 50b, Marco Saracco 172cl, Juergen Schonnop 36c, Science History Images / Photo Researchers 112cla, Seaphotoart 184br, SebastianP 124b, Iuliia Shevchenko 99clb, Sibons photography 53crb, Paulette Sinclair 37cla, Sport In Pictures 96tr, sean sprague 169clb, Kumar Sriskandan 31bc, stockeurope 108c, Stockfolio® / Stockfolio 704 78cla, Tansh 5bc, 152crb, Marc Tielemans 107c, Ann and Steve Toon 43tr, Peter Treanor 56b, Tommy Trenchard 52cra, UDAZKENA 47clb, Universal Images Group North America LLC / DeAgostini / M. Leigheb 45cl, USFWS Photo 185br, Lucas Vallecillos 144cra, Genevieve Vallee 177bl, Greg Vaughn 34bl, Tom Wagner 104fcrb, David Wall 175ca, wanderluster 88cl, WaterFrame_fba 22crb, WaterFrame_jdo 183cr, Tony Watson 71bl, WENN Rights Ltd 74cla, 113cla, Westend61 GmbH / Andreas Pacek 86cra, Ray Wilson 15cl, Jan Wlodarczyk 107cla, 121clb, World History Archive 139crb, Robert Wyatt 147cl, Xinhua 151cb, Xinhua / Luka Dakskobler 111clb, Xinhua / Sergei Stepanov 90bl, Babelon Pierre-Yves 77clb, Ariadne Van Zandbergen 76cla, Zoonar GmbH / Sergey Mayorov 138cla; **Avalon:** Philip Enticknap 104tr, © Everett 163tl, © World Illustrated 147br; **AWL Images:** Matteo Colombo 1, 154bl, Alan Copson 184ca, Tom Mackie 10clb, Nigel Pavitt 48tr, 59br; **John Bradley:** 177tr; **Bridgeman Images:** Gift of the Egyptian Exploration Society 42bl, Granger 83c; **© The Trustees of the British Museum. All rights reserved.:** 52crb; **© CERN:** 110cl; **Circus Zambia:** Greg Bruce Hubbard 69r; **Depositphotos Inc:** ajafoto 97ca, anpet2000 37bl, GekaSkr 134tr, jianghongyan 174tl, lifeonwhite 58tr, mihtiander 77b, vlade-mir 51crb; **Dorling Kindersley:** Idris Ahmed 159br, Andrew Beckett 77cl, 165cb, Ruth Jenkinson / Holts Gems 53clb, 66cra (Gem), Natural History Museum, London 52ca, University of Aberdeen 123cla, 177br, Urospoteko 126cl, Whipsnade Zoo 5tr, 5ftr, 33tr, 33ca (x2); **Dreamstime.com:** Subodh Agnihotri 136crb, Aiisha 85tl, Lev Akhsanov 112tc, Ziya Akturer 137ca, Albund 11c, Alex7370 143br, Kierran Allen 74cb, Nuno Almeida 95tl, Leonid Andronov 40bc, Andzhey 12ca, Nir Antman 136br, Anusorn62 164cra, Arsty 103cl, Kairi Aun 140cla, Anthony Baggett 120cr, Bankerok 21bl, Anny Ben 59c, Harald Biebel 84cla, Larisa Blinova 5bl, 35ca, Boggy 168crb, Brackishnewzealand 19tl, Tatiana Bralnina 40cla, Maurice Brand 121tl, Dave Bredeson / Cammeraydave 16-177 (Magnifying glass), Jeremy Brown 166clb, Ryhor Bruyeu 127cra, Zbynek Burival 114cb, Evgeny Buzov 168cla, Byheaven87 147cra, Volodymyr Byrdyak 66b, Mohammed Anwarul Kabir Choudhury 152clb, Su Chun 75cr, Jerome Cid 118cr, Lucian Coman 72cb, Cowboy54 168ca, Kobby Dagan 30bl, Daitoiumihai 125clb (River), Svetlana Day 113b, Ddkg 136tr, Deyan Denchev 147cr, Derejeb 48cb, Dianearbis 56cla, Dziewul 125tl, Cecil Dzwowa 71tl, Sergey Dzyuba 101tr, Eastmanphoto 40clb, Elenatur 133t, Erix2005 89b, Ermess 106ca, Faunuslsd 77cla, Evgeniy Fesenko 135clb, Freesurf69 123cr, Eugeniu Frimu 120cl, Anne Fritzenwanker 20cra, Filip Fuxa 78tr, Geckophotos 87cb, 87cb (beef), Giuseppemasci 84cl, Rostislav Glinsky 108br, Diego Grandi 14cr, 16bl, Green_cat 128cl, Andrey Gudkov 67tl, Pascal Halder 110cla, 110bl, Paul Hampton 66b (Elephants), Cor Heijnen 167bl, Jiri Hera 97ca (chocolate pralines), Hpbfotos 10l, Hrlumanog 158cl, Ildipapp 31cra, Imladris 97r, J33p3l2 160cra, Anujak Jaimook 169cla, Wieslaw Jarek 102cl, Jatmika Jati 166br, Jojjik 110tr, Lukas Jonaitis 91cra, Kaiskynet 156cra, Kira Kaplinski 166ca, Matej Kausitz 114ca, Mikhail Dudarev 34cla, Pavel Kavalenkau 100cla, Bryan Kessinger 12clb, Michal Knitl 114bl, Sergii Kolesnyk 42cb, Liliia Kondratenko 115tl, Kristina Kostova 96ca, Sergii Koval 50cra, 119clb, Tetiana Kovalenko 159cl, Jesse Kraft 34crb, Aliaksei Kruhlenia 119cra, Kuhar 111ca, Matthijs Kuijpers 24cra, Serhii Liakhevych 126crb, Lidian Neeleman 23clb, Lightfieldstudiosprod 132cla, Limpopoboy 73cr, Miroslav Liska 87tl, Lornet 113c, Oleksandr Lytvynenko 111cr, Maceofoto 77ca, Makidotvn 162cla, Dmitry Malov 90tr, Marko5 111crb, Markuk97 104crb, Masezdromaderi 125cl, Zdeněk Matyáš 121cra, Aliaksandr Mazurkevich 139tl, Jeff Mccollough 35c, Daria Medvedeva / Dash1502 85clb, Nik Merkulov 124tc, Mikelane45 55bc, Mikeltrako 104b, Serhii Milekhin 176ca, Milosk50 105tl, Minnystock 95tc, Borna Mirahmadian 139cra, Klemen Misic 120b, Mistervlad 100cb, 108tr, Pranodh Mongkolthavorn 175cra, Moniquesds 34tc (butterflies), Louno Morose 11cr, Luciano Mortula 99c, Mrtobin 84tr, Robert Mullan 102cla, Mzedig 142tr, Roland Nagy 162tr, Krzysztof Nahlik 93b, Natalyka 99cra, Nevinates 135cb, Nicolaforenza 106clb, Duncan Noakes 21ca, Stephen Noakes / Stevenoakes 151tc (Cricket ball), Nonmim 106cr, Noppakun 154tl, Noppharat 21tr, Elena Odareeva 156tr, Olgacov 90crb, Palinchak 97tl, Iordanis Pallikaras 5fbl, 120ca, Sean Pavone 165clb, Phanuwatn 19crb, Photostella 133cb, Pikkystock 71cra, Pipa100 40cra, Sergey Plyusnin 82c (tea), Marek Poplawski 18cla, Ppy2010ha 20ca, 36cl, 93cra, 137cla, 139cra (dish), Tawatchai Prakobkit 156cla, Presse750 28cla, 28cra, 79crb, Ondřej Prosický 129br, Pawel Przybyszewski 92clb, Subin Pumsom 160-161t, Rafael Angel Irusta Machin / Broker 101clb, David Ribeiro 103cr, Goce Risteski 116br, Rudi1976 105b, Rukanoga 92clb (petals), Rungrote 25tl, Rusel1981 114cla, Samystclair 36bl, Luca Santilli 109cra, Constantin Sava / Savcoco 108cla, Alfio Scisetti 46clb, Jozef Sedmak 114tr, Serturvetan 133crb, Sichkarenko 125clb, Siempreverde22 31bl, Dirk Sigmund / Disiflections 48cla, Silvionka 165tr, Przemyslaw Skibinski 71cr, Svetoslav Sokolov 124cl, Nuthawut Somsuk 98tc, Sova004 118tr, Michaela Stejskalova 106-107t, Stockthor 145crb, Nikolay Stoimenov 124cra, Zlatimir Stojanovic 25cl, 25cl (Half), Jens Stolt / Jpsdk 14ca (cra), Bogusz Strulak 106tr, 107tr, Swisshippo 73cra, Stephen Tapply 35b, Huy Thoai 158tr (x2), Pranee Tiangkate 53tl, Sasin Tipchai 156cl, Tomas1111 85cra, 113tr, 128cla, Vladimir Tomovic 116cr, Georgios Tsichlis 122cb, Typhoonski 141tl, 141b, Sergey Uryadnikov 63cl, Uskarp 134cra, Valentyn75 5crb, 101cb, Oscar Espinosa Villegas 64clb, Vilor 91clb, Vitalssss 15tr, Natalia Volkova 126cla, Vvoevale 66cra, Pattadis Walarput 151cl, Dennis Van De Water 124cr, Marcin Wojciechowski 88bl, Björn Wylezich 146cra, Thomas Wyness 149cra, Xantana 109cla, Yakthai 133tr, Yuri Yavnik / Yoriy 160ca, Vadim Zakirov 163cla, Hongqi Zhang (aka Michael Zhang) 75tr, Znm 70cl, 70b, Петлин Дмитрий 77tl; **EcoTec Lab:** Ousia A. Foli-Bebe 57cla; **ESO:** J. C. Muñoz / creativecommons.org /licenses/by/4.0 35cra; **Ryszard Filipowicz:** 113cr; **Fotolia:** Eric Isselee 160cr; **Getty Images:** 500Px Plus / Juhani Vilpo 66tr, 500Px Plus / Rasto Rejko 114crb, 500Px Plus / Sergey Grishin 127tl, AFP / Ahmed Ouoba 55tl, AFP / Bertrand Guay 176cra, AFP / Emmanuel Arewa 59ca, AFP / Fethi Belaid 41cr, AFP / Hannah Peters 175crb, AFP / Hussein Faleh 138crb, AFP / Jack Guez 60cla, AFP / Joe Klamar 37cra, AFP / Khaled Desouki 138cla (book), AFP / Laure Fillon 77cr, AFP / Louisa Gouliamaki 67tc, AFP / Martin Bernetti 35tl, AFP / Miguel Medina 107cb, AFP / Mohamed Abdiwahab 49bc, AFP / MOHD RASFAN 166tr, AFP / Monirul Bhuiyan 62bl, AFP / Nelson Almeida 36cla, AFP / Patricia De Melo Moreira 102bl, AFP / Pius Utomi Ekpei 56cl, AFP / Reinnier Kaze 61cla, AFP / Sergei Gapon 119br, AFP / Seyllou Diallo 50cla, AFP / Stefanie Glinski 47b, AFP / STR 47cra, AFP / Vano Shlamov 135tl, AFP / Xaume Olleros 53cra, AFP / Yoshikazu Tsuno 165ca, AFP / Zoom Dosso 55br, AFP PHOTO / Juan Barreto 28bl, Alloy / Michele Falzone 23bl, Anadolu Agency / Fatemeh Bahrami 139b, Archive Photos / Jack Vartoogian 45cra, The Asahi Shimbun 164cla, Scott Barbour 23br, 56tr, Edward Berthelot 99tc, Yann Arthus-Bertrand 55cra, Torsten Blackwood / AFP / © June Smith / Copyright Agency. Licensed by DACS 2020 / © DACS 2020 172crb, Bloomberg 168tr, Bloomberg / Simon Dawson 123tl, Bloomberg / Susana Gonzalez 17crb, 17br, Bloomberg / Vincent Mundy 126tr, Kitti Boonnitrod 43b, Paula Bronstein 148cla, 156cr, Corbis Documentary / Galen Rowell 178tr, Corbis Documentary / Layne Kennedy 183bc, Corbis Historical / Ashley Cooper 177ftl, Corbis Historical / Photo Josse / Leemage 107cra, Corbis News / Art in All of Us / Anthony Asael 21cra, Corbis News / Art in All of Us / Eric Lafforgue 73cra, Corbis Sport / Visionhaus / Ben Radford 163clb, Corbis Unreleased / Frans Lemmens 29cra, DeAgostini / DEA / V. Giannella 176bl, DeAgostini / De Agostini Picture Library 109tl, DeAgostini / DEA / G. Kiner 37tl, DeAgostini / DEA / M. Seemuller 34tr, DeAgostini / DEA / S. Vannini 76crb, David Degner 60cra, DigitalVision / Chris Nash 100cl, DigitalVision / Juergen Ritterbach 31cla, DigitalVision / Klaus Vedfelt 87crb, EyeEm / Hafizal Talib 167tr, EyeEm / Nguyen Duc Thành 2-3, 157b, FilmMagic / D Dipasupil 57bl, FilmMagic / Toni Anne Barson 14bl, Focus on Sport 17bl, Gallo Images / Mike D Kock 47crb, Gamma-Rapho / Dominique Berbain 142bl, Gamma-Rapho / Jean-Luc Manaud 5br, 46cra, Gamma-Rapho / Michel RENAUDEAU 79bl, Gamma-Rapho / Yves Gellie 141cra, Erika Goldring 13clb, Tim Graham 66cla, Hulton Archive / Allsport / Tony Duffy 109clb, Hulton Archive / Heritage Images / Fine Art Images 124cla, The Image Bank / © Ingetje Tadros 174clb, The Image Bank Unreleased / Atlantide Phototravel 91br, The Image Bank Unreleased / nik wheeler 138tr, The Image Bank Unreleased / Onne van der Wal 23cra, The Image Bank Unreleased / Timothy Allen 159tl, In Pictures / Qilai Shen 160crb, Dan Kitwood 17cra, Mark Kolbe 177cb, LatinContent Editorial / Jan Sochor 14cla, LatinContent Editorial / Sean Drakes 25br, Christian Liewig - Corbis 54tl, LightRocket / SOPA Images / Lito Lizana 65cl, LightRocket / Wolfgang Kaehler 36tr, 179cl, LightRocket / Yousuf Tushar 152cla, Linden Adams Photography 184bl, Lonely Planet Images / Jenny & Tony Enderby 175tl, LOOK / Alexander Kupka 95cb, Dominik Magdziak 52l, Maskot 88cb, Moment / © Santiago Urquijo 44br, Moment / Anton Petrus 129tr, Moment / asifsaeed313 148cl, Moment / Cedric Favero 72cla, Moment / Jackal Pan 161cra, Moment / Jasmin Merdan 140b, Moment / Kelly Cheng 30cla, Moment / Lassi Kurkijarvi 118b, Moment / Manuel ROMARIS 137clb, Moment / Michele D'Amico supersky77 65cra, Moment / Natthawat 145bl, Moment / Pakawat Thongcharoen 155br, Moment / Paul Biris 137b, Moment / Robert Lowdon 11crb, Moment / Stanley Chen Xi, landscape and architecture photographer 86cla, Moment / Tiancheng Wang 144clb, Moment / vladimir zakharov 83b, Moment / wiratgasem 157cra, Moment Open / Afriandi 158cr, Moment Open / Ankur Dauneria 151tc, Moment Open / irawansubingarphotography 174cra, Moment Unreleased / Bashar Shglila 41bl, Moment Unreleased / Geraint Rowland Photography 151cr, National Geographic Image Collection / Scott Sroka 22tr, NurPhoto / Nicolas Economou 135cra, NurPhoto / Ulrik Pedersen 162br, Minas Panagiotakis 11ca, Photodisc / PICHA Stock 68cla, Photodisc / ULTRA.F 151tl, Photothek / Michael Gottschalk 44ca, Popperfoto / Leo Mason 129cr, Premium Archive / Anne Frank Fonds Basel 96cr, Joe Raedle 12cla, Alberto E. Rodriguez 16cla, Shamim Shorif Susom / EyeEm 54cra, SM Rafiq Photography. 148br, Sportsfile / Piaras Ó Mídheach 84bl, Sportsfile / Stephen McCarthy 20cla, Michael Steele 122cla, Stockbyte / ICHIRO 165cra, Stone / Arctic-Images 85b, Stone / Gonzalo Azumendi 117tl, Stone / Harry Hook 65br, Stone / Hugh Sitton 44cl, Stone / John P Kelly 86bl, Devon Strong 32crb, Sygma / John van Hasselt - Corbis 152cl, TASS / Sergei Bobylev 125br, TASS / Viktor Drachev 147cla, ullstein bild / JOKER / Walter G. Allgöwer 94ca, ullstein bild / Olaf Wagner 62crb, ullstein bild / Reinhard Dirscherl 49cra, Universal Images Group / AGF / Francesco Tomasinelli 73tl, Universal Images Group / Eye Ubiquitous 167tl, Universal Images Group / Farm Images 64br, Universal Images Group / Hoberman Collection 75c, Universal Images Group / Jeff Greenberg 74cl, Universal Images Group / Marka 154tr, Universal Images Group / MyLoupe 57crb, Universal Images Group / VW Pics / Mel Longhurst 144cla, Universal Images Group / Werner Forman 54br, 61clb, Velo / David Ramos 98cl, Visionhaus 42ca, Visual China Group 161cb (tennis table), Nigel Waldron 148tr, Westend61 182cra, WireImage / Dan MacMedan 24tr, WireImage / John Lamparski 161br, World Rugby / Clive Rose 75clb; **Eli Greenbaum, Ph.D.:** 64cla; **Iittala:** Birds by Toikka 89cla; **iStockphoto.com:** AbleStock.com / Hemera Technologies 10ca, BirdImages 137tl, boerescul 106cla, brunoat 68bl, Corbis Documentary / Arne Hodalic 143bl, diverroy 123cb, E+ / 1111IESPDJ 83tr, E+ / ALEAIMAGE 28cr, E+ / DieterMeyrl 112b, E+ / Eloi_Omella 13cb, E+ / ewg3D 104cla, E+ / FilippoBacci 142cla, E+ / Flavio Vallenari 24crb, E+ / fotoVoyager 153b, E+ / golero 33clb, E+ / hadynyah 67cl, 157cr, E+ / Marcus Lindstrom 92ca, E+ / MediaProduction 164bl, E+ / Morsa Images 162cra, E+ / Nikada 69cb, E+ / Phooey 107br, E+ / sansubba 153crb, E+ / ugurhan 42cla, emretopdemir 65tl, evemilla 87cr, fotoVoyager 88tr, Freder 16cr, guenterguni 63br, 64cra, Bartosz Hadyniak 48br, Ahmed_Abdel_Hamid 142crb, holgs 36cr, HomoCosmicos 45tl, JGolosiy 4br, 19cra, Jorgefontestad 101cr, Burak Kara 133cr, Kardd 153cla, Katiekk2 143cra, lleerogers 110crb, marchello74 33cra, marcophotos 158cla, MindStorm-inc 183clb, Murchundra 128cb, Musat 62cla, Kylie Nicholson 143tc, R.M. Nunes 32cla, Photosensia 132cb, pittapitta 79clb, Mauro_Repossini 18cb, rosn123 70cr, Stockbyte / Visage 150cl, structuresxx 153t, SzymonBartosz 92cla, TatyanaGl 108cb, tehcheesiong 167tc, unser 100bl, urf 134crb, Urvashi9 155tl, utamaria 41tl, VUSLimited 49cla, Kirk Wester 12crb; **Alexander Keda:** 125cra; **David Kirkland:** 177cr; **Library of Congress, Washington, D.C.:** LC-DIG-ppmsca-18521 55cb; **The Metropolitan Museum of Art, New York:** The Crosby Brown Collection of Musical Instruments, 1889 63cb, Fletcher Fund, 1927 163cl, Gift of Carolyn C. and Dan C. Williams, 1984 14crb, Harris Brisbane Dick Fund, 1963 139cla, The Michael C. Rockefeller Memorial Collection, Gift of Nelson A. Rockefeller, 1965 58cla, Rogers Fund, 1950 138c; **Música Para Ver Collection:** 146tr; **NASA:** Carla Cioffi 145tl; **naturepl.com:** Bryan and Cherry Alexander 11tl, Ingo Arndt 18c, Sylvain Cordier 32tr, Bruno D'Amicis 106crb, Suzi Eszterhas 30tr, 70cla, Daniel Heuclin 57tl, 61cra, Sebastian Kennerknecht 166cra, Pedro Narra 53cla, Naskrecki & Guyton 68crb, Piotr Naskrecki 29ca, Nature Production 90tl, Flip Nicklin 179cr, Cyril Ruoso 167br, David Tipling 17tl, Robert Valentic 173clb; **Rob Nerja:** 51bl; **Nokia Corporation:** Since 2016, HMD Global is the exclusive licensee of the Nokia brand for phones & tablets 89tl; **Picfair.com:** Ines 63cra; **Pixabay:** happylism / 15 images 163cra, janeb13 / 454 images 20crb; **Press Association Images:** PA Archive / Brian Lawless 84cb, PA Wire / Ian West 59cb; **Reuters:** AAL / RCS 58cl, Salim Henry 69ca, Afolabi Sotunde 59tr, Paulo Whitaker 33crb; **Rex by Shutterstock:** AP / Andrew Medichini 108cl, AP / Charlie Riedel 13c, AP / Geert Vanden Wijngaert 121br, AP / Mohammed Seeneen 149clb, Colorsport 29br, EPA / Martin Philbey 89clb, EPA / Mauritz Antin 87b, EPA / Muhammad Sadiq 146crb, EPA / Roland Schlager 112clb, EPA-EFE / Vickie Flores 82clb, Jane Hobson 134cla, imageBROKER 16crb, Martti Kainulainen 86crb (reindeer), UIG / Auscape 178b; **Robert Harding Picture Library:** Biosphoto / Robert Haasmann 175b, Michael Nolan 85ca, Michael Runkel 53bl, 146cla; **Photo Scala, Florence:** The Metropolitan Museum of Art / Art Resource 57clb; **Science Photo Library:** Massimo Brega, The Lighthouse 51tl; **Shutterstock.com:** Chris Allan 25cra, Yevgen Belich 91cla, Bondart Photography 103b, Radek Borovka 71clb, CKP1001 120tr, Digoarpi 115cla, Dijise 120cla, Ba dins 166cla, Grzegorz Drezek 104cra, Gil.K 76bl, Jesus Giraldo Gutierrez 117cr, Visual Intermezzo 154cr, Kota Irie 15clb, Katiekk 159cra, Heracles Kritikos 133tl, Chintung Lee 162clb, macka 43cra, Martchan 47tl, Anamaria Mejia 30crb, novak.elcic 119tl, RHJPhtotoandilustration 147clb, s4svisuals 115b, Sergey-73 66ca, Mohamed Shareef 149crb, Sopotnicki 73br, Alexey Suloev 12cra, Keith Michael Taylor 176br, topten22photo 156br, Vershinin89 127clb, Darek Warczakoski 92crb, yvon52 98crb; **South American Pictures:** 35clb; **SuperStock:** Alaska Stock - Design Pics 179cra, Biosphoto 45b, Hemis.fr / Paule Seux 56crb, juniors@wildlife Bildagentur G 145ca, Minden Pictures / Vincent Grafhorst 63cr, Photononstop 133bl, Prisma / Alex Bartel 59tl; **Unsplash:** Spencer Davis / @spencerdavis 137cra, Fidel Fernando / @fifernando 172cb

All country and continent maps in the book are created by DK using textures from NASA satellite imagery and Natural Earth raster data.

All other images © Dorling Kindersley
For further information see: **www.dkimages.com**

NORTH AMERICA

CANADA · UNITED STATES OF AMERICA · MEXICO · BELIZE · COSTA RICA · EL SALVADOR · GUATEMALA · HONDURAS

GRENADA · HAITI · JAMAICA · ST KITTS & NEVIS · ST LUCIA · ST VINCENT & THE GRENADINES · TRINIDAD & TOBAGO

SOUTH AMERICA

COLOMBIA

URUGUAY · CHILE · PARAGUAY

AFRICA

ALGERIA · EGYPT · LIBYA · MOROCCO · TUNISIA

LIBERIA · MALI · MAURITANIA · NIGER · NIGERIA · SENEGAL · SIERRA LEONE · TOGO

BURUNDI · DJIBOUTI · ERITREA · ETHIOPIA · KENYA · RWANDA · SOMALIA · SUDAN

NAMIBIA · SOUTH AFRICA · ESWATINI (formerly SWAZILAND) · ZAMBIA · ZIMBABWE · COMOROS · MADAGASCAR · MAURITIUS

LUXEMBOURG · NETHERLANDS · GERMANY · FRANCE · MONACO · ANDORRA · PORTUGAL · SPAIN

POLAND · SLOVAKIA · ALBANIA · BOSNIA & HERZEGOVINA · CROATIA · KOSOVO (disputed) · NORTH MACEDONIA · MONTENEGRO

ASIA

LATVIA · LITHUANIA · CYPRUS · MALTA · RUSSIA · ARMENIA · AZERBAIJAN · GEORGIA · TURKEY

QATAR · SAUDI ARABIA · UNITED ARAB EMIRATES · YEMEN · IRAN · KAZAKHSTAN · KYRGYZSTAN · TAJIKISTAN

CHINA · MONGOLIA · NORTH KOREA · SOUTH KOREA · TAIWAN · JAPAN · MYANMAR (BURMA) · CAMBODIA

AUSTRALASIA & OCEANIA

SINGAPORE · MALDIVES · AUSTRALIA · NEW ZEALAND · PAPUA NEW GUINEA · FIJI · SOLOMON ISLANDS · VANUATU